Chapel of Dreams
The Peter Wynne Story

As told to Dave Lodge
Personal Manager to the late Tommy Bruce.

Published in 2018 by Dave Lodge and Peter Wynne

© Copyright Dave Lodge and Peter Wynne 2018

All the photos used in this book are copyright, some are very old but every effort has been made to find sources, they are the personal property of the Peter Wynne Collection.

ISBN: 978-1-9160217-0-9

A Catalogue record for this book is available from the British Library.

Printed in the UK by INGRAM

Book & Cover Design by Russell Holden
www.pixeltweakspublications.com

Cover photo by Chris Weston Photography
Charterhouse recording studio, London

All rights reserved without limiting the rights under copyright reserved above, no parts of this publication may be reproduced, stored in or introduced into a retrieval system, or transmitted in any form, or by any means (electronic, mechanical, photocopying, recording or otherwise) without the prior written permission of both the copyright owner and the publisher of this book.

This book is dedicated to you Amanda. I love you dearly.
You are my best friend, my lifesaver.
I also dedicate it to all my kin.

My thanks go to so many people who have helped me though my life, too many to mention here. These wonderful people include Uncle Bill, Ron James, Bob Barratt, Hughie Green and Dave Lodge who helped make this book possible.

Peter Wynne Sixties recording artiste

Contents

Introduction ix
How it all began 1
The family together at last, Life in Broseley 11
Kidderminster New school, voice breaks, athletics, start work 40
London beckons 58
Larry Parnes 74
A change of musical direction 105
Halfords and The George Cooper Agency 114
Life as Simon Smith 146
Taking The Cabaret Scene By Storm 168
The American Dream Is Real 185
The Welsh Valleys 222
The London Dream Is Alive Again 238
The Australian Experience 267
Home again to Wales 274
Back To Australia 290
Back In The UK And On To Pastures New 303
The Musical Dream Is Revived 310
Amanda and a new lease of life 324
Inspiration and Innovation Continue 343
A Conclusion But Not The End 357
Peter Wynne / Simon Smith Discography 373

Foreword By Amanda Hazelwood

I was a divorced woman and ten years ago I met Peter on the Internet. Peter was quite a determined man and any negative thought about our age difference disappeared when we met. I already had plans to be a foster carer, which later on Peter and I did for six years. I first heard Peter sing online and I liked the song, it was called, "Miss You Already". I have always liked Elvis singing ballads and Peter sings these songs too sounding very similar. He has a strong voice, with a maturity that hasn't changed much since he was singing as a twenty years old. We were married Harrogate in 2012. Peter makes me laugh and today we have our latest Grandchildren, Henry and Meadow occupying our time. Also Peter has his art and song writing interests. We had discussed him writing his life story throughout the years, on and off and Peter is very fortunate now through his friend and author Dave Lodge to realise this written account in this book of Peter's wonderful interesting and varied life. What a gift to have this insight into Peter's career to treasure for all of us. Dave and Margaret I thank you for your time and faith in bringing this book to life.
Peter I love You, Amanda xxx

Foreword by Graham Hunter

A Wynner!

If you are an early sixties fan of the 'pop' music idiom, then the chances are that you will know all the main big hits of the recording stars, but you won't know Peter Wynne. If on the other hand you are more than just a fan, a collector of fine vinyl and a connoisseur of rare records, then you will know that records by Peter Wynne (UK Parlophone, Columbia and Polydor) are near impossible to find, and if you are lucky enough to find one it'll be at a steep price.

Singer/songwriter Peter Wynne, should by all rights have enjoyed some chart success, he had everything going for him to be a pin up/teen idol, but for the chart placings. You see in my book, Peter's career was mismanaged, on many levels too. Alas he was not alone on that score!

There has to be an element of 'luck' and some of it passed his way with him gaining a recording deal just out of his late teen years. Top recording manager Norman Newell praised his voice and it recorded well. But the song choices did little to inspire a buying public and paired with his youthful look, powerful and mature sounding voice, performing on package tours, with what where essentially rock 'n' rollers, the audiences were perhaps a little confused.

His first record a cover of The Dubs *Chapel Of Dreams* fitted the bill in principle, but to my mind Peter's talents deserved a different approach and one that he didn't have a say in. Though Parlophone did let him record his own material on occasion. History cannot be changed and as this book will attest in relating Peter's story, I urge you to seek out some of the gems that Peter Wynne has recorded and enjoy as I have.(And continue to do so!)

In conclusion, I can only say that I have been privy to hearing some unreleased material of Peter's and can only say that as a singer he was never scared in going that extra-mile. He has such a powerful range and superb pitch. Check out the B side of his 1967 single release, And *This My Beloved* (Colombia DB8213-UK) recorded as Simon Smith, the B side is a song he co-wrote with producer Bob Barrett, *I Just Can't Live Without You* and you will see/hear what I mean, if you are lucky enough to find a copy.
Graham Hunter 2018

Foreword from the author

This probably one of the most remarkable stories that I have ever been called on to write. The story of a boy called Peter Hazelwood who in the humble opinion of the author had one of the most amazing voices of his generation, if not of the whole period of music from 1900 to the present day.

For me as the author of this book, Peter Wynne would come to my notice in 1959 because I had heard him sing *Chapel of Dreams*. In those days I was a young lad who loved ballads and this song is among the best and beautifully sung that I have ever heard. I wanted to buy it, but even though I ordered it from my local music shop I couldn't get a copy. This poor distribution by the recording company, was probably the reason why in spite of his popularity with the listening public Peter Wynne did not have a hit record, with this fabulous song. At this time I had no idea that Peter Wynne was in fact Peter Hazelwood. I would not know that, for another sixty years or more. Sadly I would also be unaware that he changed his name to Simon Smith along the way. This would mean I missed many chances to see and hear this amazingly talented vocalist. His timing and phrasing of lyrics makes him in my eyes a nothing less than a vocal genius.

So musically we had hit the sixties and these would be exciting times in music for young people, like myself. Suddenly we had our own, music and Rock and Roll stars, not just the Americans, Little

Richard, Carl Perkins and Elvis Presley etc. People like Jack Good, Larry Parnes and Robert Stigwood were promoting and producing British shows and more importantly British artistes. Now because of this Peter Wynne was being seen on television shows such as Boy meets Girl and receiving standing ovations up and down the country on Larry Parnes Rock and Trad shows. With a voice like his how could Peter Wynne not succeed?

The fact was that due to a failure on the part of the powers that be in the music business, to realise just how remarkable Peter Wynne's talent was, every chance to promote him and his recordings was missed. This meant that chart success was evading Peter Wynne, yet the live audiences and his fellow performers, including the authors dear friend Tommy Bruce, who said that Peter had the best voice of all the Parnes Boys, loved the sound of Peter's voice. The promoters and the record companies were happy to simply let the popularity of youth carry the day, they did very little to promote the artistes.

Because of ineptitude or lack of interest, these people did not place Peter Wynne in the right environment, he was not being showcased to the right audiences. Peter would continue to record and perform, audiences loved him. He was making fabulous recording of classic songs and his own recording but without the proper promotion, the records were not selling. The thing was that with Peter's fabulous voice he should have been a regular on TV shows like Sunday Night at the London Palladium, he was and is, that good. If whole families could have seen and heard him, his records would in my opinion definitely have sold. But before the right people could catch on to this seemingly obvious chance to promote this young star, sadly the times as they say, were changing and by 1966 the Beatles had changed the face of British music.

I would not hear of Peter Wynne again until the early seventies, when my wife Margaret and I had met and become friendly with Tommy Bruce, starting a relationship that would last until Tommy's death in 2006. Tommy would talk to me about his time on the Parnes Tours, telling me about all the guys he had met and become friendly with in those days. One thing became clear in these conversations, Tommy Bruce was sure that Peter Wynne had the best voice out of all of them. As we became successful with Tommy's theatre shows, we tried to find Peter so that we could feature him on those shows. Unfortunately we were not successful, it was only several years after Tommy died that another friend of ours Chris Ely was able to put me in touch with Peter.

This Peter Wynne's book in its entirety, the memories and experiences are all his, Peter has been kind enough to use me as the conduit to pass his life story on to you the reader. I am very proud to have this privilege and I will endeavour to be worthy of the honour I am being afforded. During the months spent writing this book I feel that Peter has become my friend just as Tommy Bruce would have known that he would, had we had the good fortune to meet in Tommy's lifetime. Time spent with my wife Margaret, in Peter and Amanda's company has been an absolute joy, so many shared memories. Where our thoughts and memories of people and things of the time, over overlapped, I have with Peter's permission, offered my own thoughts as part of the story. I hope that these thoughts and memories help the readers

So there we have it, the beginning of a voyage of discovery for me and the readers of this book. This a great story, one that Peter has shared with us all. A story that I hope you will enjoy reading as much as I have enjoyed writing it. Peter, please let me say at the start, you are not just and incredibly talented entertainer you are a lovely man. It is one of my great pleasures in life to have met you. I hope and pray I am able to pass this important fact about your personality on to your many fans and few more people who are yet to discover the power, majesty and emotion that you have in your voice.

So let us all take our first steps together through the door of this chapel of renown, *The Chapel of Dreams* and in doing so join Peter Wynne on his amazing journey through life. We are very lucky that Peter has chosen to share his dreams, memories and his life so far, with us. It was felt that these memories should and would form part of *The Chapel of Dreams*.

Dave Lodge, author and personal manager to the late Tommy Bruce.

Dedication by the author

This book has been made possible by thelp and support of my wife Margaret, whose love is the foundation that my life is built on.

Introduction

When the late Tommy Bruce and I were working on his biography, *Have Gravel Will Travel*, we spoke of Peter Wynne often and I think that Tommy would be pleased if what he said about Peter in his own book *Have Gravel Will Travel*, could be repeated here. He would have wanted Peter and everyone else to know just how much he thought of him as a man and a singer. So I have treated Tommy's words as a foreword for Peter's book, anyone wishing to understand why, need only look at chapter nine of Tommy's biography. D. L.

Tommy Bruce, memories of my old mate Peter Wynne:

Peter Wynne has the most wonderful voice, in my opinion it was the best of all the voices on the Parnes tours and there were some good ones, Dave Sampson, Danny Rivers, Marty Wilde, to name but three. His voice had an almost operatic quality, I used to listen to him going through his scales in the dressing room before the shows and wonder, "How can this boy not be having hit record after hit record"? Peter should have been a massive star, I can remember him stopping the show with his marvellous voice on more than one occasion.

Davy and I have tried to find Peter because I would love to work with him again. It was good to know you Peanuts, great company and great times. Hopefully one day we will find you and once again hear that great voice powerfully ringing out through the auditorium. When we do find you Pete, as I am sure we will because Davy is very tenacious, he doesn't give up on things, or people, my message to you is, "It was good to know you, be lucky my old son, you will never be forgotten by any of us who were lucky enough to get to know you and work with you".

Tommy Bruce.

Columbia recording star and TV entertainer. 1937-2006

Authors note

Frank Ifield was over in the UK in May and June 2018 touring with the very talented Country singer Nikki Gillis. I am pleased to say that my wife Margaret and I were lucky enough to spend several hours in Frank's company, both watching him perform and in conversation. He remembered Tommy Bruce and I from previous occasions. More importantly he remembers the happy times at the Palladium in 1965 with Peter Wynne and gladly agreed to provide a foreword for Peter's book. When we receive it, Peter and I have decided to place this foreword ahead of the chapter in which their time working together is recalled. Since writing this Frank has emailed me the said foreword for Peters book. It is thoughtful and well written. As Tommy Bruce always said, "Frank Ifield is a gentleman". Tommy never spoke truer word.

Chapter One

How it all began

Peter Hazelwood, who would later be known as Peter Wynne a man who would go on to become one of Great Britain's finest vocal talents was born on the 30th of April 1939 in Chester Royal Hospital. His parent's were Charles Leonard and Carmen Christina Hazelwood. The maiden name of his mother had been Williams, it seems although Peter is not completely sure, that her maiden name was actually Wynne-Williams. However his mother only used the name Williams. What he is sure of is that his Grandfather's name was Tom Wynne-Williams.

Peter's father was a Canadian who had been born in Toronto. He left the family to join the RAF just after his second son was born. Charles would be shipped abroad to serve with distinction against the onslaught of Hitler's forces. From this information we are able to understand that Peter is the son of a Welsh lady and a Canadian gentleman.

In these circumstances, mother, Carmen, found herself like many other mothers of the day in the role of a single parent. Now given the fact that Britain was at war, evacuation to what was deemed a safer area for such families was common practice. So the Hazelwood family were evacuated to a place just outside Ruthin, North Wales. The exact place they went to was a farm called, Tythun Ucha. (Note from the author, Peter tells me his Welsh is not wonderful and he asks his fellow Welsh people for their forgiveness if the spelling is incorrect.) This farm was high up in the Welsh mountains. It seems that Mr Roberts, the man who farmed the land there was a friend of the children's grandfather and because of this their mother was offered a home for herself, Peter, his older brother Charles and their sister, Pamela. As Peter recalls it, they all lived happily on the farm throughout the war years.

Occasionally the children's Paternal Grandmother used to come to visit them. Apparently their Gran was a very frugal lady and in an effort to maintain her careful nature she would climb up into the hayricks in search of the eggs that had been laid by the farmers' hens. It seems that their Gran was very good at finding the eggs and because of her skill as a forager, the family would have eggs for tea or breakfast on a regular basis. Looking back Peter can recall his brother Charles, shouting to the farmer, "Mr Roberts my Gran is up on the hay loft stealing your eggs". The farmer never came out to see what was going on, nor did he ever respond to this information. Peter thinks that Mr Roberts very kindly pretended not to hear what his brother Charles was saying.

There were occasions when the youngsters would be reminded of the war, this was because they were able hear the German bombers when they passed overhead. When this happened their mother would get them all to shelter under the table, in her thoughts this action would keep them safe if a bomb fell. Fortunately they never heard or felt any explosions and were able to continue their daily life when the planes had passed them by.

When Peter was about four years old his brother Charles decided he would show him how to milk a cow. On one occasion, Charles squirted the milk from one of the cow's teats into his brother's face, it went straight up his nose, Peter didn't help with the milking after that. One of the best memories from those childhood days is that the farm had a beautiful Welsh Shire Stallion. The stallion's name was Captain. Peter gives a description of the horse at this point, "My heavens this stallion was to me a four legged giant who could run like the thunder". This clearly a very happy boyhood memory.

While Peter is remembering life on the farm, he thought this would be a good time to share a strange story that his mother told him later in life. It seems that Charles had gone walking in the mountains surrounding the farm and somehow he had got lost. Charles was crying and very afraid that he would not be able find his way home. Suddenly he saw a tall man dressed in black wearing what used to be called a stove-pipe hat. The man did not speak he just pointed in the direction that Charles assumed correctly, was the way home. Charles was not frightened by the man, he went the way the man pointed and got home safely.

Peter tells me that he himself got lost one day, when he was about three years old. On that occasion, his Gran had been coming to see them from where she lived, in Ruthin. She made a habit of walking the whole six miles. So he set off to walk out to meet her but somehow he missed her. After some considerable time had passed, Peter was eventually found by his mother.

The children's days on the farm were filled with happy memories, the years rolled by in these idyllic surroundings until after about four year the family moved to a place called Eaton Constantine. This place was near the Wrekin Hill. Because she needed to make ends meet the children's mother, Carmen took a job working for a family, cleaning, washing, ironing and sometimes cooking. In return for her work she was given a cottage in lieu of wages. She worked hard and long for her family, this was the sort of life many young wives and mothers had during and just after the war. Never knowing when or even if their husbands would return from so far away. But always striving to give them a home to return to.

This would be a good time to let Peter express his fond memories of his Mum as she made a tremendous impact on his life, as many war time mothers did on their children. His Mum was an attractive dark haired Welsh lady who loved her children with a passion. She always wanted the best for them, she may have possessed a Victorian attitude towards being strict but always without fail tried to be fair. To Peter at the time it seemed that his sisters could get away with anything. Having said that they were, all well behaved and always polite, they must thank their mum for that. Looking back he sees things in a different way, he just didn't understand how difficult being a parent was. Why should he? He was after all just a little boy.

Unfortunately during the time he was growing up Peter never felt as though his parents gave him enough encouragement, at least not until later in his life. He was always singing everywhere he went, any time of the day or night, if he was awake he could be heard singing. Practising, copying, even mimicking the top vocalists of the day. But it seemed that there was never a word of encouragement. Nobody ever said the words that he longed to hear, such as, "Your singing was excellent or even nice". As a family the Hazelwood's all kept their feelings locked up, so it is not possible for him to know if they knew how he felt. Certainly Peter never felt able to tell them, that, oh how he longed for that kind word that would make him feel that they noticed how hard he tried. Too be fair to his family they probably didn't understand how he needed some outward sign that they were proud of him.

Peter's Mum had a good singing voice, but strangely he only ever heard her sing when she was making the beds. She smoked, always had a cigarette while doing her housework, just the one, never more than one. He knows that she liked to have a bit of fun, but he feels that it was hard for her to achieve this on many occasions because, Peter's Dad always had a stiff upper lip, he always conducted himself in a dignified way, he was a proud man. Almost completely teetotal the only drink he ever took was a sip of port at Christmas. His mum liked a drop of sherry during the festive season, but she never over did it. In all his life Peter can not recall seeing either his father or his mother tipsy, never mind drunk. Sad to say his mum died in Tasmania when she was ninety three years old, Peter thinks she just gave up on life and living.

As he thinks back one of Peter's early memories of Eaton Constantine is of the day he was happily playing ships, he was doing this by floating twigs on the surface of the water in the water tank. This pastime was giving him great pleasure until, a man who was known to everyone as the Major came up to him and stopped his game. He, the Major then proceeded to splash him with water and then removed the imaginary Armada. Having done this he told him never, ever to play in the water tank again. Needless to say Peter was broken hearted, he thought to himself, "how could this man be so mean?" How could he wet him with water and confiscate his little twig ships, at that age he couldn't think why he had been treated in this way.

The problem it seems was that it was important for the water in the tank to be clean. The Major obviously did not think it necessary to explain this fact to a little boy. He merely expected him to obey, such was the way of things in those days. Peter although he was not in the frame of mind to forgive this man, really liked his daughter. She was very kind to him and would let him ride on the front of her bicycle on trips to the shops. Added to this she always bought him something small to eat, which in the days of rationing was greatly appreciated by a young boy.

When he was old enough to understand Peter's mother told him a story about something that happened to her when they were living on the farm near Ruthin. It seems that one day his mother had left the farm to go and buy groceries to feed her family from the shop in Ruthin apparently this event took place near Christmas time one year and the weather was looking a little ominous. Never mind she thought, it has to done, and so she picked up her shopping basket and set off on her walk to the village. The weather held until she had almost reached the village, but the time she had done her shopping it was starting to snow heavily. She had no choice but to set off on her journey home so in spite of the weather she carried on walking. By now the snow was sticking to the ground and becoming deeper with every step. Now she was on the hill, still some distance from the farm and she was becoming exhausted. The wind and snow was lashing her face, and the weight of her basket was pulling her down, to make matters worse the snow was now covering her shoes. Peter's Mum was starting to worry that she wouldn't be able to make it home, but still she kept going. As she walked she was saying a silent prayer, "Oh please God let me get home to my children".

By now she was really staggering, completely exhausted and losing hope of ever reaching home, she knew that she simply could not go on. Then suddenly out of the corner of her eye she saw a small light, shining in the darkness, she felt that her silent prayer had been answered. Eagerly she forced her way through the snow towards where the light was shining. As she got closer she saw that there was a small cottage ahead of her. Peter's Mum gasped with relief and surprise and almost fell down on the path that was leading her to the cottage door. When she got there she knocked on the door, and elderly lady opened the door, and when she saw Peter's mum, she said, "Oh come in my dear, you look done in". Once inside the elderly lady helped her to a seat saying, "Rest here for a while, I'll make you a cup of hot tea". His mother took the tea gratefully, as she started to recover from her frightening ordeal, she told the lady where she lived. The lady assured her that she had not got far to go saying, "Don't worry you will make it home without any problem from here".

So after she had drunk her tea and when she was feeling revived his mum thanked the lady for her kind help and resumed her trek home. She got home with all the groceries, not suffering to badly from the blizzard like conditions. None of the children were aware of her terrible ordeal, they were just pleased to see her. This kind act from a lady she did not know, helped her to be able to remain at home safe and warm for the whole Christmas period. As she would later tell Peter, it was in her hour of greatest need, she had asked God for help getting home and God listened and helped her.

The children's Grandmother used to come and stay with them quite often, they were always pleased to see her. However as he got older and more aware of things, Peter noticed was that his Gran liked to enjoy a few beers, Bass being her favourite tipple. When she found herself to be out of supplies Gran would walk to the local Inn to replenish her stock, this was a distance of two miles. Having bought a couple of bottles she would walk back. This was quite an amazing effort for a lady of her age because this made a round trip of four miles. Peter recently went back to visit the area and he now feels the walk is like a marathon for an older person.

One of the things that Peter enjoyed during his time in that area was to sit with the farm workers and share their lunch of apples and cheese. These lunches the reader may be surprised to know, were eaten in the pig sty. It has to be said that this was a very clean area as it was not occupied by pigs at this time. Over all the first five years of Peter's life were happy and enjoyable. The only thing that all the children missed was the company of their father. Thankfully that situation would soon be resolved. Because as Peter was approaching his fifth birthday there was another move for the family, this time to a house in Broseley in Shropshire. His brother Charles and sister Pamela would be starting school there, and there was a lovely surprise for them all when they moved.

L-R Leo, Pamela, Charles and me standing up. Taken at Lido Bridgenorth 1948-49

Peter's Great Welsh Grandad

Peter's Great Grandmother

Chapter Two

The family together at last, Life in Broseley

The surprise was that when the family had moved to Broseley the children's father was demobbed at the end of his military service. They were all very happy that after the best part of six years, the family was together again. Peter remembers seeing his father chewing gum, something he had never even heard of, let alone seen it or chewed. His dad gave him a piece of gum and he kept it for days. As he thinks of that piece of chewing gum now, Lonnie Donegan's popular song comes in to his mind, *Does Your Chewing Gum Lose Its Flavour On The Bedpost Overnight?* Because that is exactly where Peter kept his valuable, piece of Spearmint Gum.

There was very little in the way of luxury in this house, although what it did have was more space for the family. There was no electricity, only candle light in the rooms. There were four bedrooms, two living rooms and a kitchen. One of these bedrooms Peter would be sharing with his brother Charles. Down in the kitchen there was a gas mantle, and one side of the room was a big copper for heating water and on the other side and open fire that had a built in oven with a cooking plate. So it was not a house with many facilities, but what it was a happy house that was filled with the atmosphere of a family home.

Peter has happy memories of time spent with his father in those early days after he had been demobbed. The family would go for long walks down Willey Drive, this walk led them to the big house that was owned by Lord Forrester. They were walking through really lovely countryside, it was quite flat, not in the least hilly so it meant that they could enjoy leisurely strolls. In fact the only rise that could be seen in the surrounding terrain was "The Wrekin" this a local landmark that can be seen in the middle of Shropshire. Peter thinks that he was six or seven years old on the day this particular event took place. The family were on their usual walk when Peter's dad picked up a piece of wood, saying, "Oh look, this piece of wood is shaped like a cowboy's Colt 45". Taking the piece of wood from his dad, Peter ran off, as though he was riding imaginary horse and raced ahead of the others. At various intervals he would hide in the bushes or behind trees and any other cover he could find, then he would jump out firing his pretend gun as he ambushed his family. He kept up this exciting game until he tired of it. In those days children played for the fun of it, not as they seem to now with expensive electronic games. To Peter's mind that simple piece of wood was a fantastic find, it needed to be treasured and played with again. So with future games in mind Peter said to the others, "I am going to hide my pretend gun so that I can find it and play with it again when come on our walk again".

This was a good plan, but one that did not bear fruit, because they went on lots of walks over a period of many weeks, during which Peter searched diligently for his prized toy. Sadly he searched without success, because he never ever found that cowboy gun as he called the piece of wood again. Who knows maybe it is still there perhaps tucked under a tree trunk or a bush along Willey Drive, having waited more than seventy years for an adventurous and imaginative child, like Peter was then, to find it and play that game with his own family. It is a nice if perhaps not very realistic a thought, it is though for Peter, is a flickering happy memory of childhood and family that some, if not all people are blessed to have.

Another happy memory of that place and that time that Peter cherishes is of the time that his school friend, a fellow pupil from Broseley School, called Neil Beddows and Peter found a tiny fox cub, that seemed to have been abandoned by its mother. The two boys took it in turns to carry the cub back to Neil's house. They took the cub there because Neil lived nearer to the woods. When they got to the house they put it the cub in the garden shed. In there they were able to keep it warm and fed for a few weeks. Time went by and the cub was growing bigger and, stronger, it was now more able to fend for it's self so, they decided to let it go. Quite excited about returning the cub to the wild they put it in a large cardboard box and carried it to a field near Willey Drive. When they got to the field they put the box down on the ground, and started to carefully open the top, as they did so the little fox jumped out and ran for freedom, disappearing across the field and into the woods.

Peter remembers feeling rather sad to see the fox go, but he consoled himself with the thought that it would find a parent fox who would look after him. That is part of the joy of being young, because you have not had the simple pleasures of childhood clouded by the sometimes cruel treatment that you can become aware of in adult life, as a child you could see the good in every situation. If you are lucky like Peter and the author of the book, you retain that naïvety if you can call it that and still see the best in all situations, no matter how upsetting they seem to be. Anyone who doubts this philosophy only has to go on You tube and listen to Peter's recent recording of *One Pair Of Hands* to know that his belief in that ideal is a strong today as it was then.

So the family found that their life was different now that they were all living at 51 Church Road Broseley. There are things that Peter clearly remembers about the place, for one thing they had to light underneath the big boiler so that their mum could do the weeks washing and he clearly remembers night times when the gas mantle would be burning dimly in the kitchen. The low glow that came from the mantle would create shadows in the room, this looked rather strange and in some ways exciting for small children. Peter remembers one night in particular, when their Gran came round to visit, she was carrying two little chicks.

Being a very considerate lady so that the chicks would be warm she brought them in to the kitchen and put them down in a cardboard box beside the fire. As soon as the box was put down on the floor one of the chicks jumped straight out of the box and landed in the fire. Luckily the fire had only just been replenished with fresh pieces of coal to boost theat in the kitchen and the chick landed on a piece of this fresh coal, the chick was quickly grabbed from the fire and put back in the box. This incident was the source of great excitement for the children, who were jumping up and down shouting for the chick to be rescued.

Although Peter feels that he never really knew his dad very well in his early years, he thinks this was because of the time he had spent in the RAF. One thing he does remember is that his dad was quite a tall man, nearly six foot in height, he thinks, although it could have been slightly more. But on a more personal note he also remembers that his dad was a very quiet and reserved person. He was a man with a strong sense of duty and he was very hard working. His dad was a skilled tradesman, his job was that of an upholsterer, he was able to work from home and he used the front living room as his workroom. This left just one downstairs room and the kitchen as living accommodation for the family. You could hear his dad's hammer banging tacks into webbing or the sound of the Singer Sewing Machine humming a gentle tune as their father made loose covers for a settee or, a three piece suite. One day as Peter was getting older and more capable of performing tasks, his father asked him to come in and help him. Peter didn't want to help him and so was resentful, as he wanted to get out and play with his friends. So he became impatient ripping and tearing the old material off the chairs, instead of doing the job as his dad had shown him to, by easing the material off the wood with a chisel. This destructive behaviour was taboo in his father's eyes so he told him to get out, adding that he didn't like the temper that was being shown by Peter, telling him that he would need to grow out of it.

Having said that temper was something that father and son had in common, because although his father was a quiet man he had a bad temper and was prone to being moody. To the extent that if he had a little argument with the children's mum, he would go upstairs to the bedroom and lock himself in there. On some occasions he would go out to the cinema, on his own. There was one occasion, that Peter recalls being told about, that his father sat through the whole of Disney's version of Pinocchio, because he didn't check what was showing before he went in. Part of the problem seemed to be that Peter's father had grown up as an only child, because of this he seemed to be used to his own company. Then when he found he had an aptitude for the work he had followed his mother into the upholstery trade, meaning that he would spend more time in his own company. Peter's Gran was very capable and she cleaned upholstery and refurbished items that had become worn.

Something else that Peter recalls being told was that when his Gran was younger there was an occasion when she had completed a job for some high rolling company. Naturally expecting to be paid for her work she went for her payment. However when she got there there was some unpleasantness and the boss refused to pay her. Why? You may ask, well it seems that it is the usual story of a rich married man having his way with an attractive young single girl and then deciding to get rid of her. That would have been fine but his Gran, who was expecting a child, as a result of this liaison, Peter's dad, threatened to expose the boss to his wife for his infidelity. This infuriated the man and he threatened to inform the police about her attempt to blackmail him and have her arrested. So Peter's Gran panicked and did a runner, taking a ship to Canada where she gave birth to her son. The exact place of his birth being in Toronto.

Peter doesn't know how long his Gran stayed there in Toronto, but when she did finally return to the UK she found herself being arrested as she disembarked from the ship in Southampton. As a consequence of this, when she went to trial she was convicted of attempted blackmail and she spent six months in a women's prison. Her son, Peter's Dad was brought up during that time by his mum's sister, this experience seemed to have affected his father in some ways, throughout the rest of his life.

A few years later when he had grown up his dad crashed his motor-bike and broke his leg, jaw and ribs, as a result of the accident he also suffered from concussion. These injuries left him left him prone to occasional fits in later life. There were several continuing consequences of his injuries. Many years later Peter remembers one night when his mother and father had a small argument over something or other. His father left his mother and went to sleep in another bedroom. Later Peter heard his mother calling out frantically for him to come and break down the door as his father was having, as she put it one of his turns. Peter did break down the door, cutting his eyebrow as he fell through, catching it on the electric light switch.

When he recovered himself he found that his father was in a daze, breathing deeply and hanging half out of the bed. Peter lifted him back on to bed and made him as comfortable as he could. Afterwards his father had no memory of anything that had happened. After living an eventful life, during the course of which he served in the Royal Air Force and lived in more than three countries, Canada, the UK, Australia and Tasmania, Peter's father sadly died of Emphysema at the age of seventy five, while living in Tasmania.

Returning to the time of Peter's childhood the kitchen in the house in Broseley only had one window which was five feet up from the floor, if they could have seen through it, they would have had a view of the bakery that was situated just behind the house. However the children very often couldn't see the bakery, the reason being that the bakery had a ton of coke, for their ovens, delivered every week. So the pile of coke was standing a foot higher than the window sill. This meant that all the family could see out of the kitchen window was the top of the coke heap which was piled against the kitchen window.

Peter's school day's started while he was living in Broseley and sadly his first day did not turn out to be a happy one. The reason being that when he walked into the school yard that first morning, a slightly older boy accosted him and for no reason at all began to call him names and saying "I can beat you in a fight"! As he was five years old Peter felt brave enough to reply, "No you can't". The two boys started to fight and Peter's brother Charles was standing there watching the event taking place. To make matters worse he was shouting to other boy, "Go on Johnny hit him"! The shouting continued throughout the fight and Peter became upset and started to cry. Not because of the fight or because he was being physically hurt but, because he just couldn't understand why his brother wanted him to be hurt, or why he wasn't supporting him.

Charles should have been on Peter's side and to this day he doesn't know why his brother was against him, instead of standing up for him. Wanting to give Charles the benefit of the doubt, with the benefit of age and hindsight, Peter now thinks that his brother was frightened and thought that the bigger older boy might start hitting him when he had finished with Peter. Judging by their relationship in later life it is impossible to believe that Charles would have wanted any real harm to come his younger brother, they clearly thought a great deal of each other.

As Peter looks back on his childhood, it is clear that there was certainly fun to had for the children in the kitchen of their home in Broseley. Most of the fun that they had was when their mum was out and their dad was busy working on some furniture in the front room. They really enjoyed playing games then. Particularly when Charles had a friend of his, called Peter Jones round at the house to play. On one of these occasion Peter had tried to make a parachute out of some old rope that the children had found somewhere. They cut the rope into four pieces one for each corner, then using a piece of cloth about the size of a tablecloth, they tied the rope to it. When they had done this they found that they had made had quite a realistic parachute. Having made the parachute they would then take it in turns to leap out from the old copper boiler.

There were lots of games to be played with thelp of this old piece of rope. One game involved each of the children taking turns to be tied to an old rocking chair, then they would struggle until they managed to unfastened the knots and then they would start running round the kitchen, making their escape from whatever situation had caused them to be captured in the first place. Children had good imaginations in those days and they were able to make up some great games, those games would keep them happy for hours. Nowadays it seems if there isn't an expensive electronic toy of some kind to play with, children are bored. Looking back our generation feel that, our times were the best.

There were many occasions when Peter would go across to the local abattoir and while there he would watch the butcher making sausages and black pudding. He found that it was very interesting to see how these things were done and it was a good learning experience for a young boy. The other thing that Peter was able to do was play football with a pig's bladder that had been blown up for him by one the men who worked there and then tied, to stop it going down. He enjoyed kicking the bladder up and down and all around the immediate area of his home and the abattoir. As Peter says, "Who needs and expensive football when there is such a marvellous substitute to play with".

One day Peter was invited to a girl called Kath Wedge's birthday party at the farm house in Church Street Broseley. It was only a short walk from where he and his family lived so he was allowed to go on his own. Kath's father Mr Wedge was the Mayor of Broseley and Peter remembers the farm house well. He recalls that the grounds, which he thought were fantastic were surrounded by a large wall. Part of the wall was also the property dividing line of Peter's friend Colin Shaw's family home. The two of them were good pals in their youth, but when it came time to make their own way in life Colin would take holy orders and become the Reverend Shaw. After years of doing things together Colin's choice left Peter to go his own way, we all know now where that would lead him, to a musical career. Returning to his description the grounds of the farm house Peter remembers that when you went through the gate, you went up a long lane and that after a while you would come to a massive field that had apple, plum and damson trees in it. He used to climb over the wall into the field and get himself a hand full of plums, Peter says that even now he can remember that they were lovely, they tasted so sweet.

The farm house itself was a fine building, it's rooms were large and well furnished. After all Mr Wedge had a reputation to uphold, he was an important man, so everything had to be just so. Anyway Peter was about five years of age at this time and in his immature way he really loved Kath Wedge. Unfortunately for him this feeling was not reciprocated, in fact she never displayed any feeling of any kind for him at all. However we digress, returning to the party all the children enjoyed a really lovely time, then Peter's sister Pamela arrived to tell him it was time to come home. As he was saying his goodbyes, Kath's Mum, Mrs Wedge said to her, "Give Peter a kiss and thank him for coming" Kath looked absolutely mortified by this idea and ran to her mother who lifted her up in to her arms and there she stayed, until Peter had left.

As he thinks back to that day now, he can remember that it was raining and that there was thunder and lightning when he started to walk home. Having said that even though he was we have previously said, only about five years old at that time, the storm didn't frighten him. He just thought how beautiful the lightning was, the thunder didn't then and still to this day has never frightened him. It seems that he has always been comfortable with all the amazing things that nature brings and shares with us all.

There was a big change coming in Peter's life indeed a change for the whole family. The reason for the change became clear when one day in 1946, a lady who looked like a nurse came to the house, after she had been there for a while heard a cry. It was amazing to him as this cry signalled the fact that his mum had had a baby, his sister Leonora had been born. It seems that the lady who looked like a nurse was a Midwife, Peter asked her where the baby had come from. She looked at him and then she pointed to a large tin with blue writing and a picture of a babies face on it, saying, "Out of that tin". For Peter that was it, the mystery was solved, six years old and he now knew where babies came from. As he looks back now Peter realises that the tin was not big enough to hold a baby, but at the time he was completely sure that he knew, it was true, all babies came out of a tin.

As a young boy Peter loved living in Broseley, by the time he was eleven he could go into the woods and fields to run and play. He remembers the sense of freedom that he felt running and jumping over fallen trees and brooks, they were great days, Another memory of Broseley is of the lovely Cottage Hospital, where Peter's talented, and much loved brother Terry was born. Terry would go on to become an excellent guitarist and singer, we will hear more about him later, as in the future, there would be significant happening for Terry and the whole family.

Although up to now things might not have been great school, there were better times to come. When Peter was ten or eleven years old he and Charles auditioned to sing in the schools Christmas choir. The song that they sang at the audition was 'The Holly and the Ivy" and both of the brothers succeeded in being chosen to sing a verse in the boy soprano voice, during the planned concert. When the auditions were over theadmaster called Peter over to the piano and while playing a tune that Peter recognised he told him that he had very good voice. Peter started to sing the melody of the tune being played, on hearing this theadmaster told him to go into another room and keep singing, which he did.

After being told that theadmaster could still hear him singing perfectly and clearly in the other room he sang with great gusto, he loved to sing. Because of this theadmaster told him that he should continue singing because in his opinion, Peter had a great future with such a fine voice. From then on Peter sang everything at every opportunity including, the page next to baritone in 'Good King Wenceslas'. Not to mention the other carols that would be needing to be sung.

Sadly in life people who give support to others can be flawed and so it was with theadmaster As much as he supported Peter and encouraged him to follow his dreams as singer, this man had a darker side. He would go on to assault several young boys, he even attempted this with Peter, who was able to rebuff his advances. As a married man with children of his own, this man who in all other aspects of his life was considered to be a pillar of the community found himself unable to live with the shame of his actions. He took his own life, by putting his head in the gas oven, he could see no hope in life where he could not comply with the law and so he ended it all.

Peter did not dwell on these unfortunate matters, he was after all only a boy, so he carried on singing throughout his school days. While still attending school he entered a talent competition at the Central Cinema in Kidderminster. He took his music with him, he remembers that there was a picture of David Whitfield on it. He was unable to read music and he assumed that he would sing the song in the same key that David Whitfield sang in. So he asked the lady pianist if it was a high key, she replied that it was and he was for the time being happy that all would go well.

When it came to his turn, the pianist played the intro and Peter started to sing. The key was so low that he was struggling to hit the notes, he made some remark, he thinks it was, "Blimey wrong key"! The audience were in fits of laughter and he had never felt so embarrassed in his life. As a result of his lack of musical understanding he came nowhere in the competition. But he took his apparent failure in his stride, he would not allow himself to be diverted from his chosen course. Nothing was going to stop him fulfilling his dream, he knew that he was destined to be a professional singer, so just he kept on practising his art at home in the cellar. He was making use of a jam pan as his microphone, with it hanging from the rafters, he would put his head in the pan to create an echo.

When he was down in the cellar he could be Frankie Laine, Al Martino, Tony Bennett or David Whitfield, whoever he dreamed of being. These men were all big stars then, and they are still remembered today. He would go on to perform on the same stages they had appeared on, he just knew it. How right he was, because he went on to appear in all the major theatres throughout the UK including the London Palladium, to great critical acclaim. As we are all aware the chance to succeed in your chosen field is there for all who dare to pursue their dreams.

Even though Peter enjoyed his life in Broseley there were some sad times. There was a very upsetting and really sad occasion that came about when Peter was about eleven years old. His best friend in those days was a boy called Brian Instone and they naturally spent a lot of time together, getting to know each others family. Now Brian had a younger sister called Marlene who the doctor had diagnosed with chest problems, wrongly as it turned out. Brian's sister had to stay in bed with steam kettles paced all around her, throwing out hot vapour. After she had been in bed for a few days, Peter went to see how she was, only to be told that she had died.

This news was a terrible shock for him because Briand Peter used to take Marlene and her sister Maureen for walks when they were just small children there is no doubt that he was terribly upset by the news. It was a great shock to everyone in the neighbourhood that knew the little girl, when they heard that she had passed away. Peter and Brian were asked to be bearers, at the funeral. Carrying that coffin to the church was a heartbreaking experience that Peter has never forgotten. He stayed in touch with Brian's parents and even more than twenty years later he would still call to their home and see them

As we all know life has to go on even when we lose people that we care about, we don't forget them, but somehow we keep going forward. So it was with Peter and as the months went by life returned to normal and he was just doing the things that young boys do. There was a really enjoyable treat in store for Peter, because in 1952 he went to summer camp with the two upper classes from Broseley School. He feels that this experience is one of his best memories from youthful days. They travelled as a group with teachers to guide them and as he says, "Keep us all in line".

They set up their camp at a place called Nash Court near Hereford. Peter thinks that he was about twelve years of age, going on thirteen, and he was surprised to find that there were girls camped on the other side of the field. However there was a rule in place that said that, no one from the boys camp was allowed to go into the area of the girls camp after 7pm. The trouble was Peter had seen a very pretty dark haired girl, who he wanted to get to know better. Even after all these years he still remembers her name. The reason he remembers is because it was Marlene, the same as his friend Brian Instone's sister. The other thing he also remembers about this girl was that she came from Shrewsbury. They got on with each other straight away and they talked and laughed together all the time. Out of their pocket money they would buy each other little presents, from the local shop, they quickly became as we used to say an item.

On the last day they had decided that they would meet up later that night, after the 7pm curfew. So after they had all been sitting round the camp fire singing songs, the youngsters all returned to their tents and settled down for the night. Not Peter, as dusk fell, he slipped out of his tent and then crawled across the field, on his stomach, as he thought like a commando. He had to be careful because the teachers who were supervising the camp were still up and about. To avoid being seen he had stop his manoeuvring across the ground occasionally. The classes were all in their tents and after he had been cautiously crawling for quite a while he reached Marlene's tent. She had clearly been watching out for him ad when he got there she came out to greet him. The other girls very kindly pretended to be asleep, so the two of them kissed and cuddled for about ten minutes. When it was time to say goodbye for the last time, they promised to keep in touch. Peter doesn't remember if they did, it was all so long ago but as he says, "The idea of that romance is a lovely memory of childhood innocence".

Peter would become friendly with a few girls while he was living in Broseley those he remembers include, Marion Welsh, the Rooney girls who had originally come from Dublin. One girl in particular who keeps coming to mind was is Kath Wedge. The reader will remember her fifth birthday party when she was mortified at the idea of having to kiss him. Her mum and dad, who was also the Mayor, ran the local bakery, and they delivered their bread in horse drawn carriages. It was a truly lovely sight to see a horse pulling a coach full of fresh bread, just after sundown and as Peter recalls, "Oh the wonderful smell that fresh bread gives off, it makes a person hungry just thinking about it". These were very happy days, that included the milkman coming on his rounds with his milk in a big churn, he would fill peoples jugs with milk that he drew from the churn. With the large jug that his family had, Peter collected many pints of milk for his mum in that way.

Now Peter's school days were passing quickly but not always happily. He remembers that one day when he went into his classroom, early for a lesson, Peter found a young lad sitting very quietly on his own. The boy looked very thin and pale, when he asked the boy why he wasn't outside playing, the boy replied "I am not allowed to". At this point Peter realised that the boy must have been very ill indeed if he wasn't allowed to play. After that first meeting he took the time to spend time with and talk to the boy, and this new friendship continued for a few months. One day when he went to meet and talk with boy as usual, Peter found that the lad was missing from school, he was rather puzzled by this because even though the boy was poorly he always attended school.

He would find out later that the lad had tragically died, as you might expect this was shocking news for him. Peter was aware that the lad lived in Ironbridge, so he felt that he ought to go and visit his friends family so that he could express his condolences. It was with a heavy heart he walked to Ironbridge, taking the path that he knew through the woods. When he got the boys home he found that his mother, was naturally in a state of great distress. When she opened the door and saw Peter standing there she invited him in and showed him her sons' coffin, when he saw the coffin, he was very upset. As he thinks back about the event, Peter remembers that he and the boys mother cried together.

Authors note: Sadly as those of us who were around in those days were only to aware that it was all to common to have a classmate die. Peter was clearly a very kind and considerate boy, who showed great compassion as to my knowledge no pupil from my school ever visited a bereaved parent, even though I can remember three children who died during that time. Having said that although I was not at the same school as David Hare, I did visit his parents after he died following an unsuccessful operation to remove a brain tumour. Like Peter I found the experience devastating. Although my feelings were nothing compared to those of David's parents.

Time moves quickly when you are young and Peter's sadness at the loss of his young friend was behind him by the time Christmas came round. He remembers that Christmas in Broseley was a very happy time, it always seemed to snow and at night the moon lit up the crisp white snow with a lovely glow. That particular year, the boys were wishing out loud for their presents, Charles was keen to have a racing bike and Peter wanted a bow and arrows and maybe a small dagger. Their sister Pamela wanted, well Peter doesn't remember, although he is sure it would have been some thing that a girl in those times would like, perhaps a doll or a pram. There were just the three of them wishing for their presents that Christmas it was before younger brother Terry was born.

As he looks back Peter remembers the joy he felt on that Christmas morning when he opened his eyes and saw leaning there against the wall, in the corner of the bedroom a real bow that stood five feet tall, it had three beautiful arrows, with all the trimmings. Even though he was really excited he remembers his dad telling him that the arrows were very expensive, 18 shilling and 6 pence each, he feels that would equate to about £10 each in today's money. He was delighted to find that he also had a small sheath knife in its scabbard. His dad told him to be careful where he fired the bow, warning him to always make sure that there was no one in range of where he was firing his arrows.

He couldn't wait to get out on the long field near the church so that he could test the strength of his bow. When he did get out he took a mate with him so that he could watch Peter try the bow out. He was absolutely thrilled, he and his mate went in to the long field and they spent the whole morning shooting, each firing an arrow in turn. After a while Peter wanted to try something more difficult, looking around he could see that there was a tree that was at least in his mind 100 feet tall. He said to his mate "I am going to shoot an arrow over to that tree, to see if I can hit". He stood up as tall and erect as he could, then he notched the arrow in his bow string and pulled back hard on the bow, when he felt ready he let the arrow fly. They both ran to the tree, eager to see if he had hit, when they got there they looked all around searching the tree trunk and the ground but they couldn't find the arrow even though the grass in the field was well cut.

Peter was starting to panic, how could he go home and tell his dad that he had lost an arrow on the first occasion that he had used the bow? He was feeling anxious, his mouth dried up, which is a sure sign of stress. Over and over he asked the silent question, "What could he do"? Then his mate said, " I know let's go to church, we can pray about it". Broseley church was only about half a mile away so they collected the other arrows and the bow and then they set off to walk to the church. When they got there they went inside together and knelt down to say the Lord's Prayer, when they had done that Peter asked God for his help in finding the lost arrow.

They remained in church on their knees for some time, then they decided to go and have one last look for the lost arrow. As they got back to the tree Peter gave a cry of relief, there in sticking in the ground at the base of the tree was his missing arrow. Think what you will readers, but for these two boys, God had granted them a miracle, for them there could never be any other explanation. There is no doubt that this was a Christmas to remember, because their faith in God had been strengthened.

While we are remembering Christmas times in Broseley, we should be aware that by the age of ten Peter was an established member of the church choir. Indeed he was the lead boy soprano in many of the solo recitals. Always present on Sundays he also attended on Saturdays and when ever he had free time, in order to ring the church bells. This skill is not as easy as it may look and one occasion, when someone Peter does not remember their name, was ringing one of the big bells, they missed grabbing the sally as it came down, the person was dragged up to the ceiling banging his head. This person was very lucky indeed as he did not receive any serious injuries, after that Peter was always very careful when he was carrying out that task.

There was something that Peter and his brother Charles always did at Christmas time, they used to go out carol singing, mainly for the older people who really appreciated hearing a carol or two at

Christmas. On the occasion that he recalls Peter was about ten years old and his brother was about thirteen years old. They had tried to coax their sister to come out with them but all to no avail, she felt she had better things to do with her time. So on the day he remembers, brother Charles and his friend Peter Jones had an idea, they would spin a coin to decide whether they would walk out in a northerly or southerly direction. Right they said, "If it lands on heads we will all head south if it lands on tails we all go north".

They spun the coin and it landed on tails, in their mind that was pointing them to Bridgenorth, Now Bridgnorth is about six miles from Broseley but filled with boyish enthusiasm Peter said, "If we get there, I have enough money for our bus fare, so we can come back home to Broseley by bus". At this point Peter Jones got nervous saying, "I don't think I can go that far, I have to be home for my lunch in about half an hour". Going on to say, "No, I can't come". So the two brothers said cheerio to their friend and set off to walk to their destination.

They walked and walked, becoming very tired, thinking to themselves, will we ever get there. Eventually they reached the outskirts of Bridgnorth. They had been walking for at least three hours, they kept walking until they saw the Broseley bus stop. With a great deal of relief at having reached the end of their epic trek, they waited patiently for their bus home to arrive. There would be no carols for the elderly that day. Well where the two boys in for a shock because when the bus pulled at the stop, they saw their mother on the bus.

She was sitting in a window seat looking out at them with a face like thunder.

In their naivety the brothers wondered what could possibly be wrong, why did their mum look so annoyed. After all they had set out with such good intentions and at least they had not got lost. Well they didn't have to wait long for answer, because their mother met them as they boarded the bus, saying to them in a very firm voice, "Where have you boys been for the last four hours"? "How dare you go off like that without a word to anyone, not even telling me or your father where you were going". She carried on, " You are in very serious trouble, with your father, just you wait until you get home"!! There were a few more words from her delivered in a similar vein. When the two boys arrived home, they were already filled with apprehension. Things got worse when they were greeted by their fathers stern face, because they could see that he was holding a cane in his hand. This sight made both boys feel very nervous indeed. It was just too much for them to be able to comprehend how things could have gone so wrong.

Although their father was clearly very relieved to see them home he endeavoured to maintain a serious expression as he delivered his rebuke for what he termed their disgraceful behaviour. "You can both get upstairs to your bedroom, there will be no tea for you tonight". Then he added, "Before you go one of you can hold out your hands", Peter did as he was told and each hand was swiped in turn, his brother Charles received the same punishment. As they both said afterwards, "Wow that certainly stung the fingers"! They both trudged upstairs feeling a bit hard done by, after all they were very hungry but they had not been given any grub, what a way to end to the day. Feeling that they had been quite hard done by they tried to go to sleep, but hunger pangs were keeping them awake. However they felt quite a lot better and all misery soon drifted away when about an hour later their mother crept upstairs with soup, bread rolls and loads of butter. They asked themselves, "When had food ever tasted so good"?

As it is with most families the Hazelwoods found during the course of their daily lives that there were ups and downs to contend with. There were mixture of happy and sad events that transpired while the family were living there. The loss of his friends sister and they boy from school who died are all too real reminders and memories of how hard life can be. But it is not possible for a young boy like Peter to always dwell on sad times his thoughts more often drift to happier memories. Sometimes as he looks back Peter remembers the happiness that visits from his Gran brought him, she was always doing little things that made him want to spend more time with her.

When she came back to stay with the family he used to come in from school to smell the scent of her Benson and Hedges snuff pervading the air. He recalls liking that smell very much, but that he probably liked it more because smelling that, meant that his Gran was there. She always brought little treats for the children when she visited. There would be sweet treats when she came, usually a box of meringues or sometimes chocolate éclairs would be in her bag. The sweetness was so welcome and seeing her brought a thrill that was almost too much excitement for a young boy. There is no doubt that Peter loved his Gran very much.

As we read earlier his grandmother was a cleaner and repairer of furnishings, she gained work by calling on certain houses that looked respectable if a little worn. She would knock on the door of such a house and ask if their furnishing needed any cleaning or repair, three piece suites or chairs usually. If a chair needed patching or a leather settee needed any refurbishment she was more than capable of making good the damage. Because of this she invariably came home with goodies for the family, the only downfall was that she loved to have a drink and if she had been paid she would sometimes imbibe more than she should.

One day she when came home, Peter thinks that it must have been about 9pm in the evening and it was clear she had been drinking too much of her favourite tipple. One Peter's sisters friends had called in and they were standing talking at the bottom of the stairs. Gran walked up the stairs from behind them carrying a very large bottle of cider that she was taking up to her room. Suddenly there was a loud bang, Gran had dropped the bottle of cider, then when it hit one of the stairs it burst it's top and cider sprayed all up the wall. Then the bottle rolled down the stairs and down the hallway coming to a stop at his sisters feet, leaving small river-lets of cider, that were running across the hall floor. The shock was too much for his Gran, in despair at her loss she had to be escorted to bed by his Mum and Dad, the memory of this event still makes Peter smile.

There was another incident to do with Peter's Gran that still makes him laugh out loud. This memory involved an incident with his brother Charles even now as he recounts it, Peter really laughs at the thought of it. There was a local bully, whose nickname was Leather arse, Peter has no real explanation for his nickname, but no doubt readers may think of one or two. He came from the area down Foundry Lane, he always pushing people around. On this occasion Leather arse had given Peter's brother Charles a good hiding. This action enraged their Gran, because she just wouldn't stand for anyone hurting any of her grandchildren. So she waited in the lane for this man to come home from work. When she saw him coming on his bike, she shouted "Leather arse"! He alighted from his bike saying to their grandmother, "What do you want"? Without another word she ran towards him produced a willow stick that she had surreptitiously hidden up her sleeve and proceeded whack Leather arse all the way home to his house. It was great fun for Peter to see his Gran carry out this action and there no more trouble from Leather arse for the Hazelwood family.

As he looks back now Peter seems to think he was a bit of a clown during his school-days. So much so that his teacher used to get him up in front of the class to do impersonations of relatively well known people of the day. People like Winston Churchill, the King and sometimes, Country singers. He did his best to copy these people, he looks back now and thinks that maybe his impersonations were not as good as he thought at the time. Having said that his school friends seemed to like the performances he gave, unless they were just being kind. On one occasion the school decided to present a play for the parents of the children in the class, the script was made up and the children were excited by the idea of entertaining their mums and dads. The show would be presented at the Town Hall, rehearsals began. There would even be miming, unfortunately there were no props or scenery, in Peter's case the only help he had was a chair.

Eventually the great day arrived, all the parents including Peter's mum came to the Town Hall. He and the other children ad-libbed their acts and in the space of half an hour the play was finished, Peter was sure that this was the beginning of a great acting career, he would be the next Laurence Olivier. On the way home he was full of enthusiasm, holding on to his mother's hand he looked up at her and waited for her praise. There was none to be had, all his mum said about the show was, "I thought you would have had some scenery". That was her only comment, Peter was completely deflated by her apparent disinterest and he completely lost all ambition to be a great actor. As Peter says now, "In support of my mum, the show was very amateurish and it really wasn't well presented or performed, I don't think her disappointment was in me, more in the school".

Not long after this none event the family would move again, this time to Kidderminster in Worcester. There was another addition to the family now, Peter now had a little brother Terry who had recently been born. They clearly needed a bigger house so their dad had found them what turned out to be a much larger house with four bedrooms, having said that the house did not have an inside toilet. They would have to walk over a lane to an outbuilding, when they wanted to go to the toilet. The house did have a lovely large garden with an apple tree, this tree produced lovely Bramley apples. Over a period of time their father had a garage built, and he would use this building as his workshop. Parties would also be held in the garage, although it was a cold place and very hard to heat. In spite of the cold Peter recalls that the parties were always fun.

Chapter Three

Kidderminster
New school, voice breaks, athletics champion, starting work.

This was a good move for the family who were very happy in their new home on Bewdley Hill, Kidderminster, Worcester. Peter and his brother Charles were on the top floor sharing a bedroom across the landing from their sister Pamela. Their parents had one of bedrooms on the landing below, because he was still only a baby they shared their room with Terry. All in all there was more space for the family and having a garden to play in was a dream come true for the children. Mum, Dad and the children were pleased to have this very comfortable place to live.

So it was that 1951 Peter started at Sladen Secondary Modern School in form 3b. He was a likeable boy and he fitted in very well and quickly made many friends. He also proved to be diligent in his studies and was soon upgraded to the upper fourth form. Academically and socially Peter was doing very well in the environment provided by Sladen Secondary. Of course he still loved to sing and this was the time when his voice started to break, giving a hint of the fabulous voice he would have when he matured. For Peter the voice breaking was a gentle process and he hardly noticed that it was happening until he tried singing some songs that he knew well and found that he was unable to reach some of the higher notes.

Because he always had his planned future career in mind Peter thought that the way to overcome this change would be to concentrate his voice into a tenor range so he practised that. He was very pleased to find that as time progressed he was very comfortable, vocally, when he was singing in this register. When we hear his remarkable voice today it is strange to think that as a young boy Peter was able without any real musical knowledge at the time to recognise the development path his voice needed to take.

During Peter's time at Sladen Secondary Modern School he would excel in several sports, he won the short burst runs, sprints as they are called today 100 yards and the 200 yards by some considerable distance from his competitors. (There were no metric measurements in those days). He also won the Discus, High Jump and Shot Putt. In 1954 Peter represented the County of Worcestershire at the All England Championship, which were held in Ashington Northumberland that year. He competed in the Shot Putt, with unexpected success, given that some of the other competitors were older and bigger. He was showing great promise for the future in this event and as with everything he has ever attempted Peter put 100% effort in to improving his ability to putt the shot..

One day having spent the whole day practising on the large playing field with the shot putt he passed the Worcestershire record and then the All England record. His PE teacher asked him how long he had been practising for the event. Peter replied, "About two months". The PE teacher was amazed that he had done so well so fast. He needed to be sure that the shot was the correct weight so he had the shot weighed at the local grocers, it was only six pounds in weight. Now the correct weight of a junior shot at that time was 8lbs 13oz, this meant that Peter had been practising with a shot that was 2lbs 13oz under weight, so it was no wonder with his great natural strength and improving technique that he was achieving such distances.

The bad news was that the championships were only two weeks away. He started to practice with the correct weight but it felt heavy, in comparison to the one he was used to, and he didn't do very well, coming eighth in the championships. Peter was mortified, the practice with the lighter weight was blamed and the phrase that he used at the time was "if only"! This set back was soon forgotten as he went on to break three records and became the schools athletics captain. The school had a great 4x100 yard relay team, comprising Peter, Bob White, Tony Wright and Neil ? Sadly Neil's surname escapes Peter now, but this team won most of the 4x100 yard races that they competed in throughout his time at Sladen Secondary Modern School.

All to soon it was time to leave school and start the preparation for adult life. Peter was unable to settle in any job that he considered mundane. This meant that, he went through several jobs in a very short time. Those jobs included being a lab assistant. During the time he worked at the science lab he would sample things like the lanolin content in sheep's wool, they also gave him several similar tasks. However he soon got tired of this job, finding it really boring, so it wasn't long before he left. However leaving jobs on a regular basis was not a problem at that time, because jobs were easy to come by in the 1950's. So Peter, having entered the world of science, was very very quickly able to find another job, this time at Hepworths Tailors. Again he would soon leave there for employment at Burton's the Tailors, he was developing a very nomadic outlook to his work.

Peter was employed in the tailoring industry until he was fifteen and a half years old, but he was still a long way from finding his vocation. It was at that point his friend and former athletics team mate, Bob White asked him why he didn't join the local Police Force as a cadet. He thought this sounded like a good idea so he signed up, looking back he enjoyed every minute of his time as a police cadet. Peter went on to spend two years in the Motor Patrol Department, only leaving when he made the decision to join The Grenadier Guards. His intention was to do three years as a guardsman and then return to the Police Force when he was demobbed. He felt that in this way he would have some real experience of life outside the police force which would stand him in good stead later on. Of course he still hadn't lost sight of his real ambition, he still wanted to get up on stage and sing.

So Christmas was approaching and Peter just knew that it would be the last Christmas he would spend in Kidderminster. He decided to spend the last night with his friend Bob White. He invited his friend to the house and Bob rode his bike to Peter's home at Bewdley Hill, when he arrived there everyone else had gone out, so the two friends had a drink of Peter's mum's port, to celebrate Christmas and wish each other luck. Bob was staying on as a Police Cadet and when they parted company it was in a snow storm, Peter really wondered how Bob was going to get home on his bike, but he would be on a train to London the next morning so he just had to trust that Bob was home safe.

When he arrived at the Guards Depot, Peter's first impression was that it looked like a prison camp, it was nothing like what he had imagined. Right next door to the Depot was a Mental Hospital, great thought Peter, if I don't make it as a Grenadier Guard they can shove me in next door. When he and other new recruits arrived they were greeted by a trained soldier at the gate of the depot, this soldier took his details without giving him so much as a smile. Peter wondered what sort of life he was coming to. The soldier then pointed them in the direction of the accommodation blocks, the barrack rooms and somehow they found themselves in the NAAFI canteen, where they waited for a guardsman to find them and tell them what to do next.

When the recruits were finally found, they were feeling quite unwanted and wondering why they had bothered to turn up. The first thing that happened was that they were taken to the stores where they were issued with their kit, the usual things, boots, gaiters, khaki drills and all the rest of the normal equipment for new men. The first instruction was to burn the leather dimples off their boots. Peter says that he was stupid enough to ask "How"? "With anything you can find", was the reply. The new recruits were just left to fathom a way of doing it, the whole situation was bewildering.

It was with some trepidation that they all acquired spoons from the canteen and someone found some candles which they lit, then they started to heat the spoons over them. When they were hot they then applied them to the boots. This was a painstaking job, because they were only able to burn off an inch diameter of the dimples in about two hours. The following morning it was reveille at 6 am, then they were all marched down to the canteen with their cutlery clasped behind their backs, at a very quick pace. Afterwards they came back at a the same pace still without any clue as to what was going on, or happening to them.

Now when he attended Sladen Secondary Modern School, Peter boxed for the school. He never really liked the sport, although he did appreciate the dedication that boxers need to succeed in their chosen sport. He never lost a bout while he was on the school team, so it was a simple step to join the Grenadiers Boxing Team. They had a guy called Peter Priseman in their squad, he was the North London Champion. They were sparring partners and one day Peter released a right cross that made Priseman's nose bleed, he apologised profusely, hoping that the guy wouldn't take offence. He had seen peoples jaws dislocated in the ring, this was something that he did not want to happen either to him or an opponent. There was no problem with

Peter Priseman, who understood the risks that came in the ring. As it turned out Peter only fought once while he was serving in the Grenadiers and the fight was stopped in his favour, Peter Hazelwood was more than happy to retire undefeated.

Time was passing with his training and Peter thinks that he must have been at the depot for a couple of weeks when from his point of view disaster struck. On the occasion in question, he had gone into the barrack room for some recreation time. When he entered the room he found that it was empty, except for one trained soldier, so called because they had some service in and therefore had the ability to help the sergeant, with the training of recruits. As Peter entered the room the trained soldier threw a rugby ball to him, he caught it and threw it back, The ball was returned to him this time with a looping pass that was lobbed high, Peter caught that and thought "Right, I will make him dive for this one".

He swiftly sent the ball back, it was flying across the room but as it was travelling it's flight took it across the middle of the barrack room table, the ball was low enough at this point to knock something over on the table. Unfortunately for Peter it did, the ball hit a bottle of black marking ink that had been left open on the table. The ball sent the bottle flying up into the air as if it had been propelled by a rocket, the black marking ink was emptied all over the table and the floor. To make matters worse it sent a few drops through the air and they splashed on to a freshly pressed and ironed uniform,which was hanging over a locker waiting to be worn.

"You did that on purpose Hazelwood"! The trained soldier screamed, "No it was a complete accident". Replied Peter, truthfully. The trained soldier ran across the room to inspect what damage had been done. The damage was considerable, the table and the floor were considerably stained, not to mention the damage to someone's uniform. Peter remembers asking himself at the time, "Oh God why did I have to throw the ball back"? He was really in trouble, "Well you can F***ing well clean up this mess, get a razor blade and scrape the floor" came the order. This meant that Peter was on his hands and knees scraping away at the ink stain for at least an hour. His efforts had no effect, except to make the wood look a shade lighter. Eventually the trained soldier, seeing that the task was hopeless, told him to stop, which Peter did immediately and gratefully. Not for the first time he was questioning the wisdom of his decision to join up.

There was a really nasty incident that occurred on the square at Caterham Guards Depot. Everyone was on parade and the recruits were being drilled by the Regimental Sergeant Major. They were all trying to obey every order that he yelled at them. Peter can remember one soldier being yelled at and put under close arrest for some mistake he had made. So he was determined that he would not to suffer the same fate. With full concentration Peter marched on to the parade ground, he was primed, on red alert, he would follow each instruction to the letter. He heard the order, fix bayonets ring out, he did this no problem and for the next few minutes they drilled with their bayonets fixed. Then heard the words, "Halt stand easy, unfix bayonets". He was struggling to unfix his bayonet, he struggled but as he says, "I just couldn't get the bloody thing off".

He was really panicking, then horror of horrors heard the awful sound, the words that he had been dreading, the sound of the Sergeant Major bellowing, "Put that man under close arrest"! He stood there and casually removed the bayonet, he couldn't believe it after all his struggling it eventually came off. Now it was free in his hand, he was resigned to his fate so he stood and waited, hearing the sound of boots marching towards him. Peter was feeling very sick as he waited, because he did not know what happened to a Grenadier, after he had been marched at full speed to the guardhouse. But suddenly it was all over, and thank God it wasn't happening to him, it was some other poor sod standing directly behind him. He had heard that the Sergeant Major who was nicknamed 'Hawkeye', never missed anything. Well to Peters great relief he missed something that day, Private Hazelwood struggling in great distress. Thank God he missed that!

Peter had a wonderful surprise when his Gran came to live in Caterham which was just down the road from the camp. Her presence in the area was much appreciated by him, as she would provide him with cigarettes and other items that were hard for him to either get or afford at this time. The recruits were always short of certain items, things that were used by everyone. For example the TS would make use of certain things including methylated spirits and even he would run out. So one occasion the TS asked Peter if he could get him some methylated spirits, well he couldn't, but when he asked his Gran to help him find some she was able to get some for him.

When he handed over the liquid to the TS, too his great delight he was rewarded with a pass, enabling him to go out of camp for a few hours. He met up with his Grand they took the opportunity to go for a few beers. He thought it would be a good move to bring a couple bottles of beer back for the TS back to camp with him. When he got back to the depot, he threw the bottles of beer over the 8 foot fence where they could land on soft grass. He did this because he knew that the guard on the gate would confiscate them, if he tried to carry them in. When he got in to the camp he retrieved them and he gave them to the TS. The beer was well received and Peter thinks that by this time the TS had forgiven him for the accident with the marking ink. In fact they seemed to be getting on quite well.

The new recruits practised their drill in the big square in Caterham and also on long marches around the local countryside. For these marches the recruits had to wear greatcoats, for those readers who have not served in the armed forces a greatcoat is a long overcoat. They did not wear their Khaki drill trousers. On that particular day the only thing they wore apart from their greatcoats were socks and boots. While they were out they had to pass the local hospital for the mentally infirm, when they did there would always be some of the inmates watching them. As the soldiers were marching past, some of those inmates would mimic the soldiers by marching along the perimeter fence with a hoe or a spade over their shoulders. The recruits found this mimicry quite amusing in a rather sad way.

One day they were doing some running as an exercise and for some reason Peter wasn't sure whether the sergeant had a liking for, or maybe even a dislike for him. He would gee him up comments like, "Keep going Hazelwood". Or. "Don't drop behind"! This annoyed Peter so he approached the sergeant when the exercise was over saying, "Why all the mickey taking sergeant"? "You know I could beat you in a 100 yard sprint"! An argument ensued, the sergeant saying, "You think so", Peter replied, "Yes I do" They were being egged on by the rest of the squad who were mostly on Peter's side, he was wearing army trousers and plimsolls, so the sergeant said, "Prove it"! They both lined up and then someone shouted "Go". Peter went as fast as his legs would carry him and he seemed to be in front by the 50 yard mark, but then in his peripheral vision Peter saw that the sergeant had pulled slightly ahead, then suddenly the race was over, the sergeant had won.

This defeat left Peter feeling a bit forlorn, because he had felt confident of his ability to win the race. The disappointment was almost too much to bear, he was after all a multiple schoolboy sprint champion, who had no reason to doubt his speed. However his spirits were soon lifted because heard later that the sergeant was the Grenadier Guards 100 yards dash champion! This news took away any disappointment at the defeat, because he had come very close to winning, so his confidence was restored. However there would more altercations with this sergeant over the next few weeks, not because he treated Peter badly but because he would bully a certain lad in the squad unmercifully. This behaviour appalled Peter and he was never slow to tell the sergeant in no uncertain terms what he thought of his behaviour. Authors note: As Peter has told me in his own words, "I despise bullies in every way, I have a real deep rooted hatred of them". This an opinion, one of many that he holds, that I find that we both share.

There were times when Peter and the other recruits would be sent to the coke bunkers to collect coke for the stove in the barrack room. On these occasions, his mates having heard him sing before, would call out "Sing us a song Pete". So he would climb up on top of the black heap of coke and sing, "I'll walk with God". This can be a very apt choice because sometimes when life is not going as we hope, this hymn is very inspirational. Authors note: Very apt indeed because this song has been an inspiration throughout my life. From time to time the recruits would be allowed a small party. On these occasions were they would be allowed to wind down a bit and let off a bit of steam. Entertainment would provided in the form of the band, now there was a recruit from the Coldstream Guards who would always get up and sing a few songs, he had a very pleasant voice and he pleased the crowd. Peter himself would be encouraged to sing, something as we have learned, he always enjoyed. This reference to the two vocalists leads to another story, one that Peter says he will tell us later in the book.

One day the recruits were told that there was to be a full kit inspection, this involved a well made bed and all kit laid out in good order on that bed. After the inspection a thirty six hour pass would be issued to all the recruits all who passed. But, anyone who failed the inspection would not be issued with a pass and would have to remain camp. Peter really wanted to go home, as he said in his own words, "Oh how I wanted to go home"! He was eager to impress, and determined to succeed, he missed his dinner in order to get a good bed made up and laid out with his kit. Everyone was rushing round, they all knew how important this inspection was. The one piece of kit Peter didn't possess was a button polisher, but someone had a spare and they kindly said that they would lend it to him for the inspection. When they handed the button polisher over to him, Peter placed it in a nice position his bed and then he eagerly awaited the inspection.

Later that day a young Lieutenant entered the room and went round inspecting the specially laid out kits. When he got to Peter's bed he picked up the button polisher and examined it, in great detail. Horror of horrors the item was marked with a fingerprint on the inner side. The response of the officer seemed out of proportion to such a minor indiscretion Peters bed and it's contents were immediately thrown over onto the floor. Peter had been standing to attention, during the inspection, at the point were his bedding hit the floor, he suddenly felt an overwhelming blackness engulf him, his legs started to buckle and he ran forward, he had no control over his legs or his feet and he crashed to floor in a dead faint.

The next thing he knew he was sitting on a chair by his bed, the first words heard were from the sergeant who was saying, "You won't be going home today Hazelwood". "Why not sergeant"? Asked a dismayed Peter. "Because you are not well, you just passed out". The sergeant replied. "But I'm OK, I just felt a bit faint, I think it was because I missed my dinner". "Well you will have to prove that you are fit by running up the stairs from the bottom to the top, with your full kit on. "I'll do it Sergeant"! Replied an very anxious Peter. This task he was able to achieve, no problem, so thankfully Peter got to go on his Thirty six hour pass. Once again, he thanked God.

Peter had already met the lady who would become his first wife, her name was June. He had been introduced to her by her sister Ann, he liked Ann's then boyfriend, who is now her husband a lot. This chap was a very good pianist and had played piano on a recording that Peter made in a studio in Mill Street, Kidderminster. June was still living at home with her mother on a small estate in Wilden Top near Stourport. At this time she was sixteen and Peter was seventeen, so they both felt that they were ready for love. Because June was a real tomboy, Peter found that she was great fun and added that he found her very attractive. He remembers that she was fond of walking around in her bare feet and Peter thinks that if it had been the 1960's rather than the late fifties, she would have been a hippy. When they had been going out together for a few months he had surprised her with the news that he had enlisted in the Grenadier Guards. Having told her the news, in September 1957 they had said their goodbyes and he left to join the Queens Regiment, he was sure that was the end of their relationship.

Peter having enjoyed the opportunity to go home soon found himself with another reason to feel faint because June, the young lady that he had been courting from Stourport had some unexpected news for him. She told Peter that she was pregnant, so being a thoroughly decent chap and a true gentleman he resolved to marry her. In order to fulfil his intention as a serving soldier he would need permission to enter into holy matrimony. So when he got back to camp he asked the Sergeant for leave to get married, permission to do this and explained the reason why. When the sergeant heard this news, permission was duly granted. Peter was give a forty eight hour pass and wearing his guardsman's ceremonial uniform, red tunic, dark worsted trousers, peaked cap, and a great blue cape he set out to get married. He looked absolutely magnificent and with his lovely bride at his side they made a splendid couple. After the ceremony the time passed by so quickly, his forty eight hours of freedom were up and Peter soon found himself back in the depot ready to start another days duty.

By now Peter was spending a lot of time wondering if he had done the right thing by joining up. He was very homesick, he really thought that he should be at home, he was feeling unhappy and didn't know what to do. As he looked for the answer to his dilemma he realised that the lads that he was training with all thought he must have been crazy to not to have stayed in Civvy Street and tried to get on the route that would lead to him climbing the ladder to singing fame. The more he thought about it, the more he agreed with them so with his fellow recruits advice in mind Peter, not without a feeling of trepidation, approached the sergeant and asked about the possibility of buying himself out of the service.

The sergeant was disappointed when heard that Peter wanted to get out saying, "You should stay in", Then he added, " If you stay in you will be promoted within six months". He went on to say, "I do like your voice but I really think that you should be guardsman". The reason the sergeant was able to comment on Peter's, voice was that he had been given an acetate of two songs that Peter had recorded at the age of fifteen, titled, "Two Different Worlds" and "It's Almost Tomorrow", so he was aware of the vocal talent that this recruit possessed. Peter asks the rhetorical questions, "I wonder if he or his family still has those recordings"? "Will I ever know"? Anyway the result of their conversation was that Peter bought himself out of the guards for the sum of £25. He said farewell to his mates and some of the drill soldiers who he had got on well with and set out to pursue his dream. Authors note: Just to give the reader some idea of the value of £25 back then, it was equivalent to about five weeks wages for me and many others.

So there he was out of the guards at eighteen and a half years of age, needing to make a fresh start. He had no home of his own and he had no job, no source of income. They were living with his seventeen year old wife June's mother and this was not a happy arrangement.

Looking back now Peter realises they were both much too young to settle down and start a family. Having said that he does know of other young couples who were able to make a go of it, but he and June were not ready for total commitment. Looking back now, he realises that he did not try hard enough to do anything or get anywhere with his life at that time. He didn't even try to find them a home of their own, he had one dream and it was music, he wanted to devote himself to that, nothing else mattered.

Looking back Peter knows how selfish that must seem, but as he says, "Hindsight is a wonderful thing". Would he or could he have done things differently? Who knows? At that age none of us are able to make all the right decisions, he only knows that he did his best and that he has never set out to deliberately hurt anyone. To make things more difficult their daughter Katrina had been born by this time and they were all living in one room – not a great start. The close proximity to each other made things very tense, and he and June were really struggling to get along.

It was clear that their marriage would not last long in these circumstances and that assumption was not long in being proved right. Something that Peter remembers enjoying at the time was walking his daughter, in her pram across the common. This break from the oppressive atmosphere he was feeling the house, gave them some quiet time together during this time he would sing to her. One day he was singing to her as they sheltered from a rainstorm, as usual a few of the local kids had followed him and they listened as he sang.

It seemed to him that the pleasure they obviously took in the sound of his voice was telling him something, he resolved to take some action and speak to June about the future.

So one day, quite soon after he came to this decision, when he was out walking with June, Peter asked her if she thought there was any point in them staying married. She replied that she didn't think there was, in fact she thought they should part company as soon as possible. Because he agreed with her on this point their break up was an amicable one, with Peter offering as much maintenance as he could manage for Katrina's support. Peter felt very sad when he left June and Katrina but he hoped this parting would be the best thing for them all. He got in touch with his Uncle Bill who was living in the Maida Vale district of London, telling him the situation that he was now in. Eager to help him his uncle said he would try and find Peter a job and somewhere to stay, if he moved down there. During the time he was waiting he made friends with his brothers girlfriend. In fact they became got very close, but he made it clear that as he was leaving to try and find work in London and hopefully make a career in show business, the relationship might not last. The young lady seemed happy to accept this basis for their relationship.

Chapter Four

London beckons

The time passed by and the news that Peter had been waiting for eventually arrived, and he found himself on the train to London. His uncle met him on arrival and let Peter stay with him while he was looking for a place of his own. Uncle Bill had found him a job as a trainee chef at the Victoria Servicemen's Club. Having said that the job title was a bit grand, in reality he was just a glorified veg preparer really, peeling spuds and carrots etc. However he stuck at the job and he soon became proficient at providing breakfast for all the people who came in. He also found himself able to take a couple of eggs home with him in the hood of his duffle coat, for his own and Uncle Bill's tea.

Peter and his Uncle Bill fitted in well together and many happy evenings were spent in each others company, they even enjoyed the occasional game of chess, that was of course when they weren't busy talking and planning Peter's musical career. One night his Uncle Bill was reading the evening paper and he noticed an advert which read, "Singing Competition at the Kingsbury Ballroom, first prize £20. He pointed it out to Peter, Who said "I must try for that", while saying that he was noting the date and the time, it was a Saturday, it would be a momentous day, it was the beginning of changing times, his musical dream would be getting a kick start.

So on that Saturday, Peter and his Uncle Bill made their way to the Kingsbury Ballroom. When they arrived he gave his name and the title of the song he had chosen to sing to the organisers. The song would be Gigi, this was a lovely number from the film of the same name. We will all remember that the film starred, Leslie Caron, Maurice Chevalier and Louis Jordan. Peter says, "Maybe I am being a bit big headed because I never actually saw the film, yet I can still remember most of the cast". I personally, as the author having got to know Peter, rather well, can tell you that he has never been big headed or arrogant about anything. Any way getting back to the story, it would seem that it was around this time that Peter adopted the stage name of Peter Wynne in tribute to his uncle Furness Wynne Williams who had been an outstanding Operatic singer. Furness' it should be known had been principle tenor at Covent Garden for three seasons. He also sang at La Scala in Miland in the major Operatic Theatres all over the world. Furness or Peter as he was also known in the Operatic world became a close friend of the great Enrico Caruso.

We return to the contest, It seems that there were about ten entrants one of whom was a young and very good looking girl, who seemed to have brought many friends or admirers with her. The show started and the young girl went on about sixth in the line up, Peter is sure that she sang a Shirley Bassey number. The audience gave her a really loud ovation, Peter recalls that he thought to himself, "Wow, I don't have much of a chance against her". "I certainly haven't got her following, I only have my Uncle Bill with me". He was in for a surprise because the audience really got behind him and he received the loudest applause. Much to his great surprise he had won, in what was only his second attempt at a talent contest. Peter had the Twenty quid first prize as well. He was so pleased with the win that he took Uncle Bill out that night and treated them both to sirloin steak at Lyons Corner House at Marble Arch. He was following his dream and after this unexpected success he had no doubt that a life in show business was on the cards for him.

One of the things Uncle Bill and Peter had been talking about was the idea of going on stage as a duo or a trio. The reason for this was that his uncle was still quite young and more importantly Bill had a really good baritone voice, plus he was a very healthy and fit man. They were filled with enthusiasm for this idea so they auditioned a girl who worked at Marks and Spencers for the third place in the trio, however this idea was not a success. The reason being as Peter says, "After rehearsals it became clear that without being too conceited, she seemed to be more interested in me than actually singing with the trio that we were trying to set up". He spoke to Uncle Bill and they agreed that they should let the girl go. When the band had left the rehearsal Peter told her their decision. She was not at all happy with this turn of events and to demonstrate her displeasure, as she was leaving she hit Peter over thead with her brolly!

While Peter was living with his Uncle Bill in Maida Vale area, he really wanted his own space so he found and moved into a small bedsit. When he had moved there, because he still enjoyed athletics, he remembers that he found that there was a local park nearby and that it had a running track. Once he found this out he would go the park and run during the late evenings during the summer. He changed his time to the afternoon when the days were getting shorter and darker. The park also had facilities for Javelin, Discus and putting the Shot. Although Peter was not great Javelin thrower he did spend time trying to conquer the skills required for the throw. It required a fast arm and a throwing technique that he found himself unable to master. So he decided that he would lay down the spear and concentrate on the Discus and Shot. On one occasion after he had been training with appliances for a good hour, he decided to go on to the track and run a fast 400 metres. Having done that, thinking that it was a lovely day, Peter decided that he would go for a stroll through the park and cool down.

After Peter had been walking for a while he saw a wooden bench at the side of the path, so he decided to lie down and relax for a while. As he lay quietly with his eyes closed and the warm sun on his face, he was disturbed by two children, who had stopped while passing by. He could hear their voices, so he opened his eyes and saw that they looked to be about twelve years old, they seemed to be very interested in Peter. "Are you 'Ivanhoe'" one of them asked. Of course he had to reply "No I'm not". Having said he did find it very flattering, to be likened to Roger Moore as he had always admired his humour and his tongue in cheek style of acting. Peter thought that Roger Moore was a really great person, sadly no longer with us, may he rest in peace.

Another person who Peter met during his time in Maida Vale was Dick Katz, who had formerly been a pianist with the jazz great, Ray Ellington. He lived in a flat just down the road from Peter's bedsit. One day he was invited to Dick's flat, so that Dick could play some songs and listen to him sing. They got along very well, but unfortunately nothing came of the time they spent together. Dick Katz other claim to fame was that he was Marion Ryan's manager at that time so perhaps he felt he had enough on his plate looking after her interests. Incidentally apart from apart from being a lovely lady and very talented vocalist in her own right who had top five hit with the song 'Love Me Forever' in 1958, Marion Ryan was married to Lloyd Sapherson in 1948. Marion and Lloyd are the parents of twins, Paul and Barry Ryan, Barry recorded that great song written by his brother Paul, *Eloise*.

Sadly as far as we know only Barry survives from this very talented family. Returning to Dick Katz Peter got on well with his daughter, he remembers that they enjoyed a few laughs together and that she was a really nice person. Dick Katz, who was a serious musical talent in his own right would go on to be involved in the careers of numerous artistes, including Engelbert Humperdinck.

Also by that time Peter had found himself another day job, he was working in a garage storeroom, keeping the books and handing out different car accessories, he enjoyed his job but show business was his target. He kept reading the paper looking to see if there were any other opportunities to showcase his vocal talent. The next thing that came to his attention in the paper was an audition for Hughie Green's Radio show, which was soon to be a TV show, Opportunity Knocks. So he got in touch with organisers and was given a time to attend rehearsals/auditions, he would be singing hoping for the judges approval again. As he felt that Gigi had previously been a lucky song choice for him, Peter decided that he that this was the song he would choose for this audition. He sat waiting excitedly for his turn with at least thirty other hopefuls.

At last Peter was called on stage and at that point he was introduced to the great man himself, Hughie Green. Hughie was in a control booth or more accurately, a sound control department that was almost like a recording studio. Then Peter stood at the microphone while the pianist arranged his sheet music, when he was ready the pianist nodded to Peter and started to play the musical introduction. When Peter began to sing, he was only about thirty seconds into the number, before Hughie Green stopped him saying "Sorry I'm just going to make a phone call". After a couple of minutes he said, "Right sing that again". Peter did, he had only got halfway through the song when Hughie spoke to him again, telling him to stop singing and come into the sound booth saying to him, "Hi Peter I'm Hughie Green, I'm on the phone to Norman Newell at EMI, here please take the phone, because he wants a word".

Peter took the phone and Norman Newell, spoke to him saying, "Peter I want you to come to Abbey Road studio and sing for me tomorrow". He found it very hard to sleep that night, because all he was thinking of was, "What's going to happen in the morning". The next day found a very excited and nervous Peter at Abbey Road studios, meeting the redoubtable Norman Newell. As Peter says, "Norman was very smartly dressed in a dark suit, he seemed a very sweet man" He made him feel at home and helped Peter to overcome his nerves, Norman engaged him in conversation, getting him to talk briefly about himself and where he lived.

Authors note: To have been involved with Norman Newell, was Peter said to me, "A great honour". The reason being that Norman Newell during his time as a record producer and lyricist had a reputation that was second to none. While he was head of EMI's Colombia label he worked with stars of the calibre of Shirley Bassey, Petula Clark, Vera Lynn and Russ Conway to name but a few. For the name Peter Wynne to be added to this list was an amazing boost to this young singers career. Using the name David West, Norman Newell would have a hand in writing, The English lyrics for Petula Clark's hit *Sailor, I Reach For The Stars*, a massive hit for Shirley Bassey in 1961, Steve Conway and Dorothy Squires would along with several others, enjoy great success with *My Thanks to You*. During his illustrious career Norman Newell achieved three Ivor Novello awards, a Grammy, an Emmy and a Golden Globe. He was also honoured with the OBE just before his death in 2004. It seemed that with this remarkable man involved in the production of Peter Wynne's début recording *Chapel Of Dreams*, success wassured.

We return to Peter's memory of the occasion, after he had been in Norman's company for a while, there was a knock on the door and in walked Russ Conway, Russ as many of you will know had hit records with tunes such as *Side Saddle* and *Roulette* . Russ was an excellent pop pianist and he was also a very nice congenial guy who said to Peter, "I am going to play for you so that Norman can get a better sound than he got over the phone, when he originally heard you. Peter sang and Norman Newell immediately offered him a contract for four records that would be released on Parlophone. This seemed unbelievable, needless to say Peter was ecstatic and he thanked Norman profusely. He was then told that they would meet up at EMI to sign the contract the following day.

After another sleepless night he went to EMI where he met Norman who introduced him to a guy called Bob Barratt who became a very close friend. Peter and Bob went on to be the co-writers of some of the songs they later penned. Then Peter was ushered into Norman's office were he signed the contract, he was on his way. After that he was handed a song sheet which was going to be his first release, the song was called *Chapel of Dreams*, this was and is a great song, it had the potential with Peter singing it to be a massive hit. The year was 1959 and Peter was just twenty years old, he was taking his first tentative steps towards a career in show business and that elusive and tantalising dream, stardom.

Authors Note: As a big fan of doo-wop singers I can tell you that my first knowledge of *Chapel of Dreams* came in 1959 when a friend in the USA sent me a recording of it by "The Dubs'. This group was made up of former members of The Five Wings and The Scale Tones. I believe that they may also have recorded as the Marvels without success. *Chapel of Dreams*,was I think on the GONE label, it had been released the year before but did not get into the Hot 100 chart. The group released the song again 1959 with more success. I believe the line up of the group was, Richard Brandon, Lead vocal, Cleveland Still, first tenor, Bill Carlisle second tenor, James, known as Jake, Miller baritone and Thomas Gardner, bass. Thomas Gardner may have been replaced by Tommy Grate at the time of the re-release, I am sure he joined the group in 1959. *Chapel of Dreams* by The Dubs is now regarded as a Doo-Wop classic. It was and is amazing. That may be, but in my opinion, Peter Wynne's recording far exceeds theirs, I just love it, I believe that this song was meant to be sung by him.

At some point later in the recording session Hughie Green wasked to choose a song for the B side of the record. The song Hughie picked was one that he thought would suit Peter's voice, it was called "Twilight Time". this song had been a hit for American vocal harmony group, The Platters a couple of years previously. Hughie was right in his choice because the musical arrangement really gave Peter the chance to shine vocally, this was an opportunity that he took with both hands. Both recordings gave what turned out to be an eager public, the chance to hear just what a fine voice this likeable young man possessed. Unfortunately the recording was not well promoted and the record shops had difficulty in supplying it to the public. A very disappointing state of affairs, chart success eluded Peter, when this recording should have taken him to the top of the hit parade.

One of the problems Peter and many other talented young performers around in those days had, was that they didn't understand what they needed to succeed, they relied on people who they believed in, who were already in the business. In his case he had the voice but no representation, none that was worthy of the name anyway. At the time he signed his recording contract he didn't have an agent or manager, or even the idea that he needed one. Hughie Green a very astute operator could see the problem that Peter had so said he would introduce him to a man called John Hayman, he was a film producer who Hughie felt might be interested in managing him.

In fact it soon became clear to Peter this involvement with John Hayman was more of an idea of Hughie Green's to help his friend John than a considered or constructive way to further Peter's career. But initially Peter went to meet John Hayman, filled with enthusiasm for the future, this enthusiasm being further encouraged when John said that he could, indeed would handle his business affairs. Now Peter had already been signed up to appear on Opportunity Knocks and it seemed in the opinion of those in the know that he stood a more than good chance of winning. When the show was broadcast he won the studio audiences approval but, when the listeners vote was counted he just lost out coming second to a young girl, whose name escapes him now.

The time spent with John Hayman as his manager did not really bear fruit, because although John was a clever entrepreneur and had produced some great films, he had no idea how to promote a talented but naive young performer. He simply did not apply himself to the task in any meaningful or productive way. This lack of effort was disastrous for Peter who believing that success in his chosen vocation was on the horizon, had given up his day job in expectation of the gigs rolling in. This meant that now there was no money coming in he was completely broke, he was becoming desperate and frustrated.

As time passed by things were so bad that on some occasions in acts of consideration and kindness John Hayman would would raid his fridge to give Peter things that he had cooked and refrigerated. One day he went home with a full cooked chicken in a shopping bag. If it were not for John's kindness most of the time Peter had nothing to eat. To be completely truthful things were really bad financially for Peter during his time with John Hayman. Having said that Peter did like the man but it was clear that he had no abilities as a theatrical agent, he never found any work in any theatre venues or on TV for Peter at all. Because of this failure by John Hayman to do the job that he was being relied on to do, Peter had no choice but ask John to break their agreement and part company.

Things were looking rather bleak at this point in Peter's career. His recording of *Chapel of Dreams* did reasonably well, in spite of the absence of any promotion or personal appearances but failed it to make the top forty. There were a couple of problems one was that the record wasn't being played much on the radio, the other was if anyone did hear it and try to buy it, the record shops did not have it, The distribution network was non existent. Added to that John Hayman had failed to provided any TV work at all. If he had then both the artiste and the song would have been promoted, this in turn would have provide sales and generated more work. This would have meant an income for Peter and commission for John. It seems that John was to short sighted to see that Peter Wynne was a potential goldmine for him. It is the old story in show business of chances overlooked and opportunities missed. Sadly John passed away recently, we wonder if during his long life he ever thought of the chance he missed to be a major part of British musical history by properly promoting Peter Wynne's career.

   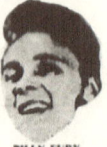 

Rock n Trad promotional poster, 1961

Peter in his trendy jacket age 21

It is significant that Dean Webb did not appear
Johnny Gentle and Peter filled in for him

Peter in the Police Cadets 1957

Various contemporary posters featuring Peter Wynne

Larry Parnes and the Parne's Boys (Peter 2nd left, Billy Fury, centre with Larry Parnes, Georgie Fame sitting in front, Vince Eager second right)

Peter Wynne backstage

Signed photo of Peter

Photo shoot for the Cyril Stapleton orchestra, 1962

Peter Wynne 1966

Peter in 1960 wearing a suit that was a gift from Marty Wilde

Chapter Five

Larry Parnes

Now in order to support and feed himself Peter had no other choice, he had to take a another day job. After looking around for various forms of employment, he thought himself fortunate when he found employment at Lyon's Corner House. The job he was employed to do involved taking confectionery to the different parts of the shop area. Because singing gave him so much pleasure, he used to sing various songs of the day while he pushed the cake trolley. The patrons of Lyons Corner House clearly enjoyed listening to this cheery young man with the remarkable voice, as he regaled them with everything from light opera to popular music . One day a lady customer, stopped him in tracks, she said, "Young man, you shouldn't be working here you should be singing for a living". Well, Peter did not know it at the time but the lady was musical entrepreneur Larry Parnes mother. At that time the way to success in the music industry seemed to be through auspices of one of three men, Larry Parnes, Robert Stigwood or Joe Meek. Musical history records that these men were both innovative and creative in their approach to the business. So an introduction to any of these men was extremely valuable to any aspiring artistes.

After the lady had gone home it seems that she told her son about the young man with the wonderful voice, who was working in Lyon's Corner House. Never a man to waste time Larry Parnes sent Hal Carter in to see Peter. Hal Carter was a remarkable man in his own right, who having been Billy Fury's manager would go on to form the Hal Carter Organisation, one of the leading entertainment agencies in the world and who many years later in conjunction with Flying Music would put out the successful Solid Gold Sixties tours. At the time he came in to see Peter, Hal Carter was a trusted associate of Larry Parnes, so he was keen to see and if possible hear Peter sing. When Hal met Peter he politely asked him to come and sing for Larry Parnes. Never being one to miss an opportunity Peter decided to take a chance and agreed.

So it was that Peter went along to see Larry Parnes asked him to sing for him. Peter chose to sing a ballad, the song in question was a song that had been recorded by Mario Lanza, called 'Be My Love'. "Thankfully" says Peter, although in the author's opinion not surprisingly, Larry was very impressed by Peter's voice and he took him in to his office and once they got there a contract was signed for Peter to be paid £35 a week. Now that may not seem like very much now, but back in the 1960's it was has been previously said, "A lot of money in those days". The dream was starting to come true again, once again Peter had something to believe in.

Larry Parnes office was on Oxford Street near Tottenham Court Road and they went over there so that Peter could meet the other guys who were signed to Larry's agency. When he met up with some of the guys including Marty Wilde, Peter learned that Marty was getting married and to his great surprise he was invited to attend the reception. The reception was to be held at the Lotus House, this was a Chinese restaurant that was at that time frequented by most of the countries top entertainers. There was also the news that Larry had booked Peter to appear on Boy meets Girl, this being a show that starred Marty Wilde who also introduced the other acts who were being featured on the show. It really looked as though things were starting to happen for Peter Wynne.

After some time had passed, Larry invited Peter back to his apartment, ostensibly to have a chat and talk about TV work. However Larry, as some people will be aware was gay and he had to find out if Peter was inclined to reciprocate the feelings of attraction that he was feeling for him. So with this in mind when they got there Larry sat down the settee next to him and very clumsily tried to put his arm around him. This unexpected action made Peter sit up straight, he couldn't get out of the apartment quickly enough. Because this was an untimely reminder of the incidents with theadmaster when he was at school. Thinking quickly he made up an excuse about having to meet his Uncle Bill who would be waiting for him. Larry although somewhat disappointed allowed him to leave. Peter just hoped that his clear aversion to anything of this nature, would not mean he did not get the hoped for gigs that were on offer. Larry Parnes was an astute businessman who always saw the bigger picture, so he knew that there was money to made from Peter's talent so he did not apply any work sanctions on him.

As he gives his own thoughts on this incident, Peter is hopeful that he managed to make his escape without embarrassing Larry. He just needed an excuse to enable him to get up make his farewells, and leave. It was a worry that Larry Parnes, was inclined in this way, and he could only hope that his refusal to give in to Larry's advances, would not stop him from working in the music industry. He now realises that he needn't have worried on that score. Because whatever his faults in how he may have treated some people, Larry was entitled to his own preferences. Fortunately Larry Parnes was first and foremost a business man and he recognised that Peter Wynne had talent. Still as Peter says, "It was a worrying time". Really the only bright spot for him during all this time was his involvement with the sister of his brothers girlfriend, Colleen. The two of them were getting on very well and she kept his hopes up when he naturally found himself feeling a little disillusioned.

Things were moving along very slowly and once again Peter was wondering if his career would ever really take off. Then one day Larry Parnes took a phone call, the caller told him Gene Vincent had fallen ill. This meant that he would need to find a replacement for the show that was taking place at Manchester Hippodrome that night. Luckily Peter was in the office that day so Parnes immediately made arrangements to have a seat booked for him on the next plane flying out of Heathrow Airport to Manchester. He then phoned the person who had phoned him and told them, "There is no problem, I am sending Peter Wynne to replace Gene Vincent for this show and any other shows until Gene recovers".

So Peter found himself on the plane, he had never flown before so he was understandably nervous about making the journey. However once he was aboard the plane everything was fine, the time in the air passed in a blur. It was surprising to him that the flight and a taxi ride from Ringway Airport, where he landed, had him at the Manchester Hippodrome in forty minutes. So he had arrived in more ways than one because this really was a big step on the road to stardom. To paraphrase the words of a well known song he was, "Ready willing and able to do the show, that night".

His performance was a sensation, the audience was completely blown away by the voice of this tall good looking young man, indeed they recognised that he had incredible voice. I know because although Peter doesn't know this at the time of writing, I was in the audience that night, having gone to see Gene Vincent. Please let me tell you that neither I or anyone else in the audience was disappointed by Gene's absence once Peter Wynne came on stage. The packed auditorium was quite simply in awe from the moment he opened his mouth to sing his first song, that amazement at his talent lasted until his final encore. As Peter says, "When I came off stage, the area around the stage door was packed with excited teenage girls wanting autographs and photograph". It seems that all these girls were allowed into Peter's dressing room and they all ran in screaming and shouting his name, a great publicity shot, that was not missed by the photographers, who Larry Parnes had arranged for the evening!

The following day the Daily Express carried the banner headline "The Golden Voice of the 60's!! The write up that followed theadline wasn't to well received by Gene Vincent, he didn't think Larry had handled his absence in the right way. He wasn't happy with Peter Wynne either, even though he had no say in what was written. But it has to be said that for once the reporters had got it just right, because every word they had written was true. I have to say that I personally was amazed by Peter's rendition of all the songs, what a voice! But I was knocked out by his performance of "Chapel of Dreams" I could not get the song out of my mind, I sang it, badly all the time for about a week, while I was travelling to work and while I was working. Sadly I struggled to buy it though, because the local record shops weren't carrying it. I did order the record but the order was never fulfilled. I have a copy now and I still play it to my wife Margaret along with Peter's other recordings.

After the show Peter went back the Imperial Hotel where Larry Parnes who flown in with him had booked a double room with two single beds. This arrangement really put Peter on edge wondering what he would do if Larry tried to proposition him. Larry himself was getting very excited about the fact that a film was being made in Australia and it would be primarily set on Bondi Beach, lots of people running about in swimsuits. (These days we would think of Bay Watch.) It seems they had asked Larry to find athletic young men to star in the film, so he asked Peter if he would mind posing for some photographs in his underpants.

This Larry said was so that the casting department could have an idea of how he would look in swimming trunks, he said if Peter would pose he could get the photos sent off to Australia the next day, this would give him a better chance of getting the part. This quick action would mean that there would be no delays. A very excited Larry told Peter that part was good as his. Authors note: As Peter said to me, " So like the naive young fool I felt, and was, I stood there having a couple of photos taken by Larry, thinking to myself, I might be getting part in a major film." "Needless to say nothing ever materialised". "Ho Ho, as if, it was just Larry being Larry, he was trying to engineer a situation for his own benefit". These photo's would cause Peter problems in the future, in a way he could never have imagined, we will hear of these problems later.

Peter remembers different things from his time on the Parnes tours and sometimes whilst the memories are crystal clear, understandably after so many years, it is not always possible to remember an exact date for them. One such occasion is when the tour reached a Cardiff theatre, now at that time Peter seeing a young lady who had recently finished her relationship with a previous boyfriend, apparently the lad in question made his living as a film extra. Now the young lady, it seems that her name has slipped away in the mists of time, told Peter that she had ended the relationship about two weeks before she had met him. However she said that her ex had called her on the phone that morning, to tell her that he was on his way to Cardiff with a few mates, to sort things out. Well needless to say Peter was not to happy about the situation, but he told the girl that he would be prepared to speak to the lad if it was really necessary.

As the two of them were walking down to theatre from the digs that they were staying in, a large black car pulled up alongside them, there were three men in it. The driver opened the passenger side door and shouted at Peter get in! At the same time one of the two men in the back of the car opened the door and told Peter's girlfriend to get in. They both got in and they were driven to theatre when the car stopped Peter and one of the men, who he then realised was the ex boyfriend got out and they went into theatre and back to his dressing room, with the girl following behind them. The lad began talking going on about how much he loved and missed this girl. Not really what Peter wanted to hear when he was preparing for show.

As the lad was speaking he suddenly pulled some kind of pistol from his pocket and laid it on the dressing room makeup table. Peter remembers that the pistol was never pointed at him and he never felt threatened or afraid in that situation, even with the pistol there in front of him. Looking back he thinks that the weapon was just for effect, in any event whatever it's purpose was, it didn't work. The lad asked the girl if she really meant it when she said that they were finished. She replied that she did, going on to say, that the relationship was over. Then she told him that he should leave without any violence. He mumbled and moaned on, about things for a short time and then he left theatre. As far as Peter knows the lad was never seen or heard from again. This just another example of the complexity of human relationships.

Now there were always things that were going on in the background with Larry Parnes and something that Peter found out during his time with the Parnes stable amazed him. It seems that Larry had thoughts of sending him to Italy to have his voice trained for Opera. Peter would have been up for such an opportunity because he has always known that Opera was his forte. This not a just a foolish notion his part anyone who has heard him sing songs like " And This Is My Beloved" and "Be My Love", knows that with the right training, it would not have been be a great stretch for him to achieve the position of Lead Tenor in an Operatic Company. He has always loved to attempt operatic arias, he was and is natural tenor, but singing popular songs he has had to hold back the drama and sing in lower keys than he is clearly capable of, in the hope of recording success. With this in mind he was encouraged to follow the style of other pop singers of the day. However he has always sung in a style that is all his own, he is right to do so as there are some things that can not be comprised and individual talent is one of them.

The reason that Opera was such a feasible idea was because of the fact that his uncle the previously mentioned John Williams aka Furness Wynne Williams, was one of the leading operatic tenors of his generation. The downsides of this idea of going to Italy for him were that Larry wanted to travel to Italy and stay with him while he was over there. Peter would never have agreed to that for obvious reasons. Added to that Larry wanted to promote him as him Pedro Wynne, the great Welsh/Italian Tenor this was a farcical idea in Peter's eyes. Quite apart from anything else, Pedro as we all know is a Spanish name, Larry had clearly not given any serious thought to this idea, it was just a ruse to find a way to spend time alone with Peter. In the light of Peter's hopes and dreams, it was cruel of Larry's to hold out the hope of this dream being fulfilled

Peter appeared on the previously mentioned TV show Boy meets Girl several times and he remembers one occasion very well. While he was singing *It's Only Make Believe* the camera panned round the audience and focused on a young girl who was crying, he found out afterwards that her name was Linda Brannigan, she turned out to be a really nice girl who became Peter's Fan Club secretary. She ran the fan club from her home town of Manchester. He would also become friendly with a few of the artistes that he appeared on the show with, there were two in particular, one being Michael Cox who sang and had a hit with *Angela Jones*. As those of us in the business are aware Michael Cox would later emigrate to New Zealand, they lost touch at point and Peter has never heard from Mike since.

The other singer who became a good friend was Peter Elliot a very athletic performer who used to do a backflip while he was singing this looked very impressive. He was married to a well known singer and actress by the name of Maggie Fitzgibbon who came from Australia, he was a great guy but once again he and Peter lost touch,when he moved to Australia. Peter has tried even using the internet to search for them without success, he thinks Peter Elliot will be in his eighties now and Mike in his seventies. Authors note: I have no clue as to Peter Elliot's whereabouts, but hopefully I will be able to give Peter Mike Cox's address in New Zealand as I have been touch with him for some years since he moved over there.

Peter Wynne has appeared in many theatres up and down the UK, venues as far apart as The Colston Hall in Bristol and the Glasgow Empire in Scotland. He remembers the Glasgow theatre well, as he says, "It is a lovely old building with baths next to the dressing room where you could go and lie in warm water and relax before the show." He has memories of one night in particular at that theatre although in some ways he would like to forget it. The show had been going well until Billy Fury came on stage and started to sing, of course the young girls went crazy, they were shouting and screaming, "We love you Billy" and other endearments. The young Glaswegian men were not so keen, they were a bit jealous Peter thinks, anyway some of them ripped the ashtrays off the back of the seats and threw them at the stage.

Although they were clearly aiming at Billy, one of the ashtrays hit the drummers cymbal and took a chunk out of it. Red Reece was the drummer that night, and he decided that discretion was the better part valour so he got up and very slowly and furtively moved off stage into the wings. Then Billy's bassist backed of stage, then the lead guitarist, clearly they were taking no chances with either themselves or their instruments being damaged by flying missiles. The ash trays were still being thrown, the ill feeling from the young Glaswegian men was continuing unabated. Billy refused to be intimidated, he just stood and looked at the audience with an expression of slight disgust on his face, then he turned and slowly walked to the side curtains and left the stage.

In Peter's opinion Billy Fury stood seven feet tall that night, as he says "How cool was that"? Peter was waiting in the wings to go on next, but the safety curtain was dropped, the show had come to a premature end, he would not be performing. The management told the lads not to leave theatre for an hour while they cleared the mob of very angry teenagers away from the theatre. These angry young men would have been after all the entertainers hides, if they could have got to them. When the lads entered the High Street all the angry people had gone, so with just a few girls and other ordinary people wandering about doing their own thing, the disappointed entertainers made their way back to their digs.

Jealousy from the girl fans boyfriends was common in those days, emotions would run high and the young lads in the audience, would want to show the girls that they were just good as the lads on stage. Perhaps we may think they were just being silly now, but ours was a generation who were experiencing this kind of extreme adulation for performers for the first time.

Those of us growing up after the war, were unlike our parents who had suffered through the depression in the thirties, when there was no work, no money and then they had to endure six years of war. So unlike our parents, our generation were dreamers and we believed that anything was possible, we thought then that we had it all. People like Peter Wynne, Tommy Bruce, Clem Cattinni, Marty Wilde, Johnny Gentle, Joe Brown, Brian Poole, Helen Shapiro, Tony Crane , Billy Kinsley, Kathy Kirby, Billie Davis and many others, including the author of this book took every opportunity that came their way. None of us have been disappointed, because the only disappointments come from regret and we have nothing to regret. Even now in our seventies and eighties we still think, I can do that and try as hard as we can to fulfil that dream. We will be that, 'can do' generation till we reach the end of our lives. We still have it all, everything we try for. Any setbacks we have met along the way have only made us more determined to keep going and stronger in our will to follow our dreams.

Going back to the story and Peter's memories there was another occasion that Peter remembers very well. This event took place in the summer season of 1960 when Larry Parnes booked the Queens Theatre in Blackpool for five consecutive Sunday matinees titled "Idols On Parade" The the cast consisted of Joe Brown, Tommy Bruce, Lance Fortune, Nelson Keene, Georgie Fame and Peter. Larry Parnes decided that it would be a good idea to dress the boys up as girl soldiers in a uniform that consisted of blouse, tie, short skirt all topped off with a pigtail wig. When Larry told them what he expected there was uproar, Peter was incensed by the idea He said, "I have no talent for comedy, I can't act funny, I would feel too embarrassed, On top of that I'll look such a prat". Larry Parnes reply was, "Do it or leave the show"! "Where is the short skirt"? Was Peter's response.

So all the boys got dressed up and went on stage. As Peter recalls, "It was so funny seeing Tommy Bruce in pigtails, a short skirt and his Annelo and Davide boots, trying to sing his lines like a woman with his deep gravel voice. Joe looked like a character from the Beano. They all had a laugh in the end, so did the audience, Authors note: Tommy shared this experience with me about fifty years ago when we first met, he told me that Georgie, Nelly, (which was Tommy's nickname for Nelson Keene) and Lance carried it off very well, but Joe was, as Peter said like a character from the Beano. Tommy and Peanuts as he affectionately nicknamed Peter had been the funniest of them all, because Tommy said that he, himself looked and sounded like a drink raddled lady of the night and that Peanuts bore a very strong resemblance to Elsa Lanchester in The Bride of Frankenstein. Incidentally this show toured all the Granada venues around the UK, with great success. This sort of thing was a downside of working for Larry Parnes, because no matter how silly his ideas might be he would brook no argument. It was his way or the highway!!

When the Blackpool show came to the end of it's run, Peter was sent to join the summer show on the pier at Great Yarmouth. This was good news for him because another great mate of his Johnny Gentle was on the bill. They had shared digs before, becoming close friends and they got on like brothers. There was another act on the bill a very talented performer, a big man in every sense of the word Vince Eager. Now Peter recalls that he and Vince were never the friendliest of chums, but they were always polite to each other. There could have been a problem between them on this occasion because Peter had been closing his act with the song, "Only Make Believe", This was the very same song that Vince was closing his own act with. Always an amenable and versatile man Peter started closing his act with that great song from the musical Carousel "You'll Never Walk Alone", this choice to change his final number without argument, diffused a potentially volatile situation. Everything went well with that show but all to soon the summer season was over and it was time to return home.

Before we leave his memories of the 'Idols On Parade' tour Peter would like us to hear of an incident that he wasn't proud of then, or now. But it has to be said that this incident was instrumental in helping him become the professional artiste that he became and still is. The show was at the famous 'Liverpool Empire and the lads in the show found that they had some free time to enjoy, before it was time for the curtain to go up. Georgie Fame suggested to the lads that they go to a place he knew were they could get a drink. Looking back Peter thinks it was a 'Yates Wine Lodge'. As he recalls the incident he is fairly sure that Johnny Gentle and Duffy Power tagged along. Well of course as can be the case with young lads one drink turned into a few and then a few more. Peter remembers that he had been drinking schooners of Sherry, several of them, although he didn't feel any effect from the drinks until he went outside.

Then it was a different story because, as they walked slowly back to theatre Peter began to feel terrible. He could not keep to one side of the footpath, he was weaving and staggering from side to side and he was feeling very queasy, to say the least. When they arrived back at theatre, they all went up the stairs to their respective dressing rooms, he didn't quite make it all the way to his dressing room, nearly falling into the toilet. Where he remained kneeling with his head over the toilet bowl for about five minutes, he was feeling absolutely dreadful, in the circumstances he thought that he might never get up again. At that point he suddenly heard someone shouting, " Pete, you're on mate"! Now he had no choice he would have to try to get up and go to the stage and perform. Still heaving and groaning he dragged himself on to his feet and wiped the sweat from his face, with a towel or cloth, it had to be something, he just doesn't remember what. As he made his way to the wings he was trying desperately to pull himself together.

Somehow, Peter will never know how, he put one foot in front of the other and stumbled down the stairs, as he did so heard the intro to his first song. Pulling himself together as best he could, he slowly walked on stage, to this day he still has no idea how he got to the end of his spot. He does know that his notes were shaky and he is sure that he must have sung sharp and flat during his performance. Now at that time they had a lady stage manager and she told Peter and others in no uncertain terms, that if they ever turned up to go on stage in that condition again, then they would be thrown out of the show. Such a course of action would very likely end a performers career! It will come as no surprise, to anyone when they read this, that Peter never allowed anything like that to happened to him again.

On their return to London The Parnes Boys as they had become known heard the news that two top stars would be arriving from the USA. To accommodate them a full package tour that would be taking in all the cinemas and theatres in Great Britain. The artistes were Eddie Cochrand Gene Vincent, these two performers were in the vanguard of Great Britain's new Rock and Roll culture. Needless to say there was a fever of excitement generated just by the news that these acts were arriving. Even more exciting for the lads was the declaration that Peter and several other members of the Parnes stable were to be booked to appear on regularly on these shows. As Peter says, "I was ecstatic about the idea that I would be working with two of the Rock and Roll Greats". Gene of course had appeared on Parnes shows before, and we know that he was already aware of Peter Wynne.

Larry Parnes went ahead and booked Peter on a great many of the Gene Vincent and Eddie Cochran Concerts. One he remembers in particular took place at 'The Finsbury Park Empire' The reason that he remembers this show so well is that Tony Sheridan was on the bill and he had a band called 'The Silver Beatles' backing him. Now when Tony left the UK to appear in Germany this band followed him out there. When they returned their name had been shortened and they were now called 'The Beatles' and the rest as they say, is British musical history.

The time that Peter spent touring with Eddie and Gene was a great experience for him. He learnt a lot and he enjoyed most of his time with them very much. Things were going very well on the tour, it was all good fun and all the young lads enjoyed a laugh. That is until one night on the tour bus there was a very nasty incident. It all started when Peter got on the bus and sat on the seat in front of Gene Vincent. He was feeling a bit weary he decided to try and get his head down and take forty winks. That was the plan but he would have no such luck because Gene was thumping repeatedly on the back of the seat.

Peter tried to ignore the banging but it got worse and worse, just a continuous repetitive bump, bump, bump against the back of the seat. In desperation Peter got up, turned and faced Gene Vincent saying, "Gene, please, would you mind not banging on my seat? Because I am trying to get some sleep" Gene looked up at him and then screamed, "Are you talking to me"? "Yes I am"! Replied Peter. Gene's response to this was , "Well don't talk to me, talk to Henry!" Then he shouted repeatedly to everyone on the bus, "Get me Henry! Get me Henry!!" Finally someone brought him Henry, this Henry was not a person it was a big, long vicious looking Sheath Knife. Gene took the sheath knife and banged it on the seat, "Now", he said "Talk to Henry"!!

By this point Peter had realised that Gene had been drinking heavily, so not wanting things to get any worse, he slowly turned his back on him and tried to ignore him. But Gene was determined to escalate things further and he began sneering at him, Saying, "Who is the guy who has pictures of him in his underwear, hanging on Larry Parnes toilet door"? Peter was shocked and devastated to know that this was what Parnes had done with the photos, that had been taken in the Manchester hotel, months before. This must have been what had sent Gene into a maniacal rage, the idea that Peter might have been Parnes's particular favourite. Peter thought to himself, how can I go into a big explanation about how the photos had come to be taken? He was feeling really embarrassed.

Luckily he didn't have to think of an explanation because somebody made the mistake of laughing. Gene thinking he was being laughed at, not Peter, turned round and went up to that person and using Henry, cut the pocket on the guys jacket, things were now starting to get out of hand, because Gene was losing his grip on reality. Eventually a black American entertainer called Davy Jones, who was a lovely guy, stepped in and calmed Gene down. This had been a very worrying incident, which could been much worse if Davy hadn't stepped in. Gene Vincent apologised to Peter the very next evening, asking him to have drink with him, Peter did and because he took such magnanimous attitude towards the incident they were able to carry on appearing on the tour together.

As is to be expected when group of young lads are cooped up together, travelling, performing and living together, there were other incidents that took place during the tour. There was one in particular that could have turned really nasty, this was an incident that occurred when the tour got to the Glasgow Empire. For once all the lads on that stage of the tour had been booked into the same digs. Peter remembers who was there at the time very well, the cast included Billy Fury, Joe Brown, Johnny Gentle, Duffy Power, Peter and Davy Jones, the American performer previously mentioned, who should not be confused with the 'Monkees' group member of the same name. There were also two roadies, one was called Allan, the others name cannot be remembered now. They were all in the dining room of their digs sitting round the table, some drinking coffee some drinking tea while eagerly waiting for their evening meal.

Suddenly without any warning Joe Brown leapt to his feet, spitting into his handkerchief, then shouting, "Who has put bloody salt in my tea?!! Well the roadie Allan was the first one to giggle and Joe taking that as an admission of guilt threw his tea all over him. Allan was enraged by this and he jumped to his feet and threatened to punch Joe in the face. Now Allan was quite a small bloke and Peter has no doubt that Joe would have crushed him if they had actually come to blows. So he decided it was time to play peacemaker and as he thinks now rather foolishly, he jumped in between the two protagonists, hoping that his intervention would save the situation from turning even nastier than it already had.

Unfortunately he found that he had gone face to face with Joe, it was a stand off. Peter could see that the likely outcome of things now would be that he and Joe would start trading punches, it was a bad feeling and nothing he could think of would prevent them fighting.

Luckily Billy Fury chose that moment to admit that it had actually been him who had spiked the tea with salt. Luckily things calmed down after that and the unfortunate fracas came to happy end, it was only then that Joe finally saw the funny side of the situation.

Peter would just like to say at this point that it is nearly sixty years since he met Joe Brown for the first time, during all that time he has liked him as a person. He has great admiration for Joe's abilities as a musiciand was delighted to meet up with him again backstage at the at The Grand Ole Oprey House in York in 2011 after Joe's performance there. Peter feels fortunate that he, his wife Amanda and her son Daniel were able to visit Joe in his dressing room. Joe's first words when he saw them coming through the door were "Blimey, Peter Wynne"! They both enjoyed a good chat about the old days and the great times that they had enjoyed together. We can fast forward another seven years to when having painted a portrait of Joe. Peter heard that Joe would be appearing in Newbury, so he took the painting to theatre there and left it back stage in his dressing room for him. Imagine Peter's great delight when the following day, he received a phone call from his old workmate Joe Brown. During that call Joe said that he loved the painting, thanking Peter so much for it, he ended the conversation saying, "We really must get together again sometime soon. This most welcome contact was a real boost for Peter whose health had not been good at the time.

There is something quite important that Peter remembers about those days, that is that Eddie Cochran didn't ride with the other performers on the tour bus. This was because his girlfriend Sharon Sheeley had come over from the United States so that she could be with him during the tour. This arrangement meant that they always travelled together by car, their decision would have tragic consequences for both of them as it put them in harms way in a manner that neither of them could possibly have foreseen. The last night of tour in April 1961 was at the Bristol Hippodrome, although it should have been a day later because the show was billed to appear at the Liverpool Stadium. Allan Williams a Liverpool promoter was co-promoting the show there with Larry Parnes, but at the last minute that show was cancelled.

The reason that the final show was cancelled was because Eddie and Gene wanted, in fact they needed a break. They had arranged to go back to America for a week or two for some much needed R and R. Anyway after the Bristol show Peter went to Eddie's dressing room to say his goodbyes. When he got there Eddie was playing his guitar and he called Peter in and asked him to sing a song. He doesn't remember the tune that he sang, but what he does recall is how good Eddie was on guitar and that he really enjoyed Eddie's company. When it was time to go and Eddie asked Peter what he would like bringing back from the United States, he couldn't really think of anything so he just said, "A pair of jeans, please". Eddie agreed to bring them and Peter thanked Eddie, thinking, how will he know my size? But he left it at that, saying no more.

Later that night Eddie asked Peter's mate Johnny Gentle, "Can you give me, Sharon and Gene a lift back to London"? Johnny had to refuse because he had already arranged to take Peter home with him. The reason for his refusal was because Johnny and Peter lived quite close to each other and their journey was a convenient one. Added to that there simply wasn't enough room for three adults on the back seat of a Ford Anglia. Eddie said, "OK no problem" and arranged a taxi for himself Sharon and Gene. Then everyone said their goodbyes and they all left The Hippodrome to start on their journeys back to London.

While Johnny and Peter were on their way back to London Peter noticed the fuel gauge was getting low, so he asked Johnny if he knew of any petrol stations in the area, but he didn't. They were getting worried that they might run out of petrol, so when Peter noticed a police car parked at the side of the road, they stopped and asked the policeman if he knew of any gas stations that would be open. He replied that they would all be closed by now. But he said that there had been an accident further down the road and to prevent a fire the petrol had been syphoned from the tank of the car involved and that they might be able to have some of that. The lads were out of luck the car and the fuel had been taken away by the time they got there, so there was no petrol available to help them on their way. There was nothing else they could do but drive slowly but surely home they just made it with the car running on fumes.

The next day Peter heard the devastating news that Eddie Cochran had been killed in a car crash in Chippenham and that the other passengers, Sharon Sheeley and Gene Vincent had been injured. There were conflicting accounts of what had truly had happened but it seems that a tyre had blown out on a bend and the car had skidded and hit a lamp post. The tragedy of it was Eddie Cochran had died. Peter thinks that it must have been the accident the policeman had told them about. Authors note: The policeman on the scene at the accident was my dear friend the late David Harmon, who went on to be Dave Dee of the group Dave Dee, Dozy, Beaky, Mick and Titch fame. Dave retrieved Eddie Cochran's Gretsch guitar which amazingly had not been damaged in the accident. The guitar was later returned to Eddie's family.

This would not been the only accident that the Parnes boys would become aware of involving other entertainers. Tommy Bruce turned his car over while travelling home from a gig, on a country lane. Fortunately Tommy and his passengers walked away from the accident without injury. There was another time when Tommy had to drive Billy Fury home to Liverpool in Billy's sports car which had a twisted steering wheel. This damage had come about when Billy had crashed the car, He then asked Tommy to drive it the rest of the way because it was hard to keep it on the road with a sore shoulder.

Indeed Peter would be involved in one crash himself, not long after Eddie's Cochran's tragic death. This accident occurred during the weeks following the Chippenham crash. It was at this time that

British artiste and good friend to us all, Ricky Valance had a hit with the song, "Tell Laura I Love Her". Larry Parnes decided put Ricky and Peter out the road to do some shows together. Although as is the way with accidents fate takes a hand, because in this case Peter did not have to be in Ricky's company at the time of the crash. He was not booked on the show that Ricky was travelling back from.

At the time we are talking about Ricky was living in Clapham with his wife Evelyn, Colleen who was at that time married to Peter went with him over to Ricky and Evelyn's house. When heard that Ricky would be going off to do some gigs that Peter was not booked for and not having anything in the book decided that he would travel with him and keep him company on his journey. Just as a matter of interest for the reader, Ricky was driving a Ford Anglia in those days. It would seem that the first gig was somewhere near Sheffield and after an uneventful journey they arrived at the venue. Ricky ran through his act with the local band in the afternoon, made sure all was in order, he did the gig later on and then they left after the show to make the journey for the next gig which was the following night in Scotland.

They arrived late and booked in to a hotel near Glasgow, which Peter doesn't remember the name of, after all these years. The next night Ricky did the show and afterwards they were invited by a guy they had met and his wife to come back to their place for sandwiches and coffee. They soon found out that the couple were swingers and the wife had a yen for Ricky. Of course she had no chance, because

Ricky was and is one of the good guys, he is a non smoker, a non drinker and married then and now to the lovely Evelyn, he is definitely as Peter puts it, a non cheater.

So because there was no chance that he would ever be unfaithful to Evelyn, there would be no swinging done in that house on that night. So they unable to get away quickly enough from the situation they found themselves in. As hastily as they could the two flustered young men, bid the couple a polite good night and set off on their journey home. They should really have booked in to a hotel because they were very tired, but Ricky is a very frugal man and there was no way that he would spend money on a hotel, unless he thought it was really necessary and on this occasion he was sure that he would be able to drive home without problems. Famous last words as they drove away, "We can make it home no problem".

Well they had been driving for a while, and Peter thinks that it must have been about five O'clock in the morning. He is not sure about the time because he had fallen asleep in the passenger seat. What he didn't know was that Ricky had also fallen asleep and he was at the wheel. The next thing they both knew was that they heard an almighty bang! Suddenly they were both being thrown around the car as though they were in a washing machine. There were no seat belts in cars during those days as we are all aware so no restraints meant you could be thrown all over place. With blood running down his face from a wound sustained when he had slammed into some part of the interior Peter was stunned and completely disorientated.

The car came to sudden stop as it stopped rolling, it was lying on it's roof. Ricky had somehow been thrown from the front seat into the back and he was crying out in pain, he was groaning and saying that his chest had been hurt.

Coming to his senses Peter knew that they had to get out so he kicked out what was left of the windscreen with his shoe and crawled out of the car through the small space. As he was crawling out he managed to pull Ricky out with him. He remembers that the back wheels were still spinning as he looked at the car. There was liquid running around them by the smell he presumed that it was petrol that was leaking all over the road. Just then a large articulated lorry pulled up and the driver got out When the driver saw that Peter was covered in blood and also hearing Ricky moaning with the pain from his chest, he decided that he would take them to the nearest hospital. Looking back the trip in the lorry was not a journey that Peter would want to repeat as he was feeling pretty ropey.

When they arrived at the hospital, Peter was taken to a room to be examined and Ricky was taken for an X-Ray. Peter needed to have his forehead stitched up, the wound required six stitches. He was told that the wound was going to be stitched without any anaesthetic, so he clenched his teeth together while it was being done, basically as he says, "It really hurt". After a short time heard that Ricky had not suffered any broken ribs. So they decided to call their respective wives to tell them what had happened, but not to worry they were both OK.

Then they left the hospital and headed for the railway station to catch a train home, needless to say, Ricky's car was write off. They later heard from the garage that the recovery guys were amazed that no one had been killed, given the state of the car. There could have been some good publicity for Ricky if he had thought of it because his song "Tell Laura I Love Her" was about a car crash, theadline could have been "Tell Laura singer in near fatal car crash". It has to be said that Ricky missed out on that opportunity to promote himself. Authors note, Ricky Valance is one of my closest friends and he told me about this crash saying, "There is no doubt that Peter saved my life that night, If he hadn't pulled me out I would have still been in the car when it caught fire".

After some time had passed, following Eddie Cochran's sad demise, the previously cancelled Rock and Roll show, from the end of the Eddie Cochran tour was put on at the Liverpool Stadium. While he was at the venue at the venue Peter met George Harrison and he thinks Paul McCartney, although it may have been John Lennon from the soon to be massively successful Liverpool group, The Beatles when they came back stage to meet Gene Vincent. It seems that as they were being managed by Allen Williams at the time they had expected to appear on the show, but Larry Parnes apparently vetoed their appearance on stage, by saying that they were under rehearsed. In those days no one questioned a Larry Parnes decision, so The Beatles did not appear.

Speaking of Allen Williams he owned a venue called the Jackanda, this was a small bar, where he would put on live acts to entertain the punters. He also own another venue a nightclub Called 'The Blue Angel', Peter was booked to appear there on numerous occasions. One night after the show he was introduced to that wonderful singer, Danny Williams, who had recently had a massive hit with the song "Moon River". Danny and Peter would become good friends and spend pleasant times in each others company.

From time to time Danny and Peter would do a little drinking together usually late at night after they had finished their respective performances. One night Danny had a great idea he thought they should go out and do something together and so he asked Peter what he thought about ice skating, hardly waiting for a reply he went to say, "There is an ice rink nearby, let's go skating". Peter agreed but when they got to the skating rink, it was just about to close. However when the management saw who it was that wanted to use the rink they agreed to stay open for another hour.

Well it was clear that Danny was pretty good on skates, he was soon speeding round the rink. Unlike Peter, who had never skated before and thinks he must have got an extra large pair of skates, with a mind of their own because as soon as he got on the ice his ankles buckled, he just couldn't stand up. They stayed on the ice until the rink closed, but no matter how he tried Peter couldn't even walk on the ice never mind skate. As he says, "The things we do to have fun". Authors note: It is I think worth mentioning that Danny

Williams apart from being a great singer and a wonderful man, was talented and gifted athlete who excelled in many sports. These sports included, Tennis, Martial Arts and of course ice skating.

Later in the year Peter was part of a grand tour where all the artistes on the show sang an Eddie Cochran number in tribute to his memory. For Peter it seemed to be a very poignant farewell to an era, not just to his friend, because his sad demise had coincided with a change in the direction music was taking. This meant that it was not just a farewell to Eddie and the memories both he and his music evoked, but it was also a farewell to the style of music and performance that Peter had become used to. He was finding as were the other Parnes boys that they would have to change with the times if they wanted their careers to progress. To that end with his wonderful and exceptional tenor voice, Peter was probable better equipped for the shift in music and performance than some of the other guys in the Larry Parnes stable. Who knows, he thought this shift in music, might just take me into the charts. This was not to be, but he was able to make a living from his music, where some of the others like Duffy Power, Sally Kelly, Danny Rivers, Dudley Heslop he was more of a Jack Good discovery,otherwise known as Cuddly Dudley, Dave Samson, Nelson Keen, Johnny Gentle, Keith Kelly and others like them could not. They were denied the opportunities that their talent deserved. These lads and Sally Kelly, Parnes's token girl singer were part of British musical history and they deserved better from the business, that for a few years they had graced, with some distinction. Incidentally having seen Sally Kelly on stage and bought a couple her records,I have to say she really did deserve more success than just being the only girl singer on the Parnes tours, Her Decca recordings included. "He'll Have To Stay". This as we all know the reply to the Jim Reeves hit "He'll Have To Go", Sally Kelly was another performer who given the breaks could have been right up there with the likes of Susan Maughand Clodagh Rodgers.

LtoR: Billy Fury, Dickie Pride, Peter Wynne, Tommy Bruce and Johnny Gentle looking at Tommy's jacket.

Chapter Six

A change of musical direction

One of the many reasons for the change was that was the year that Jack Good's other rock show for TV 'Boy Meets Girl' had come to its natural conclusion. It was replaced by another show called 'Wham' this show featured most of the rock and roll and pop singers in Great Britain over it's time. Now over that period of time Peter and the other the other Parnes Boys were doing one nighters, it was very frustrating time in their careers, Peter in particular felt that his career had stalled, he wasn't getting anywhere. When he tried to raise the subject with Larry, there were constant rows, arguments about money, they argued about everything really. In the face of this unpleasantness he knew that it was clearly time to call time on his relationship with Larry Parnes.

So Peter moved on to the next stage of his musical career because by the time he left Parnes he had matured into a very versatile artiste. One of the first things that happened to enhance his career was that his talent as one of the most talented ballad singers to come out of the Rock and Roll era was being recognised. His remarkable voice was coming to attention of orchestra leaders and he received an invitation to sing with The Billy Ternent Orchestra at The Festival of Britain Theatre. Now at that time Peter was leaning towards singing ballads from Musicals, so he remembers that on that night he sang "If I loved You" and "You'll Never Walk Alone". Both of these songs come from Rodgers and Hammerstein's great and unforgettable musical 'Carousel'. The only person who was shocked when he received a standing ovation was Peter himself, as he says, "I was shocked and pleasantly surprised by the audience's reaction to my performance".

Authors Note: If you have ever heard this lovely and modest man sing you will know how effortless he makes the most difficult key change or note sound. Because of that you will know as I do how much he deserves a standing ovation for every song he sings. You may say that I am biased, if I am biased, I am more than proud to be so, because I have been a fan of his voice for nearly sixty years since I first heard his him sing "Chapel of Dreams" in 1959. But what I did not know then was that he is a such a lovely gentleman, who both Margaret and I will now consider to be our friend for as long as we live.

Just after that successful show at The Festival of Britain Theatre, Peter heard from an old friend of his, drummer Jimmy Nicol. Jimmy had played on several rock shows with Peter and was a great admirer of his voice. Incidentally Jimmy's other claim to fame was that he was a stand in on the drums for Ringo Starr with The Beatles. His services were so much in demand that when The Beatles toured Australia he was there on tour with them. As we return to the story, Jimmy told him that The Cyril Stapleton Orchestra had and opening for a singer who had the versatility in his voice to be able to sing Jazz, Ballads,

Rock and Roll, basically all music genres, he asked if Peter was interested. Of course he was, so Jimmy arranged for them to meet, and eager to help, he really built Peter's voice up to Cyril Stapleton.

To such an extent that when Cyril Stapleton asked him to sing, Peter thought "God I will have to live up to the build up that Jimmy has given me". Well he needn't have worried. Because he did sing for Cyril Stapleton and he made a great impression. Cyril could clearly hear that there had been no exaggeration in Jimmy's description of Peter's voice and he had no hesitation in giving him the job as resident male singer with his orchestra. The terms of employment came in the form of a verbal agreement, in those days as with Tommy Bruce and the author, a gentleman's word was his bond and a handshake was more binding than a signature on a carefully worded piece of paper. Of course we all know that there were charlatans who abused this code and made money out of artiste, while the artiste made none. But these miserable excuses for human beings, do not deserve to named or remembered by anyone.

While he was working with Cyril Stapleton and his Orchestra, Peter met another singer, his name was Paul Merrell. Peter remembers Paul as a great ballad singer, in fact he still is, because although he is now in his eighties he is still treading the boards, still singing. Paul got on very well with Peter and they became good pals. There was another male vocalist with Cyril's band, Paul Murphy, he was also a friend, who as you will discover later in the book was responsible for taking Peter to Hamburg, in Germany were he recorded two great songs, "I'm A Fool To Want You" and "Lonely Town". As Peter says himself, "These are really great songs, released on the Polydor label, they really should have done better". He hopes you will take the time to listen to them, should you get the chance. If when you see Peter perform, as we hope you will, please say hello to him and tell him what you think of him and his songs. He has always enjoyed his fans because they are the people who helped fulfil his dream of a career in music.

There came a time later on during Pete's tenure with the Cyril Stapleton Orchestra when a young female vocalist joined them,. Her name was Jand she was a very energetic performer, with a fine voice/ Peter hopes he remembers her surname before we finish the book because he greatly admired her as a performer. Working with the Cyril Stapleton Orchestra was Peter recalls, a vocalists dream. The line-up consisted of a Brass section, Woodwind section, Rhythm section and on occasion Cyril himself would give virtuoso performances on the violin. To have that depth of musicianship behind him was for Peter an absolute dream. To make things even better the whole ensemble got on very well together and they enjoyed great times in each others company.

With these happy memories in mind Peter recalls occasions when he was in the company of the lead trumpeter Johnny Harris, and Paul Merrell they all enjoyed a drink and the occasional spliff. It was after one these occasions that the three of them were enjoying a jam session, this something that musicians like to do when they are relaxing, basically they play what they feel. Peter was playing the Tongos, which are a large percussion instrument similar to the bongos, when for some reason during a musical break Johnny Harris said, "Wow Peter, you are playing better rhythm on those things, than I have ever heard before". Peter thinks that maybe the spliff was affecting Johnny's hearing. He doesn't really know because it is a habit that he has never cultivated, those things just got passed around in those days.

Having said that Johnny Harris went on to become one of the UK's leading conductors, providing backing for artistes of the calibre of Tom Jones, Englebert Humperdinck, Petula Clarke, Lulu, Richard Harris, Paul Anka, Lynda Carter, (Wonder Woman) and the great Shirley Bassey. In fact when Peter toured with Shirley in the late 1960's Johnny Harris was in the band. Johnny Harris had suffered from Polio as a child, being left with bad limp. But with great strength of character he overcame this difficult start in life, and went on to be a very successful musician, who enjoyed a long career.

So it was the resident male singer Peter did his first gig with the orchestra at the Lyceum Ballroom, this venue is now a theatre, then he appeared at The Leicester Square Odeon. They went on to open Streatham Ice Rink and had a month long residency at The Hammersmith Palais. During that time Peter would make many Radio broadcasts, these included programmes such as 'Twenties to the Twist" and 'The Winifred Atwell Show'. He would also go on to make numerous appearances on TV shows. Peter and the orchestra appeared at The Royal Albert Hall where they were on the bill with The Ted Heath Orchestra and The Springfields, who of course had the incomparable Dusty Springfield on lead vocals. These were wonderful days for Peter because, he was being given the opportunity to display the full quality and power of his remarkable voice.

There would be other changes for Peter, not just in his music but in his life as well. Because while he was appearing in summer season at The Alexandria Theatre, in Weymouth with the wonderful Ruby Murray. Ruby Murray was a fabulous performer who was the only British artiste to have five hits in the top twenty at the same time. Readers will recall that only Elvis Presley and Madonna have achieved this feat. This show had a stellar cast which included such luminaries of the show business world as Vic Oliver who was in those days was a very famous violinist, he was topping the bill, a Welsh Comedian, the very funny Wynn Calvin who was known to us all in those days and fresh from their appearances on TV shows such as The David Nixon show and The Good Old Days, remarkable magician Michael Allport with his glamorous assistant, Jennifer, who also happened to be his wife. There was also a dance troupe, but their name eludes Peter at this time.

Now at this time Peter was married to Colleen who also happened to be the sister of his brother's girlfriend, We mention this just to show that it can be a small world when it comes to romance and because Colleen would join Peter during his time in Weymouth. There were problems with the show though, in spite of the fact that

Peter and many other people thought that Vic Oliver was a great violinist and Wynn Calvin was a very funny comedian, both Vic and Wynn's popularity was starting to wane, audiences were looking for something new. This meant that audiences were not at the expected level, because of this the promoter decided that there would have to be changes. Peter remembers a notice going up in theatre, it was signed by the big man of the entertainment world in those days, Bernard Delfonte, so the cast had to take notice. This notice declared that all the artistes on the show would have to take a cut in their wages, otherwise the show would be terminated. The notice caused quite a bit of bother among the cast but, the cuts were duly made, meaning that everybody kept their jobs, the best possible outcome in the circumstances.

During that summer Peter and Colleen became good friends with Ruby Murray and her husband Bernie Burgess who was accompanying her at that time. It should be stated that Bernie was a fine entertainer in his own right, he was a singer who had appeared as one of "The Jones Boys, during the 1950's. As Peter says, "Bernie was an ace guy in every way", he was always very friendly and both he and Ruby took to Colleen and Peter, so much so that they were often invited to dine with Ruby and Bernie. They also stayed with them at their home on occasion and Ruby was always available to spend time with and make life easier for the expectant mum Colleen.

Peter remembers one evening in particular when, Harry Worth a much loved comedian of the day, joined them for dinner. Harry was appearing with Edmund Hockridge and Pearl Carr and Teddy Johnson the pier in Weymouth, he remembers they all had a great time that night. Peter often stayed at Ruby and Bernie's their lovely cottage in Oxshott in Surrey. Indeed after the summer season was over Peter and Colleen were invited once again to stay with them. They had a pleasant time with them staying overnight before they made their way back home the following day.

Shortly after that Bernie and Ruby moved to an even nicer cottage in Wootton near Northampton. Peter kept in touch with them both and he received work from Bernie who by then was acting as the booking agent for two venues, The Cresta Club in Birmingham and The One 0 One Club in Northampton. Bernie booked Peter for both clubs and while he was appearing at these venues, Bernie and Ruby invited him to stay with them. As Peter has said previously he enjoyed their company, so he was happy to accept their invitation. He remembers many evenings spent in the warm hospitality of their home.

In fact Peter got on really well with Ruby, who had a great sense of humour and was a really lovely person. This was way back in the early sixties, almost sixty years ago and Peter lost touch with them both when he went of to Miami and Tennessee in the USA. He later heard that Bernie and Ruby had divorced and he thinks Bernie went to live in Spain. Peter was very shocked to hear about this because he had always thought that they were a lovely couple and ideally suited. He never heard from either of them or saw them again, that is until that is heard that Ruby had died in the 1990's, due to kidney problems that may have been alcohol related.

Authors note; From about 1988 until she sadly died Ruby and her second husband Ray Lamarr were great friends of my wife Margaret and I. During this time I was fortunate enough to work with her on shows where I was the compère. It is known that she did like a little tipple, pouring a drop of her favourite spirit from a china teapot into a china cup, she would pour this drink for herself in the dressing room with a twinkle in her eye, saying, "Only you and I know Dave, darling". Of course we all knew, and we all loved her. Her voice was sweet and true when she sang, right to the very end of her life. We miss all Ruby very much, as do all her fans.

Chapter Seven

Halfords and The George Cooper Agency

After the summer season was over the happy couple, Colleen and Peter, returned to the Kidderminster area to live in Colleen's mother's house at Comberton. The reason for them living there was that Colleen had been pregnant when they moved in and felt that she wanted to be near her mother. At this time Peter was taking a break from show business, or resting as they say. However he was not idle because he had acquired a job at the local branch of Halfords Cycle Shops. He was employed as a window dresser, in that capacity he made visual presentations in the shop window to show off the cycles that were for sale.

While he was working at the shop Peter made friends with a salesman and they would chat to each other to pass the time, no problem there you might think. Well like me you would be wrong if you thought that. The job only lasted for a couple of months because Peter fell out with the shop manager. This man had a strange outlook on workplace relationships, he said the staff were not allowed to talk to each other on the sales floor. Before he walked out Peter told the manager what he thought of him saying, "You are living in the past, if you think that people can't talk to each other in the workplace, you are going back to the days of Charles Dickens and I don't accept your opinion". After he left Halfords he soon found employment with a company called Carpet Trades, this firm was very well known in those days, the company was a large concern who sold carpets all over the world. As usual Peter worked hard but although he may have had a good future with Carpet trades, the management thought well of him, he of course had his mind set on his career in music.

While they were living in Comerton Peter and Colleen's daughter Teena was born on the 1sst of July 1962. Now just prior to her birth at some point during June Peter got a phone call from the The George Cooper Agency, he had worked for the agency on numerous occasions and he got on well with George. This call was a bit different, because it seems George had been approached by a film company who had seen one of Peter's performances on 'Thank Your Lucky Stars', They said that they liked the way Peter looked and that they were interested in auditioning him for the starring role in a film called 'Live Now and Pay Later'. The director would be one of the top directors of the day, Jay Lewis. There had not been much work offered to him at the time, so he was excited by the possibility of being in a film.

Peter did not possess an overcoat an item of clothing that he viewed as essential to looking smart and successful and he wanted to arrive looking both smart successful. This was not a big problem because his brother Charles was kind enough to lend him his. He didn't want to travel there and back in a day so Peter rang his Uncle Bill and asked if he could stay with him overnight. Always happy to see his nephew and help in any way that he could, Bill agreed that Peter could indeed should stay with him. With everything sorted out he went to station bought his ticket, got on the train and went to London. Peter was rather excited about the audition and he was looking forward to meeting the film crew, the directors and the producers,he thought to himself, "Wouldn't it be something if I could actually get the part"?

When he arrived and met the people who were casting the film, they asked him if he had ever acted before. As Peter was quite naive at that time he gave the truthful answer, "No". They asked him some other questions and finally they asked the big one"Did he think he could handle the part"? He had no hesitation in saying that he could. So they gave him the script to take home with him, saying "Take this home with you, read through it and then come back tomorrow and tell us if you still think that you can handle the part." Peter went back to his Uncle Bill's and went through the script with him, he felt very comfortable when he was speaking the lines for the part. The next day after a sleepless night and filled with apprehension, but full of confidence in his own ability Peter caught the tube to the casting office.

When he finally came face to face with the casting crew, before he had chance to read for them, they told him that they had had a rethink and decided to give the part to an experienced actor. Going on to name Ian Hendry as their choice. Peter being the kind of person that he is just thought to himself, "Yes Ian Hendry is a very fine actor, I am not surprised by their choice". After thinking for a moment, he thanked them for their time and then he left the building,. He was feeling rather deflated because this kind of disappointment seemed becoming the norm, for him during that period time. However that is not quite the whole story, Peter just needed to be patient, because there were good things to come and there were better times ahead.

Peter, went back to his uncle's and told him the result of his audition, Uncle Bill was ever supportive and told him to keep on trying, Then he caught the train and returned home to tell his family the disappointing news. He hadn't got the part, but he knew that he would have to dust himself off and start all over again. There was no point in feeling sorry for himself. Something else happened that week a guy who Peter had known on and off for a while called Roger Jackson, came to see him and asked if he knew of any contacts in show business who could help get him started. After mentioning Larry Parnes, Joe Meek and some musicians who were his buddies, Peter asked Roger to have a coffee. They chatted for a while and then armed with the names and information Roger thanked him and then he left. Incidentally Peter had known Roger from the days in Kidderminster when he used to see him, walking around with a bible under his arm, touting some religion or other, he is not sure exactly which one. Having taken the advice and going to see Joe Meek, Roger would go on to be known as Roger Laverne who became the keyboard player with 'The Tornado's'. This was the band who were famous for recording "Telstar" and for being the first British band to have a number one record both here in the UK and the USA. As Peter says and the author knows, because he and Roger Laverne were friends, until Roger passed away, Roger Laverne was a nice guy but a devil with the ladies, he loved them all and married a few, some at the same time, but is another story.

We should take time at this point to mention that one of his appearances on 'Thank Your Lucky Stars' Peter sang a great song, called *The Wall*, this song was one of his own compositions that you will be able to hear now on You Tube and on his CD. There were some of the UK's top chart performers appearing on that episode of the show, Cliff Richard was on the programme that night and he along with the other artistes on the bill was very impressed by both the song Peter sang and by the performance he put in.

No one was more impressed by the song and the performance than the renowned songwriter Michael Black, brother of Don Black who wrote many lovely songs for another late lamented friend of ours Matt Monro. When he later commented on the song Michael went so far as to say, "That is a great song that you sang on 'Thank Your Lucky Stars' Peter, I wish that I had written it". Sadly this the story of yet another chance missed because there some kind of electrical power cut across the country during the show and very few viewers saw Peters performance. This of course did not help sales of the record. Undaunted by yet another setback to his chances of recording success, Peter continued to wow live audiences wherever and whenever he appeared.

As we return to the story Peter remembers some of the were strange things that happened to him as he toured the entertainment venues around the country. On one occasion Peter had been booked to appear at in Ludlow at a pub called 'The Tally Ho'. When he arrived at the venue he was treated to information about the history of the Pub. Now on this occasion he hadn't driven to the gig in his own car, a friend of his from Chaddesley Corbett had been kind enough to drive him there. When they arrived at the venue it was a little early to go on stage, so they went to the bar and Peter ordered a small whiskey for himself and a drink for his friend. While they were standing at the bar he got into a conversation with a guy who turned out to be a lecturer who lived just round the corner from the venue.

For some reason, Peter can't imagine why the conversation came round to talk of ghosts and eventually specifically to the ghosts believed to haunt Ludlow Castle. This guy told Peter that he had been reliably informed, always a suspect phrase, we think, that one day a husband wife had been climbing the steps to make their way up to one of the turrets in the castle, apparently they wanted to see the view. As they were climbing the stairs they encountered a young woman, who was coming down.

Not wishing to squeeze past her in case one of them stumbled or fell, they called out to the young woman saying, "We will retrace our steps back down to an alcove we have just passed, so that you can get by us. They waited some time in the alcove but no one came, there was no sign of the young woman. They waited for some time, so very perplexed as to what might have happened to her, the husband carried on climbing up to the top of the stairs. There was no one to be seen, the lady had, as impossible as it seemed, completely vanished. Although there were people around who heard the story and expressed their apprehension, Peter contemplated the story without fear, because he did not feel threatened by the idea of ghosts.

Little did Peter know that he would be really frightened before he got home that night, by something completely unexpected. After giving his usual successful performance on the show, during which he was well received by the audience, he got changed and prepared to leave. Then he said his farewells and he and his friend left 'The Tally Ho'. They got into the car and they started out on what they both expected to be an uneventful drive home. Suddenly without warning they encountered icy conditions on the roads, the friend who was driving adjusted his speed accordingly but, as they were driving over the Clee Hills the car started to skid. Peter held his breath when the car started to slip out of line, by now it was spinning and completely out of the drivers control. Just as they both became sure that they would crash, the car suddenly righted itself and the driver was back in control. They continued on what turned out to be a very hairy drive back home. There were times when they thought that they would not get home alive, but somehow in spite of more skids and hazards on the road, they made it back in one piece.

This experience gave Peter cause to reflect on how people who are level headed in all things can still be frightened by happenings they feel threatened by. In his case it is not ghosts that make him nervous, with him it takes more tangible threats make him nervous or even frightened. Having said that. He thinks that this experience and other similar ones over the years, have made him more tolerant of other people's concerns and fears about the things that bother them. To loosely quote Shakespeare, "There are more things in heaven and earth Horatio, than are dreamt of in your philosophy". In other words we don't know or understand everything that happens in life, so we should always keep an open mind.

Now during this period of time Peter had been suffering from and performing with an ulcerated throat. This an affliction that will and does strike down all vocal entertainers at some time in the course of their careers. In Peter's case on this occasion the affliction got so bad that he had to make an appointment with a throat specialist. When Peter saw the specialist he said, " I am sorry to have to tell you that your tonsils are rotten, they will need to be removed". The timing of this diagnosis was terrible, so Peter was very hesitant about taking the time to have operation. The reason for his hesitation being that, Cyril Stapleton had just offered him a tour of all the major cities in the UK with his Orchestra as principal support act on 'The Shirley Bassey Show'. It didn't take Peter long to decide, his course of action, he informed the specialist that he was refusing to have his tonsils out at that time and told Cyril Stapleton that he would gladly do the tour.

In spite of his throat infection the show was a great success Peter was at the top of his game. Naturally Shirley Bassey was getting her usual rave reviews, but one of the critics who came to see the show wrote in his review, "Peter Wynne's vocal ability is in the same class as that of Billy Eckstine". This review was extremely flattering for Peter as he has always rated Billy Eckstine's voice. Receiving this written comparison lifted his spirits and helped him to continue to believe that it would only be a matter of time before his long overdue hit record, would be forthcoming. During that tour an offer came in asking him to be part of a Larry Parnes summer season in Great Yarmouth. The cast would include, Lonnie Donegan, Peter Goodright and Larry Parnes latest discovery's Daryl Quist. As part of the summer season, Peter would also be appearing on the Sunday concerts with a host of hit recording artistes that included Marty Wilde, Dave Berry, Herman's Hermits and many more.

Now on that Parnes summer season show Peter, who by now had developed in to a very versatile and accomplished entertainer would not only be doing his own solo spot. He was required to sing duets with an Australian soprano, whose name has been lost from his memory, he does remember that the lady had a lovely voice. There was also the opportunity for him to appear in sketches, when heard this he hoped they didn't require him to dress up in a skirt as he had on 'Idols On Parade'. Of course he did the sketches, but he always felt that this kind of entertainment took him away from his chosen role as a big ballad singer.

On one occasion Lonnie Donegan came to wings to watch and listen to Peter's performance, he was really enjoying it. Then suddenly realising that Peter was singing his last song and that he was due to be on next, Lonnie noticed that he was still wearing his dressing gown! He needed to get changed so the only thing he could do before running to his dressing room was shout to Peter, "Do my first number"! Luckily it was a song that Peter knew well so he had no trouble complying with Lonnie's request. Unfortunately the title of the song evades him at the moment. Anyway while Lonnie went and got dressed for his spot, Peter carried on performing making for a seamless transition when Lonnie did come on stage. Very smoothly Lonnie thanked Peter for his performance and encouraged the audience to give him another round of applause, which they did. Then he did his act with his usual own much loved style, before closing the show to rapturous applause. Professional artistes have the ability to make the audience believe that anything that happens is always scripted and that is what they believed on this occasion.

Authors note: I was lucky enough to meet and know Lonnie Donegan. We were both Peter Wynne fans and Lonnie took great delight in telling me this story. The reason he wasn't dressed was because he liked to listen to Peter singing from the wings, on this occasion he got lost in the wonder of Peter's voice, forgetting to go and get ready for his own performance. Peter is far to modest a man to have realised that a fellow entertainer held him in such high esteem. This still true today I recently attended a function and not for the first time found myself in the company of the previously mentioned Vince Eager,. I told Vince that I was in the process of writing Peter Wynne's book, his reply was, "Peter Wynne? Oh yes, I remember him, nice guy, great voice, please give him my best". Showing that even after all these years his fellow performers, still remember Peter's remarkable voice.

Incidentally, I have to say as the author of this and other books, that Vince Eager is a true gentleman, who wrote a lovely foreword for Tommy Bruce's book *Have Gravel Will Travel*. He also deservedly has a chapter in *The Long Road*. Vince Eager is still out there performing for audiences as only he can, I recommend that if you have never had the pleasure of seeing him you go along to one of his, you won't be disappointed. Vince Eager is as he has always been, one of the good guys and he is still a great performer.

Getting back to the subject, there was another occasion when Peter had to step into the breach and appear for another artiste during that summer season. Daryl Quist who Peter liked as a person and had made a good friend of turned up late for a show and stumbled on stage. Not to put too fine a point on it, he was clearly stoned. Daryl's performance was abysmal as he stumbled and staggered around the stage with no idea of where he was or what he was doing. The next day the producer having relayed what had happened back to Larry Parnes, who sacked Daryl Quist, and he left the show immediately.

Peter thinks that Daryl must have gone back home to Canada, it is certain that he has never been heard of by Peter or anyone he knows since. The director of the show asked Peter if he would do Daryl's spot with the sobriquet, Angela Eaton as well as making his own performance. Because he knew the songs, after all he had heard them every night for weeks, Peter agreed to give it a go. Lonnie Donegan used to joke with him that the show should have been called 'The Peter Wynne Show' because Peter seemed be on stage all the time. Looking back he must have been on stage for at least a couple of hours every performance.

It was while he was appearing on this summer season show in Great Yarmouth, that Peter met Justin Hayward, who would go on to feature in that fantastic group 'The Moody Blues'. They got on really well right from the moment that they met and two of them became great friends. At that time Justin was playing guitar on the Sunday matinees for Marty Wilde and his wife Joyce. Those readers who were fans of Larry Parnes, 'Rock and Trad Shows' will remember that Joyce had been one of the Vernon Girls before she married Marty. Joyce had a lovely voice and could easily have had a successful solo career if she had chosen to go down that route. Instead she chose to be a wife and mother and take care of things for Marty, as you might expect Joyce does a very good job in every aspect of her life.

At the time Peter was living in a flat on the High Street and he would let Justin, come round and have a bath occasionally. Justin appreciated this, because the bathroom at his own his digs, only had a shower and he really enjoyed the opportunity to have a good soak. When the two of them got together they would reminisce about the London Palladium days when Justin used to put his hands through the curtain while Peter stood with his hands behind his back, so that Justin could play the cords on the guitar.

The audience were totally unaware that Peter couldn't play the guitar, they just accepted that he played and sang. While he was visiting at the flat Justin who has always been a prolific songwriter would play some of the songs that he had been writing. Because he needed to have a regular income Justin had signed a contract with Lonnie Donegan Publishing, in the wording of the contract he gave away the rights to the songs he had written at that time, for a small wage, there were many people back then who did something like this and so never received the credit never mind the royalties that should have been theirs, when their songs became hits..

Now as the years have gone by everyone has come to know that Justin has penned and performed some terrific hits, but it was clear to Peter that Justin regretted signing away the rights to some of the other songs that he had written. Isn't that the way in life? We all tend to act in haste and repent at our leisure, hindsight is a wonderful thing. Making the right decisions is easier said than done when you are trying to make your way in life and you need to pay the rent and put food on the table. Justin and Peter's friendship lasted through that summer season and beyond, right up to recent times, although sad to say they have now lost touch with each other.

During this period of time Peter heard through the grapevine that he was going to be offered an appearance on TV show 'Sunday Night at the London Palladium'. He was excited about the prospect, but somehow an actual appearance on the show never came to pass. The rumour seemed to have credence because Peter had heard about the possibility from Pamela Davis, who worked on the show. Pamela had told him that she had heard he was going to be booked for the show, she usually had the right information so he was hopeful. As he says, "That's showbiz, always full of rumours, you never know what to believe" .

When the show that he was appearing in with Lonnie Donegan had finished it's run, Peter returned to London expecting that other gigs would be on the horizon. Instead he found that work was a bit thin on the ground, in fact there was nothing lined up for him by his current agent. Never one to rest on his laurels, Peter took matters into his own hands and signed on with an agency that he hoped would be able to find him some work as an extra on TV programmes, Films, Commercials, that sort of thing. This turned out to be a good idea, he is clearly very photogenic and the agency soon found him work. The first job the agency gave him was a photo shoot with a model called Sara Leighton. The film company dressed him in the most up to date fashionable clothing and then they had him pose in shots with Sara, clearly for some fashion house but he doesn't remember which one.

The shoot was clearly a great success and more work of a similar nature quickly followed. The next job was for magazines called 'She' and 'The Lady' respectively. On these photo shoots he was pleased to find himself working with the renowned theatre and TV actress

Sheila Hancock. Readers will be aware that her outstanding career has been recognised by her peers and fans alike. Indeed she has been a recipient of a Laurence Olivier award for best supporting actress in a musical for her role in Cabaret. She enjoyed a long and happy marriage to the outstanding actor, John Thaw.

Getting back to Peters memories of the photo shoot, although he assumed that the photographer knew what he was doing Peter felt that the shots were rather silly. There are two that he remembers. In one he had to measure Sheila's height for some inexplicable reason, although he does recall that Sheila is rather tall. The other photographs had her leapfrogging over his back when he was bending over, he had no idea then or now why they wanted such silly poses. Still, he does remember that they paid him very well for these acts of silliness. There were other shots taken with Sheila but Peter has completely forgotten what they were.

One thing he does remember from those days is appearing in a very funny commercial with the well known comedian Ronnie Barker famous for appearing in 'That Was The Week That Was and 'The Two Ronnie's' among other great TV shows. The other principle was the actor Tony Booth, who was appearing in a TV series called 'Catch hand' around that time. Tony who readers may be aware was former Prime Minister Tony Blair's father in law in later years, would go on to appear in other TV Shows such as, 'Till Death Us Do Part' with Dandy Nichols Una Stubbs and Warren Mitchell. Many years later

Tony married Coronation street actress Pat Phoenix, having appeared in the show himself for a time.

The commercial that the three of them appeared in was a an advert for a well known beer, it should have been an all day shoot, but for some reason Peter had to leave the set after a couple of hours. He thinks he must have had an appointment for something, perhaps an audition, but he can't remember what. Whatever it was it would have had to have been important to take him away from the set part way through filming. He does remember that the agency paid him for the full day which was he thinks of it now, a very nice thing for them to have done.

An other another occasion Peter remembers while he was working for that particular casting agency was when he was sent to appear in a cigarette commercial. He recalls that he was filming on a train with comedy actor Victor Spinetti. Incidentally Victor was a very funny character, who was famous for a variety of roles throughout his career, including his appearance in no less than three of the The Beatles films, 'A Hard Day's Night', 'Help' and 'Magical Mystery Tour. He also won a Tony award for the show 'Oh What A Lovely War' appearing in many other plays and films during what has been a stellar career.

Returning to the commercial Peter and Victor were on a train, with Peter being rather typecast in the part of a rock singer. The scene called for him to be sitting in a railway carriage with his guitar case beside him on the floor. At some point Victor came wandering through the train with an open packet of Benson and Hedges cigarettes in his hand. He proceeded to trip over Peter's foot, this caused the cigarette packet to fly in the air, it was a scene that required great comic timing on behalf of them both, Peter caught the packet, and with a nod took a cigarette out of the packet and lit. Then he returned the packet to Victor who carried on walking through train, all the while contriving to find different ways of losing his cigarettes. This commercial was only shown on the continent as by this time the advertising of cigarettes in the UK was they like to say now a 'Complete No, No'!

There were acting roles that came Peter's way during his time in London and one occasion In 1965 he found himself appearing in a play called 'A Whistle and Funny Hat' with Patrick Mower. In only a few years time Patrick Mower would become famous for appearances in TV shows such as 'Callan', going on to make several films, including 'The Devil Rides Out and 'The Cry of The Banshee' to name but two. Patrick Mower is still a working actor and has been appearing in the popular TV soap Emmerdale, since the year 2000 playing the part of Rodney Blackstock.

The two of them got on very well and became friendly, often enjoying a cuppa in the canteen. On one occasion the two of them went for their lunch together. While they were there enjoying their food, in the course of conversation, Patrick took the opportunity to tell Peter that he reminded him of a young Oliver Reed. He was rather flattered and strangely enough it seems to have been a family trait to be mistaken for this great actor. Peter says this because his brother was mistaken for Ollie Reed when he was staying at Ruthin Castle in Wales.

Despite his brother's protestations the hotel staff refused to accept that he wasn't Oliver Reed travelling incognito. This very interesting but one thing we can be sure of, Peter's amazing voice has never been mistaken for anyone else's, it is far to distinctive for that! In fact in many ways this was a very good year for Peter, because as we see in the next chapter he would be appearing win the best of company in theatre that every performer the world over, wishes for the most, The London Palladium.

It is relevant to the foreword of the next chapter that Dave, the author and his wife Margaret, were fortunate enough to spend time with and see Frank Ifield perform, during his tour of the UK in 2018. Their conversations about earlier times led to Frank's fond memories of working with Peter Wynne for three months at the London Palladium in 1965/66. This was when they appeared in the pantomime 'Babes in the Wood'. These conversations with Frank Ifield on the 1st 2nd and 3rd of June 2018 led to Frank being kind enough to write the following foreword for this book. Frank Ifield is in the opinion of all who know him a fine artiste, a man of his word and a true gentleman. We are privileged to know him, long may he continue to share his great talent with us all. One other thing, Dave and Margaret's favourite recording by Frank is "Three Good Reasons" we have to say that he thrilled us by performing it on these shows.

Even better thanks to Frank and his friend Bill, we now have this lovely song on CD, so we are able to listen to it all the time. It may also be of interest that another old friend of Peter and I, song writer Les Reed wrote this lovely song. Les has not been in the best of health of late, but I spoke to him recently and he wished Peter well in all he does and remembers him well.

Photoshoot with Sheila Hancock

Foreword by Frank Ifield:
Happy days with Peter Wynne

To coin a phrase "I Remember You" Peter Wynne as being my offsider Will Scarlett in my favourite Pantomime from The London Palladium. "Babes in the Wood" in 1965/66/ I played the part of Robin Hood and you were part of the merry men. In fact you were the most important henchman to me as you were the only professional singer of the bunch. While our voices blended perfectly it made the total group sound like the Norman Luboff Choir in songs like, "When You're Dressed in Lincoln Green" and "Down With Tyranny".

The second half opened on the song "Nottingham Fair" and in this picturesque scene, the villainous Sheriff of Nottingham, in a devious plot to lure Robin Hood out of hiding, put on an archery contest promising the winner of the contest the hand of the fair maiden, Maid Marion. Meanwhile you Peter as Will Scarlett in disguise headed up the motley team of contestants. Watching from the wings I must admit to being a little perturbed that as time went on your aim became very sharp and you would invariably win hands down in the first round.

Enter stage left "Robert The Tinker" which of course was me as Robin disguise, who would now be expected to beat the arrow that was closest to the bulls-eye. To the sound of the roll of drums I would take aim and pray that my arrow would find the centre of the target...

And most times it did, however there were odd times Mr Wynne that you would be the nearest- Quickly the dastardly sheriff would interject with, "Ahah, Methinks that the Tinker has attempted to deceive me... Lease another shaft!" While the two arrows were taken from the target. I aligned my sight again and let fly with a new arrow which obviously had no equal. Thus Robin Hood now unmasked made off with his much prized Maid Marion, followed by his trusty band of outlaws.

This may spark a few memories and maybe a slight twinge of guilty conscience with you Peter and I must admit this most memorable time still makes me smile and I feel we experienced great joy with happiness we brought to our audiences and a great deal of pride that they in turn made us feel inside.
Thanks for sharing this with me.

Frank Ifield.
International singing and hit recording star.

Frank Ifield with Dave Lodge, the author of this book and his lovely wife Margaret

Chapter Eight
'Babes In The Wood At The London Palladium

This was the year, 1965, that Peter auditioned to understudy Frank Ifield in the part of Robin Hood in the pantomime titled 'Babes In The Wood'. In the event he was cast in the part of Will Scarlet. The production befitted from a large cast that apart from Frank Ifield and Peter included famous Liverpool comedian Arthur Askey, comedy actors Roy Kinnear, Syd James and Kenneth Connor, these actors of course found great acclaim in the Carry On films. The show also featured Tricia Mooney a very attractive actress and singer of the day. One of the Babes in the Wood was played by Sharon Osbourne, daughter of the redoubtable Don Arden - she would go on to marry Ozzie Osborne of Black Sabbath fame. (These days she is known for her association with Simon Cowell's X-Factor). The other Babe was Elaine Paige, who has enjoyed great success in musical theatre, appearing in Musicals such as Cats, Evita and Chess to name but three. She now has a radio programme and who knows one day you might hear her play Peter 's recording of "This my Beloved".

There were loads of other stars playing the part of Robin Hood's Merry Men, far to many for Peter to be able to remember so many years later. Sad to recall the likeable and much loved, Roy Kinnear died after falling from a horse and breaking his pelvis while filming the 'The Return of The Musketeers'. This was in 1988, while he was reprising the role of Planchet that he had played with distinction. He actually died from a subsequent heart attack, that he suffered while in hospital recovering from his injuries, he is much missed by all his fans and all who were lucky enough to know him. Incidentally the 'Musketeers' films had a stellar cast which featured Oliver Reed in the role of Athos, Frank Finlay, Porthos, Michael York, d'Artagnand Richard Chamberlain was Aramis, The very lovely and talented Faye Dunaway, played Milady de Winter.

Returning to the pantomime, it was a box office success running for three months, attracting good audiences and being well reviewed at the time. Of course with such a lively story line and there were quite a few incidents and accidents during the run. These accidents were due to the cast being chased and energetic sword fights, not to mention arrows flying around the stage. The accidents Peter remembers include the occasion when Frank Ifield got a nasty cut on his forehead just above the top of his eyebrow. On that occasion Peter thought that he might have to go on as Robin Hood replacing Frank. But luckily for Frank it was only a minor scrape, he soon recovered after a little first aid and was able continue with his performance. Leaving Peter free to continue in the role of Robin's companion Will Scarlet.

The next accident that occurred found Peter on the receiving end, he had been fencing with one of the tower guards. The sword fight had been well choreographed but just as the scene was ending the guard unexpectedly took an extra swipe with his sword, in doing so he caught Peter off guard and struck him, cutting the top of his head. As Peter says, "Will Scarlet really was scarlet on that occasion because of the all blood that was flowing quickly down his face". With blood spurting from the wound Peter ran to his exit. As soon as he got off stage a member of the crew tried to stem the flow of blood, but it soon became clear the blood was continuing to pour from the wound, so there was no choice, he had to be rushed out of theatre and taken by car to the medical centre that was situated just off Oxford Street.

Looking back on the incident Peter thinks that he must have presented a interesting figure when he arrived at the medical centre, as he was still in costume. It would not be exaggerating to say that his tall powerful figure, clad in his Will Scarlet outfit that consisted of a red hood, a leather top which had chrome studs in the shoulder and chest piece, caused a bit of a sensation. Of course to complete the ensemble he was wearing thick red woollen tights, not the most dignified attire. As Peter says, "There was a great deal of laughing and tittering from the medical staff, when they saw me".

He was examined and it was necessary for the medical staff to put five stitches in top of his head. He was mindful that he would soon be back on stage so he did ask the nurse to shave as little hair from around the wound as possible, saying to her, "I am appearing in the pantomime as Will Scarlett, not Friar Tuck"! Ever the trouper Peter made it back to theatre in time to appear in the finale. It has to be said that looking back on the incident he does remember the resultant headache more than the cut on his head.

As he looks back on the events that took place, it is almost certain that the show would not have passed the more stringent health and safety tests that are carried out today for such productions. Having said that Peter has memories of the show that didn't involve people getting hurt. Like the times they were playing out the archery contest, naturally Robin Hood was suppose to win but Peter in the role of Will Scarlet couldn't help being more accurate with the placement of his arrows and because of this beating some of Frank's efforts as Robin Hood.

Perhaps the time that Peter had spent practising with his Christmas bow and arrows years before, made the difference who knows, for whatever reason he was at least equal to Frank when it came to judging the best bowman in the pantomime. In any event he continually hit the eagles eye on the target, in spite of the fact that Peter and the other members of the cast had all been told to aim away from the eagles eye so that Robin Hood could win. On some occasions it just seemed impossible to follow the instruction, because the arrows of Will Scarlet couldn't help getting closer to the centre of the target than those of Robin Hood.

These efforts had the audience in fits of laughter during every performance for three months. They thought it was hilarious watching Robin Hood trying desperately to win the archery contest. As Peter said to Frank Ifield after these scenes, " I'm sorry Frank, but the fact is you are from Aussie and I am an English bowman". Adding a second apology for his sense of humour "Sorry Frank, I really am only joking". He thinks that his apology was accepted, it was hard to tell because neither of them could stop laughing. Frank may not have been the most accurate of bowmen on every occasion but Peter is quick to point out that Frank Ifield had a wonderful voice, having hits with songs like "The Wayward Wind and the unforgettable, "I Remember You". He often thinks of Frank and those happy days in his company and will always wish him well.

There was a rather more frightening incident that Peter remembers from his time in pantomime that it had nothing to do with the actual show. The incident involved an off stage incident that occurred with a member of the cast. The memory concerns a rather small man that Peter shared a dressing room with. There were two of these men and one of them was playing Bonzo Dog in the pantomime. The other was one of Johnny Hutch's famous Herculean's troupe who were part of pantomime cast. Well on the occasion in question, the two men burst into the dressing room arguing furiously, they having a real go at each other. Peter, as is always his way on such occasions tried to act as peacemaker, he stood up and spoke quietly to them saying, "Come on lads keep your voices down, I would like to relax before the show".

He then sat down, as he did he felt an arm grab him round the neck from behind, then unbelievably he felt the shock of cold steel at his throat, Peter was in no doubt, he just knew that it was a razor.

Then the small man spoke, "I've got a brother who is over six foot tall, he will get you and when he does, he will slit your throat". Then the man added, rather unnecessarily, "This a razor"! Peter replied, "Yes I know" The man then took the razor away from his throat and Peter breathed a sigh of relief. The next night the same fellow was sitting by the stage door waiting for him to arrive, the bloke spoke to him and apologised profusely for the incident with razor.

So Peter ever the gentleman, accepted his apology and said no more about the incident. He really is a lovely man as is shown by the things related during this book. In my experience as the author and now I hope his friend, I can say that Peter Wynne is that rarest of men, a man who has not got a bad bone in his body. As the months have gone by having started out as a fan of his voice and his music, I have come to like and respect him very much

Just a few words on Johnny Hutch because he really was a remarkable man. A man who was one of the stalwarts of Circus and Variety shows from the 1920's right through until his death at the age ninety three. Readers of the same age as the author will remember Johnny, as a brilliant musician and acrobat, who possessed great comic timing. He toured theatres and TV shows with The Seven Volants, Johnny Hutch's Herculeans and The Half Wits. His acrobatic troupes were usually attired for stage performances in white leotards and red bloomers, sporting curly moustaches. These men were more than just talented gymnasts, they were hilarious and their performances were brilliant. Johnny himself made many appearances on the Benny Hill Show and remarkably at the age of seventy nine, won the World Circus championships, by performing a full twisting backward somersault. As Peter rightly says, "They just don't make men like that any more".

At this point the reader should know that Peter had changed his name to Simon Smith. The reason for this name change was that he wanted to become a member of Equity, the entertainers union. This was because it had come to his attention that all artistes who were appearing in theatre productions and pantomimes should, indeed had to be members of Equity. He was happy to comply with the rule so he made his application, still using the name Peter Wynne. He knew that he had previously been a member, because Larry Parnes had enrolled him. However because he had parted company with Larry a year or two previously, the subscription had lapsed. When he applied to rejoin he found that there was another Peter Wynne registered with them, so he would have to change his name.

Needing to find another stage name Peter spoke to his A&R Man Bob Barrett and they both agreed on Simon Smith. It was under that name that he recorded a song based on Borodin's String Quartet in D titled "And This Is My Beloved" from the 1953 musical 'Kismet' this being a song which had been a great success when recorded by Mario Lanza. At the same time he also recorded song written by himself and Bob Barrett "I Just Can't Live Without You" on the B side of the record, these recordings were on the Columbia label. There have been some great recordings and renditions of "And This My Beloved" and

Peter's recording stands right up there with the very best of them. Incidentally Peter sang, "And This My Beloved' to very appreciative audiences during every performance of 'Babes In The Wood'.

The unfortunate thing about the name change is that Peter, because Larry had not told him what his Equity number was could not associate himself with the name Peter Wynne. Because of this he became confused when he spoke to Equity. The thing that he did not realise was that the Peter Wynne registered with Equity was then and is now, him. He need not have changed his name to Simon Smith, to make matters worse this choice of name change was not as he now believes one of the best choices he has made during his career. Saying that he never regrets any thing that he did to try and advance his career, nor does he allow mistakes or errors of judgement to spoil his intention to go forward. To this very day Peter Wynne is still embracing change and innovation in his career and he is still moving forward in the musical aspects of his career.

Peter as Will Scarlett in Babes in the Wood 1966

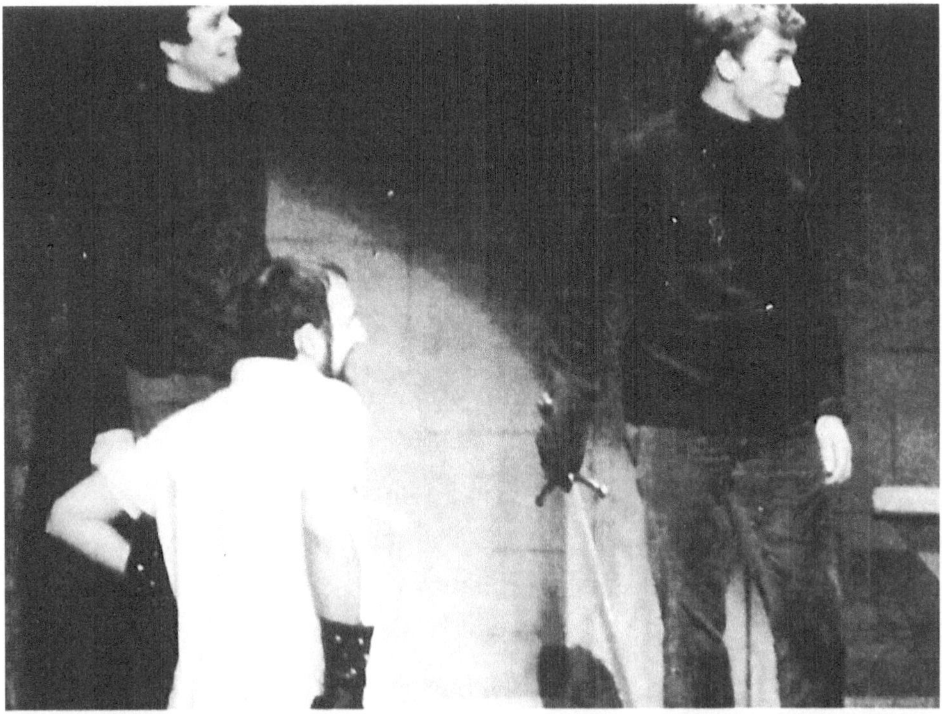

Peter, Frank Ifield and Alan Curtis rehearsing a scene with swords at London Palladium

Chapter Nine

Life as Simon Smith

Work was coming in regularly now and Peter was given a date to appear on the TV show "Stars and Garters". This was the show made famous by Kathy Kirby, Tommy Bruce, Vince Hill and Clinton Ford, to name just four of the regular cast. Unfortunately he was unable to appear on the show due to his commitment to 'Babes in the Wood' at the Palladium. It is always the way when you are in show business, regular work is more important than one off appearances. This applies even if that one off show might bring an artiste to greater prominence. Show promoters were not inclined to release popular performers from even one appearance on a long running show, so Peter had to fulfil his contractual obligations and forgo this television opportunity.

However there were plus points to appearing at the London Palladium one of these was meeting many showbiz entertainers who came to see the pantomime. Peter remembers meeting Bruce Forsyth and Cliff Richard who came backstage to speak with the cast members. Incidentally, speaking of Cliff Richard, the music for 'Babes in The Wood' had been penned by members of Cliff's backing group The Shadows.

Another interesting thing happened while he was appearing at the Palladium that was also connected with The Shadows. Incidentally the Shadows were not just Cliff Richards backing Group, they were stars in their own right, having chat success with great instrumentals like 'Apache' 'Walk Don't Run' and other lovely tunes. The interesting thing that happened, occurred during the journey Peter had to make getting home after the show each night. It came about because he and his wife Colleen had moved to an apartment in West Norwood, more on that as we go on. This move meant that he had to catch the train every night, after the curtain had come down at the Palladium. So on this particular night as he was running for the train, he bumped into an old friend, Brian 'Licorice' Locking. 'Licorice' had played bass guitar with The Shadows,when replacing Jet Harris, naturally backing Cliff on many occasions becoming a regular member of the band.

Incidentally Licorice had also appeared with Cliff and The Shadows in the film 'Summer Holiday'. Licorice had got to know Peter when he was part of the band that backed him when Peter was appearing in one nighters with Billy Fury. The two men were delighted to see each other again. They both got on the train and while they were talking Lic told Peter the surprising news that he had become a born again Christiand had retired from show business. It is good to know that Lic Locking did not remain retired from the music business and can still been heard and seen on shows,As they travelled along they reminisced about the old days and enjoyed a few good laughs.

They said they farewells and parted company when Lic got off at his station, which happened to be Crystal Palace.

As Peter has told me, he and 'Licorice' went on to become even greater friends as the years passed by. There is no doubt that their friendship still stands the test of time because they remain friends to this day and are still in touch as we write this book. In fact Lic lives in North Wales not ten minutes from the place where Peter used to live. There have been many happy occasions when the two of them get together and drink cups of tea while they reminisce about the old days. Lic plays excellent harmonica these days as well as bass and guitar, indeed he started out many years ago in a harmonica gang, called The Harmonica Vagabonds with two friends, one who didn't stay in show business called Roy Clarke, who had his own engineering business. The other very talented lad was, Roy Taylor aka Vince Eager. Who as we all know is a leading performer and like Peter made his early name as one of Parnes boys.

Funnily enough a few years ago Vince Eager was kind enough to book Tommy Bruce to appear with him in Grantham. On that show he put his old gang, The Harmonica Vagabonds back together again, I was with Tommy as his manager and had the privilege of seeing just how talented these three friends were. Peter rightly regards his old mate 'Licorice' as great musician, there are many people both in and out of the business who agree with him.

Touching on an aspect of their personal life, Colleen and Peter had found what appeared to be a grand little flat in West Norwood. It seemed the ideal place to make their home. When they walked in to view the property they were looking all round it and seeing that it was a well furnished flat. It had a big bay window which provided a grand vista, looking out of that window every morning would, it seemed be a great way to start the day. Everything was fine until they entered the bedroom, when they did Peter turned back the bed sheets and saw to his horror, about a dozen black beetles running all over the mattress. He quickly went into the bathroom where he found a bar of soap and, with apologies to those readers who love all creatures, crushed the Beatles. As Peter says, with apologies for the pun, "They literally make me crawl". They took the flat, being under the misapprehension that there would be no further sightings of beetles. However it turned out to be as serious infestation and they were woken up on many a night by the sound of a marching army of beetles as they ran down the wooden floored hallway.

Outside the flat down the entrance corridor Peter found that there was a large hole in the concrete. He decided to look down into it, when he did Peter could see water and he believed that this building fault was where the Beatles were coming from. So the following day Peter informed the estate agent of what he had found and seen. Very soon after that, the following day in fact, the agent came round to deal with the problem. The agents efforts to solve the problem were unsuccessful. Unable to stand the situation any longer, Colleen and Peter decided that they would live at that address for another few weeks until they found some other accommodation. They soon found their alternative accommodation and moved on. They simply just couldn't get used to living with a troupe of Beatles, Peter says, "Sorry John, Paul, George and Ringo".

The couple moved from the West Norwood address into a ground floor flat in Wimbledon, at least this place wasn't suffering from any kind of infestation. Shortly after they had settled in, David Firmstone, a friend of Peter's and co-writer on some of his songs, came and told him that a recording session had been arranged for him at The Deutsche Grammophon Company in Hamburg. So Peter soon found himself on a flight to Hamburg, On his arrival in Hamburg he booked himself in to a hotel near, to the recording studio.

Paul Murphy, who Peter knew from his time singing with the Cyril Stapleton Orchestra in the early sixties came to the hotel to meet him and he invited Peter to go out for a few drinks, saying, "Relax for a while and then we will go and have a meal and a drink". Then he added," I will drop back at your hotel later", Paul was good as his word, because much later after Peter had enjoyed few German beers and some wonderful cooked chicken, Paul dropped him back at his hotel. When he got up to his room Peter found that his bed had no blankets just an eiderdown, he thought this, rather strange, but being tired he just got under the eiderdown and went to sleep. He found out later when he enquired that the item was a duvet, not an eiderdown. This was an item that like most of us at that time, he hadn't come across before.

In spite of thinking that he was short of bedding, Peter enjoyed a very comfortable night in his hotel room and woke up feeling refreshed the following morning. When he got up he got ready to go to the recording studio, Paul had given him directions and it wasn't far from the hotel. The building the studio was in turned out to be a massive place, because of this he became a little concerned that he wouldn't find the studio in time. However after he had been walking round the building for a while he managed to find Paul's office. When the two got together they spent some considerable time discussing the plans for the recording session. After they had talked for a while Paul played the two songs which he wanted Peter to record. Clearly a lot of thought had gone into this recording session, there would be no time wasted going through songs to see which ones suited Peter.

As Peter says, "Paul had chosen two lovely songs", one titled "I Am A Fool To Want You", and the other, "Lonely Town". When he was told that the following day he would be recording the songs with a full orchestra, Peter was delighted, because he always enjoyed working with an orchestra. After their meeting he took the songs away with him so that he could learn them in the hotel. By the time Peter returned to the studio again the following day, he had both songs off pat. It was a large studio and he was placed in a booth that was situated in the middle of the room. He was completely in the dark, no lights at all, the reason he was given for this was that it was felt, by the production team, that in this way he would get a better feel for the music, and this feel would help his interpretation of the songs. Time passed quickly all to soon the recordings were ready to be listened to.

Paul was very pleased with recordings, telling Peter that they would be the first pop songs recorded by that studio to be released in the UK, by that company. Sadly like many other songs that Peter had recorded, the recordings were released with no promotion or push behind them. This meant that they did not get many plays on the radio. Peter thinks it was a great shame because they are two excellent songs, given the production had been given to the sound, the musicianship in the orchestra, added to his vocal interpretation, they could and indeed should have made the charts. Authors note: It seems that the record companies distribution network was inadequate, It is an old story, so many artistes suffered this way back then. Once again I will just say that if you get a copy of the CD, The Peter Wynne Story, a double album I might add, you can hear and judge the songs for yourselves.

When The Palladium pantomime run was over early in 1966, eager to continue working in theatres, by this time Peter had started to use his new stage name, Simon Smith. So it was Simon who auditioned for the role of King Arthur in a touring production of 'Camelot'. Unfortunately he was told after his audition, that the main character roles had already been cast. But, a rose by any name would smell or in this case, sound as sweet, and the producers were very impressed with Peter's aka Simon Smith's voice so they had no hesitation in offering him the chance to understudy the part of Sir Lancelot and gave him the role of Sir Lionel. Peter was pleased to accept, as he felt that appearing in this musical would be a genuine step forward in his career, one that would hopefully lead to other musicals and theatre shows.

The production was blessed with a stellar cast, with such luminaries of the musical theatre world as Bruce Trent. Now Bruce had been thrilling audiences with his voice since before the second World War and was in great demand for theatre shows between 1950 and 1970. For example he had appeared in long running shows in the West End of London, including 'Brigadoon' in 1950 and in 1953 he appeared in 'Wish you were Here'. In this production of 'Camelot' he had been cast in the role of King Arthur.

Then there was Laurence Payne, famous for both his film TV and theatre, roles, readers may remember him. In this production he was playing the part of Sir Lancelot. The very lovely and talented actress Susan Swinford had been cast in the role Guinevere, a role which incidentally she would reprise in Australian theatres, in future years. Susan who had become well known to the viewing audience who had appeared in films and many popular TV series such as 'Ivanhoe' 1958 in which she was cast as Lady Eleanor and in 1962 she played the part of Jane in 'The Cheaters'. Her theatre appearances included appearing with Evelyn Laye and Anton Walbrook at the London Hippodrome in the musical 'Wedding in Paris'.

During the run of this show Peter would meet, and become friendly with a girl singer, her name was Sian Hopkins. Sian was very a popular singer who came from Wales. Peter describes her as a Welsh Soprano, Sian had been featured on the long running TV show 'Land of Song, appearing with the great Ivor Emmanuel. For this run of 'Camelot' she had been cast in the role of a water nymph. Due to the length of time the show was on the road, their friendship would become stronger as the tour went on.

So while Peter's under the guise of the name of Simon Smith, career seemed to be moving forward, there were problems at home. This was because Colleen, who was now living in a flat that Peter had found for them in Highgate, London, was starting to appear distant and disinterested when he spoke to her. So much so that in the conversations they had when he phoned her, whenever he could from where ever he was appearing, he began to feel that her tone stretched between being icy and indifferent. It has to be said that there were no mobile phones in those days, so his calls were few and far between, really just whenever he noticed a phone box. He really felt that he and Colleen were drifting apart, while at the same time he was getting more involved with Sian Hopkins, the water nymph from Wales.

So it was that their marriage eventually broke down, Colleen and Peter parted for good during that tour of Camelot. When the tour finally came to a close, Peter made a decision about his future and went back to live in Clapham Common, for a short time. Of course his heart was always in Wales so it wasn't long before he made arrangements to move to Cardiff. He had decided to live with Sian Hopkins, they were very much in love by now and it seemed the only sensible way forward for them both. So life was changing for

Peter again, he really hoped it would be a successful change, both personally and professionally.

While he was living in Cardiff, Peter had the good fortune to meet a man who was to become one of his greatest mates. More than that he would be instrumental in helping Peter take a massive step forward with his career. This man's name was Lenny James and he had a taxi firm in Cardiff. The first time they met was when Peter called a cab to take him to a gig at The Double Diamond Club in Caerphilly. When the cab arrived Peter got in and the two men struck up a conversation about the venues that he had appeared in and the shows that he had done, his career to date really. Len was very impressed by what heard and said that he would like to bring his wife Jan to see the show, he also mentioned that she was a big fan of Cliff Richard.

Now at that time Peter was doing impressions of various artistes during in his show so having heard this he included an impression of Cliff Richard for Jan. The show was a great success and Len and Jan really enjoyed the show. When the cabaret was over Len took the opportunity to speak to Peter about his management. Peter replied honestly saying, "I don't actually have any management or representation at the moment". Then Len asked, "Do you think I could give it a go? I'll try hard and see what I can do ". He had a very strong determined look on his face, so Peter agreed to let him try. He thought at the time,"Let's just to see if he could get some good dates in the South Wales area". Len was a very resourceful man and his efforts to bring in work, resulted in more than either of them could ever have imagined, and some of that work was in places Peter could never have thought of.

Another thing happened while Peter was living in Wales, was that he and Sian had a son, they called him Simon. The lad was born on the 6th August 1967, this event made for very happy family at that time. Professionally things were happening for both of them all the time. So when that Christmas, Peter's girlfriend Sian was booked to appear in a pantomime in York, she had to go and live there for the run of the show. This meant that Peter and baby Simon were left living with Sian's mother. This was a difficult time because he was working in the clubs at night, which meant that her mother had to look after Simon while he was out. Peter wasn't getting back home and going to bed until the early hours of the morning and sometimes he didn't wake up when Simon wanted feeding. His apparent feelings in the eyes of Sian's mother led to quite a lot of banging on his bedroom door, with her demanding that he get up and look after Simon.

In the end there was one really bad argument with Sian's mother and she told him to leave. Peter didn't really mind leaving so much but he had nowhere to go. So he did the only thing he could, he asked his mate Len, "Do you know where I could find a flat"? Without any hesitation Len said, "You can come and stay with us at our house in Rumney, Len's wife Jan was happy for him to be there saying, "You can stay as long as you like Si". This couple were good people and they were very good friends to Peter, indeed as he has told me, he was really pleased to have met them.

When his girl friend Sian came back from York they were able to secure a nice flat in Newport Road, Cardiff. This meant that they were able to move out of Len and Jan's house and make a home for themselves. Although Len was still putting Peter's name round the clubs during the same period of time he manage to gain representation with The Harvey Lisberg Organisation. Harvey it has to be said was a very good manger one could go so far as to say he was exceptional. His other clients included Herman's Hermits, Tony Christie, 10cc and several other popular artistes of the day, including 10cc. Indeed he was a great mover and shaker in the business and it was Harvey who set up a recording session for Peter. Harvey Lisberg like so many other people in the business, was sure that with the right song, chart success for Peter was inevitable.

It was a good session and Peter remembers recording "Windmills Of Your Mind", with John Paul Jones. This was a great song from the 1969 film 'The Thomas Crown Affair' there was also a Graham Gouldman song, the title of which slips his mind, he thinks it was something about a train. Sadly these tracks never been released, another bitter disappointment for those who hold Peter up, as one of the great singers of his generation. As he looks back on this Peter is of the opinion that Chappell Musics executives just didn't believe "Windmills Of Your Mind" had what it took to be a chart topper. That was proved wrong by Noel Harrison, who was many of us know the son of the fine actor Rex Harrison. Noel Harrison took the song into the top ten. This would not be the first or last time that the men in suits have got it wrong, there are many recording that could and should have been hits for many artistes that were left by the wayside because of people who had no imagination.

Amazingly with the timing of things being what they are, after fifty years Peter has received a phone call from Harvey Lisberg, regarding the recording of "Windmills Of Your Mind". It seems that our friend Graham Hunter has been in contact with Harvey, to see if he knew how to obtain a copy of this recording, sadly Harvey was unable to help. However having got Peter's contact details from Graham, he was eager to speak with him. During the conversation, Harvey expressed his admiration for Peter's recording of this song, saying, that in his opinion Peter version was far superior to that of Noel Harrison, in 1968 Peter laid down a great vocal and the whole recording was of a higher standard. This recording would have beaten Noel Harrison to the punch and Harvey Lisberg could not believe that records companies did not pick the record up and run with it. In spite of his disappointment at not being able to obtain a copy of "Windmills Of Your Mind" Peter is delighted to be back in touch with Harvey and his wife Carole.

Moving on with the story, Harvey Lisberg got Peter a booking on a TV show with Hughie Green. There were no less than eight singers booked to appear on this show. The idea was that they would all be in competition with each other, to win the prize of representing

England at The Knokke Music Festival. Peter rehearsed a couple of songs, that he would sing in the show, they were titled, "Without a Song" a truly inspirational song, that had been written in 1929 by Vincent Youngmans and Billy Rose, indeed they included it the musical play called 'Great Day'. This song has been recorded by many great artistes including the incomparable Billy Eckstine, Frank Sinatra and Nelson Eddy.

It is significant, that opera singers, such as incomparable Mario Lanza and Lauritz Melchior, the great Danish/American Tenor also chose to record the song. A comparison of these recordings show that Peter Wynne's rendition of the song stands up well beside any of the other recordings. Peter also chose to sing that great song from the musical 'The Man from La Mancha' "The Impossible Dream". This song was written by Joe Darion and Mitch Leigh, and performed on Broadway by Richard Kiley and David Atkinson . The audience really loved Peter's choice of songs and with rapturous and thunderous applause they voted him the winner in the studio. His main rival appeared to be a Welsh Tenor called Allen Davies, they would both have to wait for the public vote before they knew which of them had actually won.

The votes had to be sent in by letter or postcard, there no phone votes in those days so there were no quick results. This meant that here was a hive of activity in Harvey Lisberg's office, everyone there was very busy scribbling away, voting for their man. Even Peter's friend Len and Peter Noone lead singer with Herman's Hermits helped out by writing some postcards. On the day of the result when the vote from the viewing public was counted, Peter felt that he was in with a good chance of winning but in the end, when all the votes had been counted Allen Davies was the winner.

There were no hard feeling about the result but it was a shock to every one that Peter had lost. It was a real shock to the shows producer in particular, because he had spent all the previous lunch-time talking to Peter about the many places he should visit in Knokke, when he went there after he had won. But never mind, as they say, some things are just not meant to be. He certainly didn't have time to brood on the result because following on from that show Peter was booked to appear with Little and Large at the Talk of the North nightclub in Manchester. This was a prestigious club that he appeared at on more than one occasion. Peter was told that as Simon Smith, he would be sharing top billing with Little and Large on that show, and over his time performing there he found that Eddie Large and Syd Little were great guys.

Of course it would not be right to leave this section of artistes who Peter worked with at this time without mentioning the great guitarist Bert Weedon. Peter and Bert worked together on many occasions, Bert had even played lead guitar on some of the records that Peter recorded on the Parlophone label. There was most enjoyable occasion when they both appeared on the radio show 'Workers Playtime'.

I am sure many people remember this show where popular artistes of the day were invited along to a factory to entertain the workers during their lunch break. The programme Peter remembers being on with Bert, was when they went into a sweet factory and entertained the staff. He recalls that everyone was very kind and they were given a box of chocolates each when the were paid. They also enjoyed a lovely lunch with the shows technicians that was served up in the works canteen. People in those days were very appreciative when good things happened during the working day.

There was also another show that has a particular memory for Peter because of the suggestion Bert made with a view to improving Peter's presentation of a song during his act. Bert always watched the other performers when they were on stage and was well known for his helpful suggestions. Peter used to sing an up tempo boogie style number called "Mack The Knife" this song will be known to readers as having been a successful recording for Bobby Darin. The song was about dark characters who roamed the streets, leading to murder. So Peter was not surprised when Bert suggested that he should pull out some sort of dagger/knife from his pocket on the final note of the song and throw it in to the stage Peter thought that this sounded like a good idea but, he was worried about splinters in the stage, so he never got round to trying it.

Authors note: Rock and Roll fans may remember as I do that Johnny Kidd of Johnny Kidd and the Pirates fame, did take the advice and used to hurl his cutlass in to the stage. This dramatic end to his great self penned number "Shakin' All Over" nearly had serious consequences when things went badly wrong. Johnny was unaware that some of the boards one particular theatre stage had become worn and had been covered with a steel plate. So that when at the end of the song he threw his cutlass down with his usual flair, it ricocheted of the unseen steel plate and as the newspapers reported the next day, came close to decapitating half the people in the front row of the audience, Needless to say that little stunt was removed from the act for future performances. A health and safety nightmare.

We can not leave this time frame, the 1960's, just creeping towards the 1970's without mentioning Peter's time working in Ireland. Like the time that he had been booked to appear at The Abercorn, this was a venue which had previously been bombed, this being the time of the 'Troubles' as they were referred to then. By the time he appeared there the venue was enjoying a new lease of life, it had been given a facelift and new decoration. Peter had been put in some digs just outside Belfast and the accommodations were very comfortable. His performances had been very well received by audiences and the club had asked him to come back and do a residency as the club host. In order to increase his income the club had arranged that he would also double up on occasion, with another venue just outside Belfast.

While he was considering this possibility he met a man, whose name was Danny Wilson,. This was a strange and unexpected meeting because, Danny's wife was a regular at The Abercorn and she was going home after every show raving to her husband about this fabulous entertainer, Simon Smith who was appearing there. So Danny decided to come to the club and see for himself what all the fuss was about. Well not only did he agree with his wife that there was something to make a fuss about, he and Peter became very good friends indeed. So when in the course of conversation Peter mentioned that he had been asked to come back to two of the clubs in the area as a permanent host, Danny was all for the idea, going on to say,"I will look for a house for you, Sian and Simon so that you will have a comfortable home to live in". Simon was about three and a half by this time, so he could travel without problems.

Well Danny found them a place to live, it was a house in Newcastle, Northern Ireland. The house was on a corner and Peter and his family really liked it. There were open fireplaces which he was able to have coal fires in, this was no problem as he had been used to this form of heating in some of his previous homes. Things went very well for him in his role as host, but one night while driving home in the early hours of the morning the car just stopped running, he had run out of petrol. He knew that there wasn't a petrol station the Belfast to Newcastle road, so he resigned himself to being there for the night, there was nothing that he could do until dawn. So wearily he climbed into the back seat and went to sleep. When morning broke he was able to hitch a lift to a petrol station and get a can of petrol, he hitched back to the car, then put the petrol in the tank and finally got home about ten 0 clock that morning.

On another occasion he had just driven into the parking area outside the house, he got out of the car thinking that this would be a good time to check the tires. Just as he bent down to look at the tires in the dim early morning light, heard an army sentry shout, "Halt, raise your arms"!! Peter did as he was told and then quickly explained that he lived in the house and had only bent down to check his tyres. The soldier told him to come round the car so that he could see him, when he had looked him over and listened to Peter explaining about the tyres again, he said, "Sorry mate, but, we can't be to careful" Then he let him go in to the house.

Not long after that incident an agent booked him to do gig in Dublin, appearing with Roger Whittaker, who in later years would record the many wonderful songs including, "The Last Farewell", enjoying chart success with it and many of his other recordings. After Peter had performed on the show the agent said that they wanted Peter to appear in a Christmas pantomime at the Gaiety Theatre in Dublin. So he found himself moving out of Northern Ireland into the Southern part of the country, life it seems was never dull for Peter when he lived in Ireland.

Around the time he changed his name to Simon Smith

Peter Wynne in Belfast

Lic Locking

Chapter Ten

Taking The Cabaret Scene By Storm

During his time in Cardiff Peter, once again under the name of Simon Smith was offered a six week stint in the 'Ricky Renee Show' appearing at 'The Castaway Club' Birmingham, a place Peter had come to regard as his home patch. There was some time spent at 'Apple Studios' in London rehearsing his part in the show, his set was twenty minutes long and consisted mainly of show tunes and duets. The show was an instant success, because it had the perfect line-up. Headliner Ricky Renee' was a drag artiste who had excellent comic timing, he was very popular with audiences at the time. The supporting cast included The Richard Gough Dancers, a girl singer called Jenny Kenner and the artiste who was at that time very much in demand with cabaret audiences, one Simon Smith, who as we all know now, was in fact Peter Wynne. Peter remembers that there were lots of celebrities who came in to see the show. The one who really stands out in his memory was the great footballer Billy Wright, who played for Wolverhampton Wanderers and of course England. There was a connection between Billy Wright and Peter Wynne because Billy's brother Laurence and Peter used to go scouting together in Coalbrookdale near Ironbridge Shropshire.

By this time as we have said Peter had changed his stage name to Simon Smith, this was a coincidence in the circumstances, because it seems that Billy Wright and a man who shared the name Simon Smith used to go out to clubs in the area, have a laugh and talk over old times. This Simon Smith was the sports announcer at the Pebble Mill TV studios so he had a good knowledge of football,, which is probably why he spent time in company with Billy Wright. Simon Smith seemed to quite like the idea that he and this great vocal entertainer who was wowing audiences at The Castaway Club, shared the same name.

There was someone who Peter got on very well with during his time at the club was John Reeves. A smashing guy John was actually the owner of 'The Castaway Club'. Such friendships are not always made with artistes and venue owners, but it is a very good idea if an artiste can make this kind of connection. On occasion John would take Peter flying with him in his Cessna Plane, this was most enjoyable, in fact a great experience. The other thing that John Reeves told him was that he was a friend of Tom Jones. John felt that the two singers had similarities, he really thought that Peter reminded him of Tom Jones. Because he wanted to highlight the perceived similarities between the two, he very kindly bought Peter a pair of Cuban heeled boots, just like the ones that Tom Jones used to wear.

All good things come an end and on the last Saturday night, of 'The Ricky Renee Show's' run at the club, Peter had also been booked to do the last spot at another nightclub, this venue was located in

Wolverhampton. Although it was some distance away he had to travel there after he came off stage at The Castaway Club. These booking that follow on each other were not uncommon in those days, you would often hear artistes say I've got double tonight. Indeed that is how the author came to meet the late great Tommy Bruce, more than fifty years ago, but that is a story for another place.

After he had arrived at the Wolverhampton club Peter received a phone call from John Reeves, who said, "I'm having a get together at my place, with Tom Jones, I would like you come over meet Tom and help out because there are a lot of girls here". Peter had to sadly decline because as he put it to John, "I am absolutely knackered and I have to travel home to Cardiff in the morning". So because he made the decision to rest up before his journey home, he never got to meet Tom Jones socially. But looking back he likes to think that if they had met each other he and Tom would have got on, as they are after all, fellow Welshmen. Incidentally there is a link to Peter's friend Tommy Bruce from the Larry Parnes days here, because Barry Mason, the man who discovered and managed Tommy Bruce at the start of his career, wrote *Delilah* for Tom Jones in musical partnership with Les Reed. Such links are common in show business, there are lots of unseen links between performers throughout the industry.

The following day Peter got a phone call saying, "You need to go up to Newcastle because, you may be getting an appearance on a TV Show they are making up there with Eartha Kitt, Eartha Kitt was a very sexy performer with a husky voice . She made her name in the

UK singing songs like, 'Santa Baby" and 'An Old Fashioned House'. For many years she dazzled Broadway audiences being nominated for numerous awards, She also appeared in 'Batman' making the role of 'Catwoman' her own.

Peter asked the caller, he is not sure who it was, but he thinks the call probably came from Harvey Lisbergs office, if they were sure about him getting the gig. At this point he was told that the producer wanted to see him for a chat about his suitability for the show. Because he was completely exhausted and had no stamina left, he didn't feel a maybe was a good enough reason to travel hundreds of miles, so he declined the invitation and went back to Cardiff. As he says now, "It was a great shame really, because I would have liked to have met and worked with, the fabulous chanteuse, Eartha Kitt".

He didn't have long to think about whether he had made the right decision about going to Newcastle, because work was coming in steadily. On this occasion the next gig came via a call from an agent in London called Harry Dawson. Harry Dawson had a few venues and this time Harry had been able to secure Peter a floor show style cabaret gig at The Stork Club, in London. On this show he would be appearing with the very talented and humorous, Larry Grayson and the previously mentioned Ricky Renee. This was what is known in the business as a good gig, the reason being it would have a long run and all Peter needed to do was find a place to stay, not to far from the club.

In the event Peter was lucky in his search for accommodation because managed to get digs with Larry Grayson in a big house near The Edgeware Road, they had some good times together while they were appearing at The Stork Club. Incidentally Lord Hesketh had an interest in James Hunt the Formula 1 Racing Driver, who would go on to be World Champion, was a regular visitor to the club. Lord Hesketh would buy the cast of the show a bottle of champagne every time he came in to see them. Peter would like to take this opportunity to say that Larry Grayson was a great entertainer, very talented and hysterically funny, both on and off stage. Everyone who saw him perform or met Larry loved him. Peter remembers that one night the Grades came in to see Larry perform, when they left they were very happy and most impressed by the performance that they had seen.

While he is remembering his time working with Larry Grayson and the friendship that developed between them, Peter feels that this point in the book would be good time recount one of the many funny stories that came about while they were both working at The Stork Club. Larry had a wicked sense of humour and he was just as funny when he was off stage as when he was on. As readers will remember Larry and Peter were sharing digs near the Edgeware Road so it made sense for them to travel in to work together, although for various reasons, after show guests etc. they would not always travel back to their digs together.

Anyway they would travel either by cab or bus and on the evening he is remembering they caught the bus. It was almost empty and they found two seats on the lower deck in the row behind the driver. Peter was not aware of a guy who was sitting on the long seat behind them. That was until Larry turned to look at Peter and said, "I'm in love with you Si, give us a kiss"! Puckering up his lips at the end of his request. Peter instantly turned to Larry and responded "You silly Bugger". As he did so heard the guy sitting behind them remark "I've seen it all now"!! He looked at the guy who just shrugged his shoulders, then got up and left the bus at the next stop. Larry and Peter then enjoyed a good laugh about what the guy leaving the bus was thinking, after all times were very different then.

There was another occasion when Larry embarrassed Peter, this time they had gone to see Peter's old mate from the Parnes days, Peter Elliot at a London club, the name of which escapes Peter after all this time. The landlord of the venue, Raffe, was also appearing on the bill that night and he was performing his Magic Act. Raffe reached a point in the act were he was looking for a member of the audience to help him with a trick. Larry piped up loudly, "Go on Si, help Raffe out with his trick, you know you want to". Peter just ignored him, in fact he tried to get Larry to go on stage, Larry was very raucous and he was told to pipe down. Somehow Raffe came down off stage to where Larry and Peter were sitting and succeeded in doing the trick and he thanked Peter for volunteering to help him.

After the show there was some sort of gag about Raffe's attractive young lady assistant being about 6 foot 2inches tall. As Peter says this story is a bit of anti-climax really because he can't remember the punch line to the gag. What he does remember is that he was left feeling rather silly, as he sat down afterwards he told Larry that he owed him a bottle of wine. Always a good sport Larry assured Peter that he would get one and he did.

Unfortunately for Peter there were not only good times to recall from his time at The Stork Club. For example as he was leaving the club one night the bouncer grabbed him by his tie and dragged him outside, throwing him through the door. He was puzzled by the guys action because he had just bought him a large scotch, and more to the point, he thought they got on very well together. The bouncer, Peter wishes he could remember his name, had another string to his bow, having appeared as a stuntman in some of the James Bond Films. Previously the two men would have a drink together after the show and talk about the bouncers experiences in these films. They were very interesting conversations, giving Peter an insight into the world of film, not just, the most interesting descriptions of how the stunts he took part in worked. The time spent in the guys company had led Peter to believe that they were pals, so to say he was shocked by the guys actions on the night in question, is an understatement!

Anyway although he was feeling quite bewildered and not a little upset about the event, once he was outside the club Peter just walked away. After all he thought there was no point in having a fight that might cost him his job. Unfortunately this was not the end of it, because as he was walking away wondering what he could possibly have done to cause this reaction things got worse. As far as he knew all he had done before leaving the club was speak to the girl who worked on the cigarette and other items counter as he was leaving. How could that have caused this violent action? So as he kept on walking up Regents Street he didn't know that the bouncer was chasing him, until heard a girls voice shouting at him to run!

Well he didn't run, he doesn't know why, maybe it was because he was in shock, anyway he just kept on walking. Then as heard someone close behind him, he turned round and looked into the face of the bouncer. Because he was carrying his suit bag in one hand, slung over his shoulder and his music case in the other, Peter didn't have a hand with which he could defend himself. Suddenly he felt a heavy blow to his cheek and he fell down in the gutter, he thinks he must have been knocked out for a few seconds, because when he looked up again the bouncer was walking back to The Stork Club. The only thing to do was to pick himself up and continue his journey home.

This incident troubled Peter all night, in fact it kept him awake, because he was wondering how he should approach this man when he went to the club the following night. After all there was no way he could avoid an encounter, because the bouncer was always the first person he saw on his arrival. As he made his journey to the club, the next evening he was feeling some bravado, he had decided that he would not be bullied by this man, so he told himself to take the initiative and sort the situation out as soon as he reached the club.

When he arrived at the club's entrance he was ready to take the bouncer on if he became violent again.

So he was somewhat surprised when he did arrive at the club by the bouncer's friendly tone when he spoke to him saying, "If you wouldn't mind Simon I'd like to see you in private for a moment". Peter who was feeling confident replied, "Sure, does the dressing room suit you"? It did suit him and when the bouncer came in he apologised, saying, "I am sincerely sorry for what happened, last night, I'd had a few drinks". "Yes, I know", Peter replied "I bought you one". " "Yes", the bouncer continued, "I wrongly thought that you were chatting up my girlfriend and I lost it" Then rather surprisingly he said, "While you are performing here if you have any problems with anybody, I will sort them out for you". "Great" thought Peter, "First I get thumped and now I have a minder, I can't imagine anyone else wanting to thump me". Being the man he is, with a kind and forgiving nature, Peter let the matter rest there.

When his time at The Stork Club came to an end the agent, Harry Dawson offered Peter a summer season at Lowestoft near Great Yarmouth. He agreed to do the season the understanding that Harry would also find a summer long gig for his girlfriend Sian Hopkins. Sian as we have mentioned before when she was playing the part of the water nymph in Camelot, was a popular Welsh soprano, who had featured on the long running TV show 'Land of Song' with, the talented Ivor Emmanuel a man who had lovely high baritone voice.

This programme had been made for TV Wales and was very popular in the early 1960's.

As good as his word Harry Dawson got back to him later the same day and told him that he had booked Sian in at The Tower Ballroom, Great Yarmouth they were both pleased and she was more than happy to accept the booking. They went down to Yarmouth to try and get a flat or some other accommodation. They found what was termed a 'Static Home that was 'to let' and they managed to hire it for the whole season. They were also able to obtain the services of a young Welsh woman who would be their live in babysitter, looking after Simon for most of the season.

The line up of the summer show was, beat group, The Rocking Berries, Janet Brown, who was a very talented comedienne and impressionist, John Bouchier who was a really great ventriloquist, Simon Smith and a troupe of dancers. Peter would also be appearing on some Sunday concerts with Norman Vaughan who had been the compère on The London Palladium Variety Show. On arrival at theatre Peter found that he would be sharing a dressing room with John Bouchier. Incidentally the two of them got on really well together. Another interesting thing that he found out during the season of the Rocking Berries was married to Meredith Wilson, her father was a Coca Cola millionaire, unfortunately he doesn't remember which one. It was a most enjoyable season because everyone on the show got on well and unusually with entertainers, there was no jealousy from anyone.

Having said that there were a couple of upsetting things that happen over the time that they spent in Great Yarmouth. One example of this was the day that Peter noticed that the Cuban heeled boots, bought for him by John Reeve, proprietor of The Castaway Club were missing, it seems that they had been nicked out of theatre dressing room. Peter was livid when he discovered this, because quite apart from being his stage wear, he was very fond of them for the obvious sentimental reasons. Those boots were never found and he had to replace them by buying a pair of black shoes.

Another trauma came to pass one night when he wasleep in the bedroom, Sian came in later and woke him, she said she had been followed home by one of the bouncers from The Tower Ballroom. He was still half asleep when heard the sound of glass breaking in the front door. He rushed out of the bedroom in his bare feet to face the intruder thinking, "How dare someone break in to our home and then try to push past me!" A fierce fight broke out between the two of them and during that brawl, which went on for quite some time, only ending they both got too tired to continue. The bouncer probably to his own great surprise, given that he had the confidence and the arrogance to instigate the fight, received several injuries, including a large lump on his head and he had a tooth knocked out during the scuffle.

Peter himself was not without injury having sustained a broken hand at some point in the proceedings. To make matters worse he had slivers of glass from the broken front door embedded in one of his feet. Painful and uncomfortable to say the least, it had been a very eventful night, not one he would have wanted to repeat. At some time during the fight someone, probably a neighbour had called the police. On their arrival it seems that the police knew the bouncer, this was not helpful in resolving things as they should have been favouring Peter's case. They were leaning towards supporting the bouncer, they told Peter that the bouncer was a good chap who normally didn't cause any trouble, so they could see, no reason for them to take any further action this occasion. This was hardly just or fair, after all the bouncer had broken into Peter's home and assaulted him. Surely there were serious crimes that needed to be answered for, no matter how well they knew the perpetrator.

In retrospect their attitude was reprehensible to say the very least. The brawl had left Peter having to carry on performing at theatre, for the rest of the season with a plaster cast on his broken hand. This was not a great image, for any entertainer, let alone one with such high professional standards. When the time finally came to pack up at the end of the summer season they were glad to get into Peter's Morris Minor and drive home to Cardiff, their time there had been spoiled. The uncalled for unpleasantness with the bouncer and theft of Peter's boots meant they were not sorry to be leaving Great Yarmouth behind! As Peter looks back now he wonders about the bouncer and the policemen's attitude to him. He would like to know if the police ever realised that this man wasn't the good chap that they spoke of in such glowing terms. Surely they must have known that he was clearly a very violent thug who thought he was free to do as he wished. We just have to hope that his violent behaviour was curbed before he could do someone even more serious harm than the damage he inflicted on Peter.

When they got back to Cardiff, they didn't have long to rest up because Sian was off again. Always in demand at that time she had been booked to appear in another pantomime. On this occasion she would be appearing at The Grand Theatre. This meant that Peter would be remaining at home with their son Simon during the day, while doing a series of one nighters, around the Swansea area,. An entertainers career is often taken up by one off gigs, tours and residencies although usually lucrative, can be few and far between. So as the seventies approached Peter's son was getting older, they were living in Swansea and he was having as busy life. One day out of the blue, his old friend Len James got in touch. Naturally Peter was delighted to hear from him, Len as we have been reading was a good friend who was always prepared to go the extra mile for his friend.

On this occasion Len was very excited because he had great news, something that he as sure would please Peter and enhance his career. Len told Peter that he had he had met an American lady in Sheffield, and this lady was very eager to get Simon Smith's career started in America. It seems she had been listening all of Peter's recordings, she thought that they were brilliant, and she had said to Len, "They would love this guy's singing style in the States, we have to get him over there". Peter was delighted to hear this news from Len and very excited by the prospect of success in the USA. Sian was pleased for him and very supportive as she could see that this would be a great opportunity for him.

Added to the news about the lady's enthusiasm it seems that here was a guy called Jeff Smith up there in Sheffield who was in a position to help make the dream a reality. So Len, with Jeff's help, started to make the preparations for him to fly out to the USA. A short time later the American the lady from Sheffield sent the money to him for his flight ticket, it really was going to happen. More that she was able to tell him that a crew from a TV network had been arranged to film his arrival and to greet him when he got to the USA. It was almost unbelievable, after so many setbacks and disappointments with record deals, something good was starting to happen.

Now while Len was making all the arrangements for the trip Peter was not standing idle just waiting for things to fall in his lap, he was putting together a new cabaret act. He is an intelligent man and he knew he would need something special to impress the American audiences. Peter had done his research and he was fairly sure that he knew how to present his act in the best possible way. While all this was going on the date was set for Peter to fly out from Heathrow Airport, he could hardly wait. He knew then that this big step in his career was really going to take place.

It was at this point that things started to get really hectic, he was dashing round to see his friends and say his goodbyes. He would have to go down to London because he needed new stage wear, he needed to really look the part. Sian helped him to get his clothes packed and

Peter remembers that while he was in London he bought two suits to wear on stage, one of them was a lovely grey/blue three piece dress suit, he doesn't remember the other one so well, but he does know that it was a classy looking garment. He made these purchases from what he describes as a nice high street tailors shop, located just off Park Lane. He thought the shop looked very upmarket, the suits were exceptionally smart.

There is a very special memory that Peter recalls from this time, because while he was in the tailors shop having his dress suits made, he experienced on of the most thrilling moments of his life. This was because when he walked in through the door, he saw sitting there on a seat, just waiting to be attended to was one of the greatest purveyors of songs on the planet, the incomparable Tony Bennett. Tony looked up at him as he walked into the shop and said "Hi". Peter shyly replied "Hello". Then plucking up courage he asked Tony, "What are you doing in the UK"? Tony said "Oh I'm doing some concerts and a TV show".

At that point their conversation was interrupted by the tailor, who had come to tell Tony that his suit was ready and that they would be sending it to his hotel, on hearing this Tony, looked at Peter and just said "So long" and then he left. In Peter's opinion he has to say that Tony Bennett gave off a an aura of gentleness, confidence and kindness. Peter is not ashamed to say that he loves Tony Bennett, he thinks that Tony is a truly wonderful performer. The the spell was broken and a few moments later, after Tony Bennett had left the shop Peter was informed that both of his suits were ready. He left the shop feeling elated by this chance meeting, this was surely a good omen for the future.

Finally the great day arrived, It was in November 1970, all to soon it was time to leave, he knew he would miss his family, but this was the big chance, he had to go. Len had a nice Jaguar car then and he drove Peter to Heathrow airport in it, Sian went with them . When they got there Peter went to the check in desk to show his ticket and they asked him for his visa, he didn't have one, this requirement had been completely overlooked by the American lady. It was a shock but Peter didn't blame Len, he had worked like a trooper to liaise with agents and others over in the States, so that Peter could meet them.

The lady behind the desk said, "I'm sorry sir, but you cannot enter the United States without a Visa". That seemed to be that, then Sian had a brainwave, she said that she had heard of a comic duo who had encountered the same problem. They had been able to get round it by entering America for ten days, then they had flown out to Nassau and applied for a visa to go back, from there. This was relayed to the airline and after some conversation and consideration, they agreed to let Peter fly into Miami for a ten day period.

So he was on his way he bid his farewells to Sian and Len and went through customs to the departure lounge, he didn't bother with the duty free shops, because he only had ten quid in his pocket, although he did have a bottle of champagne on the flight over. Peter with his stage name of Simon Smith was ready, willing and able as the song says, to take America by storm.

Chapter Eleven

The American Dream Is Real

The plane he finally embarked on arrived in the USA considerably later than the one he should have been on. This meant that the American TV crew, had been unable to wait for him, they had left Miami airport. So Peter came through arrivals to be greeted by two well dressed mature ladies, this was not the welcome he had been expecting. He would later discover that one of the two the blonde lady, was called Jean Henderson, she was in fact the owner of a modelling agency. The other lady was called Lady Gillette, Peter remembers that they looked very glamorous, both ladies were wearing long evening dresses and Lady Gillette also had on a mink coat.

Therein the arrivals hall, also waiting to greet him were a host of young ladies, they were carrying a huge banner with Peter's stage name, Simon Smith on it. All the young ladies wanted to have their photograph taken with their new idol. Afterwards Jean Henderson and Lady Gillette escorted Peter to a large limousine. His new entourage of young ladies were following on behind them. A local sheriff had arrived on his motorcycle and beckoned the limo driver to follow him as he rode slowly out of the airport towards the main highway. "Wow"!! Thought Peter, "I have got a police escort no less"!

When they eventually arrived at a large house, Peter had no idea where it was, or who owned the house. They went inside and he found that a buffet had been laid on but he was not very hungry, because he had eaten on the flight over. It was unbelievable, a party in his honour, amazing! He was then informed about his accommodation, it seems that he had been booked in at The Ramada Hotel. This information didn't mean a great deal in itself, but Peter assumed that it would an upper crust hotel situated somewhere in Miami. While he was in the house he saw that there were several groups of people, as well as the girls from the model agency that he had seen previously. On the record player in a corner of the room people were playing Peter's aka Simon's records as background music. It really was remarkable to find that people were making such a fuss about his arrival.

He noticed that two couples in particular, a man and two woman were listening intently to his recordings, while they chatted nodded and smiled. He took their obvious enjoyment of his songs as a good sign. He did not find out until later that they had been asked by Jean Henderson for the monies required to back his endeavours while he was in the United States. He is not sure what the outcome of their discussions was all he does know is that the end of the evening they must have come to a decision about his future, because everyone seemed very happy. As the party broke up Jean's husband Bill took Peter out to his car and drove him to his hotel. Peter found Bill to be a very gentle and likeable chap and he enjoyed his company.

When they arrived at The Ramada Hotel, Bill invited him to have a drink in the bar, it seemed a reasonable request, so Peter agreed. Looking back on the incident now, it could be that Bill might have thought, that Peter would be naive in regard to drinking habits and the cocktails being served in the bar and so was trying to get him drunk. Anyway Bill ordered him a Southern Comfort Martini. When his drink arrived, it contained a straw, which he was unable to drink through, he didn't attempt to so, because he found it awkward. He just sipped the drink from the glass and enjoyed it. Well the cocktails kept coming for quite some time and Peter kept sipping them from the glass. After he had drunk about six of these drinks, Bill laughingly explained that he had expected that after a few of these Martinis, Peter would be rather tipsy, but he could clearly see that he had been wrong. So with friendly farewell Bill decided to go home saying, "I'll see you tomorrow".

Peter went the check in desk and got the key and directions to his room. When he got up to and went in to his room, what a surprise he got because it wasn't just a room, it was actually a suite. In fact to him it seemed like a small apartment, it had a lounge, a kitchen, one bedroom, there was a separate bathroom, it really was quite a place. To his surprise he found that he was now feeling a little tipsy, this should not have been a surprise given that apart from the six Southern Comfort Martini's he had drunk down in the bar he had also had a couple of drinks at Jean and Bill's house. Feeling a bit tired and dizzy he lay down on the bed and promptly fell asleep. When he woke up later he got up and went into the lounge where he found the mini bar, and decided to make himself a drink to liven himself up. After the combination of some sleep and a drink he was feeling quite feeling refreshed so he decided to go for a walk.

After Peter had been walking for a while he found himself at the entrance of a club. Finding that there was no admission charge, he went in. Once inside he could hear that loud piped music was being played. So he ordered a drink and then he settled down on a stool at the bar. Peter just sat there for a while with his drink listening to the music. After some time had passed he engaged the barman in conversation, as they talked he found out that he was only a few miles from a place called Pompano Beach, it seemed to be a prestigious place. Before long he started to feel tired again, so he left the bar and walked back to his hotel, when he got there he went back up to his suite and fell back into bed, he was instantly asleep.

The next morning he was picked up and taken back to the Henderson's house. As it turned out the house was situated in Pompano Beach,the place the barman from the club he had visited the night before, had told him about. When he went inside the house Jean greeted him warmly and in the course of their conversation told him that she was the one who would be handling his business affairs and finding him gigs in Florida. With this in mind she said that she had already arranged a meeting at The Fontainebleau Hotel with an Orchestra Leader by the name of Lenny Dawson. It seems that the meeting would be the next evening, and prior to that she had arranged a radio interview for later that day.

The radio interview seemed to go very well, there were phone calls from the public asking questions about his career to date, where he lived, when he had answered all the usual questions, someone came up with, "Have you recorded anything"? Peter replied, telling the caller that in the UK he had recorded for EMI, Columbia, Polydor and Parlophone. The presenter then played one his recording while they were still on air. Peter thinks the song that was played was one that he had written himself called, "I Just Can't Live Without You", At the end of the show the presenter thanked him for appearing and being interviewed. Then Peter left the studio with his new agent, Jean Henderson, to prepare for his meeting with Lenny Dawson at the The Fontainebleau Hotel.

When they met the band leader, Lenny Dawson, he was taken completely by surprise because Lenny asked him what song he would like to sing. Peter had thought that they were only going there to have a talk about the future. But Jean unbeknown to him had asked Lenny Dawson if Peter could go on stage with the musicians and perform a number. The pianist had a quick run through a few songs that he suggested, they settled one that the pianist knew and was able to play in the right key, called "My Love Forgive Me". So he decided that he would just put the whole thing down to experience and get on with it. Lenny introduced him to the audience with the words, "Ladies and Gentlemen, please welcome on stage a singer from Wales, England, (Once again Peter apologises to his Welsh friends for Lenny Dawson's lack of geographical knowledge in relation to the UK) Simon Smith!! He listened to the intro and then went into the song, he included some lines in Italian, there were cheers and shouts for More! Followed by rapturous applause, which led to encores.

As a result of this incredibly successful live audition Peter was booked to appear for a week in the Fontainebleau Hotel's, Gigi Room. Before he made his first paid appearance there, all the songs for his cabaret act would have to have parts written for each instrument in the band, quite a lot of writing for the pianist. The next day Peter aka Simon went over to the pianist's house which was in downtown Miami and together they went through each of his songs. They established the right keys for him to sing in etc and where he would repeat choruses, for transitions through the songs. It was also decided that he would include his impressions of Tom Jones, Sammy Davis Junior, Gene Pitney and Mario Lanza. He had to leave out his impression of Cliff Richard, because Cliff, as we have all heard several times was not very well known on America.

Simon Smith was a great success with the American audiences and at the end of the week he was booked to do a further three weeks in The Gigi Room. By this time he had moved out of The Ramada Hotel and in to the home of Bill and Jean Henderson, as he says, "They were good people who really wanted to help him". Bill ran a pharmacy in a big store In Pompano and he was well known in the community. It seemed to Peter that Bill was a healthy man in the prime of life, he certainly looked well enough. So he was surprised when Jean told him that in fact Bill was suffering with a serious heart condition. This was not something that seemed to affect their daily life so, Peter just continued to perform to great acclaim and left Jean to look after business on his behalf.

One day Jean came to him and said she wanted him to go up to New York for a week with her, to see if some people she knew up there, could do something to help his career. He agreed to go with her and a couple of days later they flew in to JFK Airport, on arrival they hailed a cab which took them to the New Yorker Hotel. After a nights sleep they went down to try and get a spot on 'The Frost Show'. This show was of course hosted by our own redoubtable satirical master and TV presenter David Frost,. At that he was enjoying was a very successful career as a show host in the USA. Unfortunately Jean's timing was out because The Frost Show had just come to the end of it's seasonal run. However they did meet a very interesting lady who invited them to a party in the Central Park area, where it was hoped that Peter and Jean might meet people who could help to further Peter's career. Well Jean did meet quite a few influential people there who she thought may have been able to help with plans for Peter's future. During the party Peter found himself in conversation with a painter from South America, to New York to study her craft, she was being sponsored to work and learn during her time there, by someone who was at the party. Although he enjoy her company and conversation , their different reasons for being in the country meant that they did not meet again.

Jean and Peter were invited to dinner the following evening at an apartment in Central Park. They dined on a very British Sunday roast, eating their food with gold cutlery. He has to say that the food was superb, although it would have tasted just as good if the cutlery had been chrome. The next day they had a meeting with the producer of the 'Johnny Carson Show'. When they arrived they went to the shows office, as it happened the office was in the same premises that the show was televised in while they were there Peter met and spoke to two guys who really seemed who really seemed to take to him. They were impressed by him and his voice saying that they thought he would do well on the show. They suggested that he should come back and film a piece for a show that they had planned for the coming November.

Their plan being that he should sing unexpectedly and unannounced, impersonating The wonderful singing star. Robert Goulet, and then surprise Johnny Carson by not being Robert. Of course as we know both Robert Goulet and Peter aka Simon Smith had appeared in productions of 'Camelot', Robert in the part of Sir Lancelot, Peter as Sir Lionel but he had understudied the part of Sir Lancelot. This of course meant that Peter could sing with consummate ease the song from the show, that had become associated with Robert Goulet's, "If Ever I Would Leave You". The two guys in the production office thought that this would be a very funny spoof, and be a chance for the vast audience who watch the show to be made aware of Peter's talent. This was a brilliant idea and naturally peter left the office very excited about the future.

So on the face it this had been a successful trip, there were reasons to be hopeful that Peter would be heard nation wide and that his career would receive a terrific boost. Sadly this excellent promotional idea never came to fruition due to the fact that Peter was unable to sing during that November as he was suffering from a severe throat infection the evening that they had planned for him to perform. Any way after that meeting there was nothing else to do but to fly back to Pompano Beach. They arrived back feeling very tired so Jean said that Peter should stay in the spare room and they both they retired to their respective beds, with plans to talk about the trip the next day. As he was dropping of to sleep suddenly Peter heard Jean screaming and wondering what on earth could be wrong he jumped out of bed and ran to her bedroom. When he got there the lights weren't on but he could just see Bill lying on the floor by the window. He struggled to pick him up and succeeded with some difficulty, in getting him up and then lying him on the bed. Bill's wife Jean commenced to give him mouth to mouth resuscitation and pushing hard on his chest. Sadly her efforts were to no avail because he wasn't responding.

Somehow during all the ensuing moments of stress and tension, someone, Peter doesn't remember whether it was Jean or him, called for an ambulance. When the paramedics arrived and got to Bill's side. Peter returned to his own room. A few moments later Jean came to his room and told him that they were taking Bill to hospital, then she went to get dressed. While she was getting dressed one of the medics told Peter, that there was nothing they could do, because Bill had died before they before they could get to him. They said that taking him to the hospital was just a formality. Clearly Jean was in shock and in her current state she was quite naturally unable to face in the fact that her husband had passed away.

At this point following Bill's sad passing we have to return to the narrative. Just to bring things up to date it will be necessary if you will forgive us to list and write about some of the events and achievements that took place for and on Peter's behalf retrospectively. During the time he was living at her home, and when he was staying in the hotels that he performed in, Jean Henderson had spent many long hours working hard in an effort get him a recording contract. Unfortunately nothing had really come from her efforts in this direction. The thing was Peter didn't really think Miami was the best area to attempt this, so he had left her to it. His thinking that you never know what can happen, at least he knew that Jean was doing her best on his behalf. Having said that, there had been developments, because through various enquires he had been able to meet a guy called Web who would turn out to be a good friend. Web would help with the management side of things, and with him on board was clear that there were changes in the air.

It has to be said that things did not always go as planned, during Peter's time in Miami. One example of how badly things could go wrong is demonstrated by the following incident. Peter had been booked to appear on a gig with band leader Lenny Dawson. The gig in question was to be held in a baseball stadium, it was a massive venue, he thinks it could probably have seated. More than 10,000 people . Well they arrived to do the gig and set up the gear, then they did a sound check after that they waited for their audience to arrive, Peter remembers that the silence was deafening, the only way he can think of to describe it, is to say that it was like being at someone's funeral.

After waiting more than half an hour there was still no sign of an audience, it was becoming clear that someone had made a mistake, not a single person had even approached the stadium. Eventually Lenny Dawson said, "Let's pack up, I'm sorry boys, we must have the wrong venue or the wrong date, I just don't know what has happened". Peter never found out just what had gone wrong, so as he has always done in the face of adversity, he just put the whole thing down to experience. It was very strange though that no one could ever explain what had gone wrong. You usually hear something about whose had messed the booking up if you find yourself involved in a gig that goes pear shaped.

On another occasion Peter had been booked for a one night gig by a guy who had seen the show at the Fontainebleau and been impressed. He arrived at the venue with his dots, (sheet music) and went through his act with the band, there was no time for a rehearsal just a talk about the keys he sang the songs in and his act in general terms. On this occasion he had decided to open up the show with an up tempo number called, "Joy To The World", so when he went on stage he stood and waited for his musical intro, when it finally came he couldn't recognise what they were playing. As he says whatever it was they were playing it certainly wasn't "Joy to The World". He stopped the band playing and then he sang the intro himself, at a certain point in the number they started to play again unfortunately they were still playing the wrong music, the tune that they were playing bore no resemblance to the sheet music, it was clear that they were not reading musicians.

Stopping the band again he asked them to skip that number and play the second song. When they started to play he could not believe it, because their efforts on the second song were just as bad. At this point Peter was left with no other choice, he had to tell the organiser that he was unable to perform, because the band was incapable of reading or playing his music. The guy accepted the situation and apologised for the way things had turned out. Peter appreciated his candour, because in the situations there is a tendency for people to blame the artiste or his music. He has experienced situations when musicians have gone as far as to say to him, "Have you any music with pictures because I think I could play them". It really is soul destroying when an artiste hears those words, but it happens, more often the general public would think.

However in show business the artistes learn to take the rough times with the smooth and his next gig was great. He was appearing at The Police Annual Ball and he knew he was in safe hands musically because he was being backed by Lenny Dawson and his Orchestra. Peter's performance was cheered to the rooftops and he received a standing ovation. The audience were so pleased with his performance that they presented him with a plaque stating that he was 'A Member of The Fraternal Order of Police Officers', for life. This plaque is a source of great pride to Peter, he still has it displayed in pride of place on his wall at home.

During his second stint at the Fontainebleau Hotel, appearing in The Gigi Room, Peter as with his previous appearance was given a suite in the hotel. Peter learned that this was the normal treatment for artistes when they were booked to appear by the hotel. The rooms he was occupying had every gadget possible, everything was in place to make the artiste feel at home. He had a fantastic view from his balcony which looked out over the tennis courts, the beach and the Ocean. As he says , "I really had the star treatment while I was there". Anyone who has seen him perform will know that this treatment was fully deserved.

One day there was a knock on the room door, when Peter opened it, to his great surprise he was delighted to see that an old friend Allen Green, was standing out there in the hallway. He let Allen into the room and they said their hellos. When Allen was sitting comfortably he told Peter his reason for being there. It seems that he was in California on his own business and when the business was concluded he had decided to drive over and spend a few days in Miami. When he arrived in Miami he had seen a poster advertising the fact that Peter would be appearing at The Fontainebleau Hotel so he had decided to come over to the hotel and give him a surprise. Peter was very pleased to see Allen and asked him what he was doing in the States, was he working there? Allen said he had done a TV show and was now taking the time to slowly find his way round America.

Peter feels that he should explain briefly how the two of them became friends, he wants to do this so that the readers can understand why he was so pleased to see Allen. AS is often the case with Peter's friends they are either musicians or involved in some area of show business. In Allen's case he was a pianist who hailed from Manchester in England. He had played with Kenny Ball's Jazzmen and had on a few occasions played in bands that had backed Peter. So after Peter had let him in it was only natural that their conversation turned to memories about old times on the road together. They both remembered one gig in the north of England when Allen not having a gig himself, had decided to just gone along for the ride, as a travelling companion.

Anyone who has travelled the roads from gig to gig as a performer will know what a lonely life it can be. It is far from the glamorous life that most people assume entertainers enjoy. So Peter had welcomed the companionship offered by his friend. On this occasion it was going to be an early start at the venue he would be appearing in. It should also be noted that he would performing to an audience that was completely male, there were no ladies allowed in this particular club in those days. It still amazes both Peter and I just how much discrimination was allowed against women in certain venues back in the 1960's. Anyway Peter had gone on stage to perform his first spot. When heard his introduction he went into his routine, he felt that there was a strange atmosphere in the club and little response to the songs he was singing. As a popular entertainer on the club circuit, this was a most unusual situation for him to find himself in. Then to make it worse when he got the end of his act he received what best could be described as a polite ripple of applause. When he stepped off stage he was greeted by the clubs', Chairman of the Entertainment Committee, they were fond of grand sounding titles in working men's clubs in those days. This man glowered at Peter then he said the words,"I'm paying you off"! Now this phrase in entertainment parlance means, that you are fired' not the words that an artiste wants to hear. So Peter hoping he could correct the situation said, " If you would just wait until my second spot, I know what I have to do to liven them up". He looked at the Chairman hopefully, because in fact he had no idea what had gone wrong.

The guy was having none of it saying, "No after all that mucking about opening and closing the curtains, you're done"! Peter was shocked and puzzled, he had no idea what the man was talking about so he asked, "What the hell do you mean"? "I haven't been opening and closing the curtains". At point Allen who shouldn't have been doing anything because as we know he had only had only come to keep Peter company on the journey, or in case the club pianist was not a good reader and couldn't play the music, spoke saying, "I'm sorry Peter but when you were doing your impression of Billy Eckstine, I just touched this button to see what it was for and the curtains started to close, I didn't know which button to press to open them again, I eventually found it and opened them again", As Peter said then and repeats now, "What a fool I must have looked standing there singing with my eyes closed, oblivious to what was going on". Because of Allen's foolish actions he had been paid off which meant there was no chance that he would ever be booked to appear at the club again. To put it mildly Peter was far from pleased with Allen, and told him so, in no uncertain terms. However always a good natured man, who doesn't hold grudges Peter reflected on the incident later, while they were driving home and he couldn't help but laugh. The two of them laughed even louder as they reminisced in Peter's hotel room.

After they had been talking for sometime it was decided that Allen would spend the night in Peter's suite. He would be very comfortable sleeping on the settee, after all it would have been pointless to leave at such a late hour. When they woke in the morning Peter ordered breakfast and they enjoyed more memories of their time in the music business. All to soon it was time for them to part company because Allen had previously made appointments that he needed to attend while he was in Miami.

Now at that time the Fontainebleau Hotel had guests staying there from lots of the nations in the world. The reason being that 'The Miss Universe Contest' was being held in Miami. It was not surprising that some of the girls in the contest came to see Peter's act, they were all very impressed by the talented young singer from the UK. He also had two new fans, one called Jimmy Stewart, (Not the film star) and Doug Ashdown, it they had co-written some songs, and decided to try their luck with these songs in the USA. Although it has to be said Peter was not aware of any of the songs they had written. Anyway they came in to see the show and the three men got to know each other. They became friends and in the course of conversation Peter found out they had come over from Australia. It seems that Jimmy was an Australian, but Doug was British, for reasons of his own that Peter is unaware of, he had been living in Australia.

So during the last week of Peter's residency in The Gigi Room, Doug and Jimmy came in to see him again and after the show they invited him to go back to Nashville Tennessee, where they were staying, with them. Because he had a free week before, he would be appearing in his next gig, at the Diplomat Hotel he agreed to go. On the night of his last appearance he dressed for his cabaret spot and then having met up with Jimmy he walked to the lift with him and proceeded to The Gigi Room. When they arrived there he left Jimmy at the bar and told him to put all the drinks on his tab. This would prove to be a reckless thing to say, because when Peter went to collect his salary for the week he only received $100, he was surprised it should have been several hundred dollars. When he queried where the rest of the money had gone, he was told that it had gone to pay the tab that his friend Jimmy had run up. It seems Jimmy had a few girls with him and he must have used the tab to cover their drinks as well. Peter felt a bit of a mug, but only for a short time because he found out later that Jimmy had paid for his ticket to Nashville.

When the three of them arrived in Nashville they took a cab to the apartment that Jimmy and Doug were renting. They invited him to stay for a couple of days, which he did. While he was there he recorded some of the songs the two guys had written together, this was how he spent his days, then at night, the three of them visited some of the Spit and Sawdust bars that he didn't know then, but does now, are situated around Nashville. In one of the bars the three friends visited a guy tried to hustle Peter, saying, "$5 bet, I'll beat you at ball" Peter said yes, thinking well that's $5 I've lost, but to his great surprise he won. Then the guy said "Another game"? Peter thought here we go, I will definitely lose now but he won again. When he lost the guy wanted him to go on to play some sort of shove ha'penny game, but they used another coin he is not sure what, they played this game for the same five bucks bet. Peter was waiting for the stakes to be raised, but he won again and then won the next three games. At which point the guy said, "I'm done, I'm going to the bar". So Peter, shouted to him, "I'm buying". This went down very well with his new friend, as Peter has commented, "I got to know a few nice people while I was in Tennessee".

While he was down there Peter was invited to go to Tree Publishing's studio to record a song called, "I Miss You Already", he recorded a few others at the same time, as he said, "I think they tuned out pretty good" the following day he was on the plane back to Miami. He promised Jimmy and Doug that he would come back, but only if they let him stay with them, they kindly agreed to his request. Then when he was back in Miami and preparing for his gig at the Diplomat Hotel, he found out that he would be following one of his favourite singers when he appeared there, the one and only, Jack Jones. Peter took the opportunity to go in to see the show, saying, "What a great the voice Jack Jones had, it was a real treat to see him perform live". Like the star that he was and always will be Jack held the audience in the palm of his hands, with his lovely warm baritone voice. Anyone who has watched and listened to Jack Jones will know that it is easy to see why Peter enjoyed the performance that he gave.

Of course everybody will remember Jack's father, Allan Jones a fine tenor from the Thirties, Forties and it has to be said the Fifties. Allan Jones had been a great inspiration to Peter along with other great singers that he has previously mentioned. Peter also remembers that the ever popular British entertainer Petula Clark followed him in appearing at The Diplomat Hotel, she was there the next week. What a fabulous trio of vocal entertainers the patrons of The Diplomat enjoyed during that period of time, Peter was welcomed by the audience because they recognised that his voice was one of the finest that the twentieth century had ever heard. As people were heard to comment after his performances, "This Brit is phenomenal, man what a voice"!! The same people were coming in see him on successive nights, he was really popular, well worth the admission fee. There can be no doubt that if just a few of the things that Peter's American management had tried to put in place, could have come to fruition, Simon Smith would have been one of the biggest stars, to have made the crossing to what many people term 'the land of opportunity'. Nevertheless in spite of the things that eluded him, he was living the dream, the same dream that he had as a young boy that he would be a singer who could entertain all the people everywhere.

As his time to start work at The Diplomat Hotel approached Peter got word that his good friend Len James was flying in from England, more than that he would be bringing a very prestigious lawyer, Peter Mallick with him. Apparently Peter was interested in seeing him perform, he had expressed an interest to Len, unbeknown to Peter investing in his career. So the two of them had flown to the USA so that they could be at The Diplomat Hotel on opening night, to see the British sensation perform. Peter, aka Simon was very nervous that night, because he didn't want to let his friend Len down. He opened his show with"For Once In My Life", and continued with "Love Story", then he sang a couple of up tempo numbers. Then it was time for him to go into his routine of impressions finishing the spot with,"My Way". There was standing ovation to recognise his fabulous performance and the audience was calling for encores.

Peter felt that he had done a reasonable cabaret spot, always a modest man, he has never realised just how good a vocal entertainer he really is. He was happy when he left the stage and headed for the dressing room. When he came out from the dressing room Len called him over to their table and introduced him to Peter Malick and his fiancée. This young lady was really impressed by his whole performance. She had been especially pleased because one of the impressions Peter had done was Sammy Davis Junior, her favourite singer, she had loved the precise nature of the impersonation. As she, "I closed my eyes and I truly believed that Sammy Davis Junior was singing to me". Yet more proof, if proof were needed of Peter's incredible vocal ability.

It has to be said that Peter Mallick looked really pleased about something and Len was grinning like a Cheshire Cat. That night The Diplomat Hotel booked him for a further two weeks, they would be split into one week in September and one in November. Incredibly on the same night as a result of his successful performances Peter had also been booked on to The Molly Turner TV Chat Show, this was a great night's work. It was impossible for anyone who heard Peter sing to be unimpressed by him. Throughout his career he has always been in touching distance of universal recognition, a hundred years from now anyone hearing his recordings will recognise his incredible vocal ability and wonder, how it could be that such talent was not recognised world wide..

The following day was spent with Len, they had a lot of catching up to do after all, it had been a long time since they had seen each other. While they were relaxing by the pool, Len told Peter that Peter Mallick had decided that he was going to help him to promote Peter's career when he returned to the UK. Len then said he had to catch a flight home the next day, it had only been a flying visit. So it was time to say their goodbyes but Peter couldn't let Len leave until he had thanked him for all his help and support, he couldn't have a better friend.. It seems Peter Mallick would be staying the States for a while with his fiancé, there was more they wanted to see. Peter thinks that they went to visit The Florida Keys before they returned to the UK.

At the end of the week Jean Henderson, his agent came and picked Peter up from The Diplomat Hotel and drove him back to her house in Pompano Beach. When they got back there they were surprised to find that two record producers were waiting for them. The two men told Peter that they had two songs that they would like him to listen to, with a view to having him record them with a full orchestra. Well Peter heard them and he really liked them, one was "The Hole That Holds The Bones" this song was co-written we believe by record producer Bill Stith and George 'Bud' Reneau, it is anti war song and may not have appealed to everyone at that time. The B side "My Kinda Love", was written by Jerry Reed, who was a fantastic guitarist and singer who later co-starred with Burt Reynolds in the film, 'Smokey and the Bandit". So Peter agreed go with the two men to their recording studio and make the record. Things it seemed were starting to happen, dreams were being fulfilled.

The two men took Peter to a studio in Nashville, and true to their word they had an amazing orchestra waiting to play for him. What an orchestra it was, it was made up of musicians who were the cream of Nashville,the very finest musicians around. With one of his typical understatements Peter tells us that, "The songs turned out okay". Authors note: Believe me when I tell you that these recordings show off Peter voice in a magnificent fashion, the arrangements and the superb way the musicians play for him resulted in two incomparable recording. When I heard him start to sing "The Hole That Holds The Bones" for the first time, the hairs stood up on the back of my neck. It is quite amazing Peter' voice conveys an incredible level of emotion and so far I have never been able to hear this song without shedding tears". The performance on "My Kinda Love" only serves to demonstrate just how versatile Peter's vocal talent is. I strongly recommend that you beg, borrow, buy or steal a copy of the CD 'Peter Wynne The Story' and listen as I do, in complete awe of this man's versatile and quite simply incredible voice.

The recordings were going to be released on the label 'Great World Of Sound', now this was not a leading record label, just one that was launched by the producers, they made assurances about the amount of push they were going to put behind the disc. As usual the efforts to promote it never amounted to very much. To be a hit the recording was going need a lot of plays, sadly it didn't get them and another genuine chance of a hit record for Peter, was missed.

Later that week it was back to Nashville this time at Jimmy Stewart's invitation. The reason for the invitation was that "The Country Music Convention was in town and Jimmy was sure he could get Peter a spot on the show. It seems that Doug Ashdown would be appearing on the show as a singer/songwriter. With their recommendation it would be a done deal getting him on the show. So when he arrived in Tennessee Peter went to the Convention Hall to meet the shows producer it was a successful meeting, he got the gig. At that point he found out that the show was being televised, it would not only be seen in Nashville because, it was also being broadcast in Canada, this show would once again taking Peter to a wider audience.

The television spot was due to start at approximately 8pm, it was set for this time so as to give the auditorium time to fill up. Peter rehearsed his two numbers, one was the Jerry Reed song that he had recorded, "My Kinda Love", it was an up tempo number and to him it sounded like 'Hillbilly Rock'. The second was his old favourite, the one he had sung on 'Boy Meets Girl in Manchester, way back in 1962 "It's Only Make Believe", this song helped keep the country feel in his performance. There were hosts of stars on the show including his mate Doug Ashdown, as Peter has told me, Doug had written some great songs and he had a lovely voice. Doug was going to sing one of his own compositions, as well as another number that Peter doesn't recall.

The clock ticked down and while he waited, he slapped up, there was no make up lady, but on such occasions he always did his own make up, nothing excessive, just a base and a little eyeliner. The producer had told him was due to appear fourth or fifth on the bill, as he put it, "Plenty of time for the nerves to set in". So there he was pacing up and in the hallway until heard the announcer and compère of the show say "Ladies and gentlemen, please welcome on stage, one of Great Britain's greatest entertainers, the one only-----Simon Smith"!! Then heard the intro of the song, *My Kinda Love* and he was away, his nerves just disappeared as he walked on stage. It was soon clear to him that the audience must have known Jerry Reed's song, because they really entered into his performance.

When he ended that song, the audience went wild, he couldn't believe the applause they were giving him. The excitement continued as he sang *It's Only Make Believe* it was unbelievable the crowd were up on their feet, shouting and cheering, he must have had at least a two minute ovation. When Peter left the stage he was walking on air, he just could not believe that as a singer who was unknown over in Tennessee was being so well accepted by a country music audience. As Peter says, "Basically I am just a ballad singer who loves to sing and performs all types of music, I'm nothing special". There we go again he is modest to a fault, Peter doesn't know just how good he is, no matter how much adulation he receives from audiences all over the world.

After he came off stage he went to the dressing room to have a wash and brush up. When he came out of the dressing room someone, he doesn't remember who, asked him to come over and meet some people. He went across the room and was introduced to a couple, a young very flamboyant dressed man who was smoking a cigarette in a long holder, who was sitting with a lady who turned out to be the owner of Leeds Music. This company is one of the giants of the music industry, so of course Peter was very flattered by her interest. The lady spoke saying, "Simon that was a great show you did there" she then went on to say, "I am making a film and I would like you to be in it, would you be interested"? "I certainly would" he replied. The lady handed him her card, before they could discuss the any idea anymore, he was whisked away to meet someone else.

That someone was a guy called Dick Broderick, now he was the chairman of some country music association or other, Peter is not sure which. He told Peter that Capitol Records were interested in signing him to their company. He went on to say that he would look after the business side and get him the best possible deal. Peter was then taken around all the hotels in Nashville and introduced to everybody as the singer from Wales who had stolen The Country Music Conventions show. He just could not believe it, everything seemed to be happening so fast, it was dream time again. That night he went to a friends house and when he walked in the lounge, there he was on the Nashville Tennessee TV news, singing *It's Only Make Believe*, the news reader saying, this the Welsh singer, the sensational Simon Smith, who has received a standing ovation at The Country Music Convention.

Now this should have been the ideal time for 'The Great World of Sound's marketing team to flood the radio stations nationwide with Peter's latest recording, it just couldn't fail, the record would have sold itself. But it seems that they weren't paying attention to what was going on, they completely missed out on the best marketing opportunity they would ever have. This seems to have been a worldwide problem back then, the music business had highly paid executives, who never had their finger on the music pulse, missing chances and moving on to the next thing. There were so many talented young singers who had their careers destroyed by careless indifference. I could list so many here, but I am sure Peter won't mind as we are in the American part of his story, if I mention my dear friend the late Troy Shondelle. Troy wrote and recorded that great song "This Time", in a garage playing all the instruments himself for reasons to many to be listed here. Somehow it was a hit, recognised not just in the USA but in the UK as well. So Troy clearly had talent, but subsequent recording, issued by record companies failed to be promoted and so he had no more hits.

One of the reasons why so many of the talented boys and girls, especially Peter did not achieve recording success was the fact that they believed their management were doing the promotional job for them. When in fact many of these people had no idea or aptitude for this aspect of the job. It took me years to grasp the full concept of the job, basically, the way forward with your artistes career is always, if you don't know something, don't ignore the problem find out. Sadly Peter never found that person who would just put him first. Having said that he was lucky that Len James came along. Because Len really tried to do everything for him, unfortunately Len believed that some of the people who he introduced into Peter's career would do more than they did for him. Nevertheless, as the author of this book I would like to say that every artiste deserves to have a man like Len James looking out for them. Peter and I, both have no hesitation in saying, "God Bless You Len".

Always believing that people had his best interests at heart Peter decided to leave the Capitol Records negotiations in Dick Broderick's hands. It seemed like the right thing to do, after all Dick seemed to know what was going on in Nashville, the capital city of Country and Western Music. He also found out that the recorded TV show was going to be shown on Canadian television that week, so it had been sent off the morning after the show, things seemed to be looking good. So when he met up with Dick Brodrick the following day for an update on the potential deal with Capitol Records, Peter was still on cloud nine. Sadly it was not good news, because Capitol Records were not willing pay a retainer, to Peter. That would not have been an insurmountable problem but added to that disappointment was the information that they only wanted Peter to sing and record country songs.

Peter was unable to take anything positive from Dick Broderick's input so that was the end of that. Yet another offer had gone pear shaped and by now he was feeling rather flat, things just weren't going right, how could he ever break the free of the circle that surrounded him? He was being praised for great performances, audiences were giving him standing ovations, what more could he do to get that elusive record deal, that would surely lead to hit records It was clear that there were good chances to boost his career, he just didn't know how to access them. All he did know was that the people who he trusted to look after his interests, clearly didn't know the right way to go about things. Work was coming in, his performances were well received but there was no way that he could see that there was anything happening that would take his career to next level. He was feeling very deflated as he got on the plane and flew back to Florida.

He arrived back at to see Joan at Web's house in Pompano Beach where he had been invited to stay after Bill had sadly passed away following his heart attack. On his arrival there he was made aware by Joan that he had been booked to appear at a condominium.

Apparently this venue was a place where there were lovely elderly Jewish ladies in residence, these ladies, liked to be entertained. It was a very warm day when he appeared there, in fact it was really hot. He did the first cabaret spot and that was fine, although when he unfastened the top button of his shirt heard a shout of "Take it Off", He just smiled and then he carried on singing. When he came off stage at interval he enjoyed a long cold drink and tried to cool down until it was time for him to go back on stage for his second spot. He realised as he stepped back on to the stage, that he should have brought another shirt, to change into because the one he was wearing was literally soaking wet. Unfortunately when he had left the house he had not realised that the temperature would be so high, when he was on stage.

During his last couple of songs the perspiration was running off of him like a slow stream, so he opened another button his shirt, as he did so there were more enthusiastic shouts of "Take it off, take it off". At last he gave in, stripping to the waist and throwing his shirt to the side of the stage,there were loud cheers and then he sang his last number, it was, *You'll Never Walk Alone*. There was an eruption of feverish applause, when he finished the song. The applause continued as he was walking back to his dressing room.

When he got there he thankfully sat down in a chair to recover. After a few minutes there was a knock on the door, "Come in" Peter called out. The door opened and the lady who he thinks had organised the show came in to pay him his salary. She did so with a big smile on her face, then she said, "You know you really shouldn't have taken your shirt off", she paused before saying,"You could have given some of the more elderly ladies a heart attack when they saw your bare chest". He smiled awkwardly and apologised, then they both laughed out loud, it really had been a great night, they had all had fun, the ladies were happy with their new entertainer..

Now around that time Sian and Peter's son Simon had come over to stay for six months but the weeks had flown by. Unbelievably it was now almost time for them to go back home. He couldn't believe it, just as he had got used to them being there, it would only be a week before they would be on the plane back to England, Peter's plans meant that he would be staying for over in the States for another six months. So as a family they enjoyed a few barbecues together in the sunshine. They also took trips to the shopping mall so that Sian could buy odds and ends for the two of them to take back to England with them.

All to soon the time had come for them to go home, so Peter took them to the airport, he remembers that he was really sad to see his son now four years old, getting on the plane with a little toy in his hand. He consoled himself with the thought that least his family had spent six months with him and that he would be returning home to them soon. It just depended on what work came in. Basically he had decided if nothing else materialised, there would be no point in staying. Peter still had bookings at The Fontainebleau, the Diplomat and all the other hotels in Miami that were putting Cabaret Shows on, but things had plateaued. Sadly he felt forced to admit that his hopes and dreams of bigger things happening in his career, did not look like being fulfilled in America,

One day his manager and agent, Jean Henderson approached him, in fact he would say that it was more of a proposition than approach. She came up with the idea that he should move in with her full time, while she sorted out her late husband's affairs, his will and general finances etc. So Peter went round to her house to talk things over, conversation was slow and while they were playing pool, he came out and asked her, if she still wanted to handle his affairs. Jean responded in a shocked way saying, "Of course I do"! Then she stopped messing around and asked him outright to come and live with her, saying, "I only want you to help me with the taxes and protect me".

Peter was shocked by the idea and he told her that he didn't think such an arrangement would be right. His reasons were as he told her, because he was thirty one and had a girlfriend and a son, that he needed to go home to. Peter said to me, "I just couldn't do it, Jean was an attractive woman of fifty and it would have been an easy life for me, but it wouldn't have been right, so I just leaned over kissed her on the cheek and left". That week he also broke contact with Jeff Smith who had brought him over to the States and made a complete break from the Jean Henderson Model Agency. Things didn't change much on the work front because for some time he had been handling the hotel booking himself.

At one of the hotel bookings a guy came over and introduced himself, Peter can't remember the guy's name, but he does remember being invited up to his Penthouse Condominium. It seems he wanted to discuss a recording deal he claimed to have for Peter. So he went up to the guys penthouse where he was greeted warmly and introduced to the guys wife, he really was made very welcome indeed. When they had settled down, they sat and spoke about the recording deal . The guy said that he was willing and able to produce a sing-a-long type album, using songs that everyone would know and sing along with. After Peter had spent some time listening to the guys business ideas for distributing the album when it was recorded, he thanked him and left so that he could think the offer over.

Peter then went to see his friend Web and together they discussed what had been proposed. Now Web being an astute businessman was able to point out potential pitfalls. Web's opinion, based on information he had received, was that this guy was part of what that time was termed 'The Jewish Mafia' and he would expect Peter to sign a contract with him for life. The guys general attitude, his lifestyle, lush apartment, wanting to pick the songs Peter recorded, was all a bit to heavy. Without sounding conceited Peter didn't want someone else picking his songs and he certainly didn't want to be tied to any contract for life. After listening to what Web had to say he contacted the guy and refused to sign a contract with him.

As Peter looks back on the situation now, he thinks that he may have been a bit rash, maybe he shouldn't have listened to Web, but hindsight is a wonderful thing, we can all look back and wonder, what if? Anyway thinking to himself onwards and upwards, the next day he flew back to Nashville to meet up once again with his friends, Jimmy Stewart and Doug Ashdown. When he got to Nashville he found to his surprise that Doug wasn't as welcoming as he had been on previous occasions.

When he enquired why Doug was being funny with him, it turned out that he, Doug, wasn't happy that Peter had gone down so well on the country show that had been filmed for Canadian TV. Doug just couldn't understand why, when in his opinion the numbers that he had written and performed, were superior to the ones Peter had sung, he had only received polite applause. While Peter had been praised by everyone and credited with stealing the show. Jealousy is a terrible thing and has been responsible for a lot of upset and unpleasantness for many of us over the years. Anyway Peter's efforts to placate him were dismissed by Doug, this was a very disappointing end to their friendship.

When he left Nashville, not the happiest trip he had made there, headed back to Miami. Once he got there Peter was invited to stay with Helena, Chris and their family. Incidentally Helena's mother was one of the people who had backed Jean Henderson in her efforts to further Peter's career in the USA. It has to be said as we look back on the time that he spent working in the USA. His performances in the hotels and other venues that he appeared in, were of the highest standard. He was being as well received by the audiences, as

Jack Jones, Petula Clark and many other of the top stars who were working over there at the time. Audiences loved him and the people flocked to see him, his performances are still remembered today. It is fair to say that with his undoubted talent, so much more was deserved and expected for Peter than was ever achieved.

That is not to say that he did not earn public acclaim and fame in Miami and Tennessee, he did, but that acclaim should have led to international recognition and worldwide record sales. The problem was that these good hearted people, Like Jean Henderson her husband Bill, Web and Helena's mother did not have the knowledge or the know how to compete in the murky waters that can found in the music business. As the authors friend Tony Crane, lead singer of The Merseybeats has said to him, "There are are more sharks in the music business than you will ever find swimming in the ocean" But Peter always appreciative of any help and support that people have given him throughout his career does not blame anyone and more to the point has no complaints about how his career in the USA came to its conclusion.

Looking back on his time in the USA it is clear that Peter achieved some amazing things. He gave great performances in both Miami and Tennessee, did some exceptionally good auditions in New York, he also sang to considerable acclaim on a Broadway stage. Sadly he just missed out on appearing on The Johnny Carson Show, typically for Peter he had a sore throat and chest infection just before this major TV appearance. Having said that there have been other occasions were he was forced to succumb to chest infections before other important shows. It has to be said that unfortunately sore throats and chest infections are a curse that all vocal entertainers suffer from time to time. Not wishing to dwell on vocal afflictions Peter recalls that another happy memory of the time he spent in New York was actually seeing a show on Broadway, 'The Apartment',. Had things turned out differently it is not a stretch of the imagination to think he would have actually starred in shows there.

Peter really enjoyed his time while he was staying with Helena and Chris. Happy memories include trips out on Chris's boat on lovely sunny days. He also remembers Helena's kindness in lending him her Lincoln Continental motor car, so that he would at least be mobile, while he was there with them. The whole family were very kind to him and they all shared some great moments together, Chris, Helena and their three children, Gill, Andrea and Robert made his time with them very special. Peter worked The Fontainebleau Hotel again, receiving what by now were his normal rave reviews, but sadly time and opportunity were running out for his American dream.

One night he received a phone call from his girlfriend Sian, back in Wales, during the call she asked him to come back home. She said that she had found them a lovely flat in Caerphilly South Wales and she and his son Simon wanted him to come home and live there with them. Peter reviewed his current situation, he had extensions on his visa, who knew how many more would be allowed? There was no sign of a breakthrough on the recording side of his career so he thought it was probably the right time to leave. He had some people to see in Nashville, but they could wait until The New Year when he was sure that he would return. So he made the decision that seemed to be right at the time and put his arrangements in place to return home. He promised his friends that he would be back to see them all again the following year. So his flight was reserved and he soon found himself in the air travelling home.

As he travelled home Peter thought about his friend Len James who he was still in touch with. Len had said if the work gets a bit thin the USA, come home, we will find work. Len was sure of this because he was still in touch with Peter Malleck, the lawyer who had come over to The Diplomat Hotel, with Len to see Peter perform. Both of these men were very keen to help Peter re-establish himself in the UK, so he felt fine about coming home. He bought some goodies for Sian in the duty free shops when the plane landed and he arrived back in Wales on a cold, wet and windy October day in 1971.

On his arrival he was delighted to be met by Sian and Len, he was really pleased to see them both. Len who had brought the Jag, to take them home to Caerphilly, was delighted to have his pal back in the country. It felt really good to be back in the UK and Len already had ideas about what he was going to do to get Peter's UK career back on track. It seems that there was a TV show lined up with Rosemary Nobel, it would be produced by Terry De Lacy. Added to this arrangements had been made for him to be working for George Bayon, who was the owner of many clubs in South Wales, all of which Peter could appear in. It looked like things were already on the move. Once again people were ready to drive his career forward. He would go back to Wales ready to enjoy life with his family and reignite his British career.

Arriving in Miami in 1970. Lady Gillette in fur with Jean Henderson in long white evening dress.

Peter on Pomparno beach, Florida

Chapter Twelve

The Welsh Valleys

Now there were quite a few gigs that came his way at venues in and around the South Wales Valleys and Peter remembers one in particular. It was an occasion where Len James not for the first time or the last was able to show the depth of his friendship for Peter. Old style Variety Shows, with many diverse acts appearing on the bill were still popular with the public at that time. An example of this would be Tommy Bruce who by then was cabaret and rock and roll singer. Tommy often appeared on the same bill with then legendary strongman Tony Brutus, other acts might include George Formby or comedian Max Wall. Not what people today might think would be good mix, but in those days it worked and everyone had a good night out, there would often be a girl singer on the bill, who might not be so well known as the other performers but no less talented, it was simply a case of all tastes being catered for.

Well on the occasion that Peter remembers so he was appearing on a show that featured a strong man and a flame throwing act. On this particular night he was standing in the wings waiting go on when this almighty smell of burning fluid went up his nose down his throat and into his lungs. Peter was coughing and choking and he started to worry, would he be able to sing? Well he had to follow this act and he spent his first spot coughing his lungs up between songs. So after he came off stage from the first performance he went to the club manager and explained the situation. He asked if he and the strong man could swap their spots round in the second half. The manager understood and said, "It won't be a problem". Then the manager went away to tell the other performer about the change in the running order.

Well about five minutes later Peter having thought no more about the matter, found that he had an irate madman shouting at his dressing room door. Trying to keep a lid on the situation, he politely asked, "Yes can I help you?" adding, "What's the problem"? The man went into one, really losing his temper he was almost incoherent with rage, he seemed to be saying something about Peter not liking his act. Before he was able to respond Len who was in the wings, having heard all the shouting ran into the dressing room. He confronted the strongman/flamethrower and said, "What are you saying", he had to looking up at the guy, because Len is about 5ft 6ins and the other guy was at least 6ft tall.

The strongman, who was still extremely angry, began to threaten Len who was not having any of it. Deciding to take the bull by the horns Len said, "Come on then Boyo let's finish the argument outside" That took the guy by surprise and he seemed to calm down about. Peter thinks, looking back that the guy was completely amazed by the idea that anyone would have the nerve to ask him outside, clearly the wind had had been taken out of his sails. In any event, it was clear that he was taken aback by Len's bravery in standing up to him, so after all his threats and bluster he just calmed down. Then he said, "OK then you can go on before me, if your mate feels so strongly about it". As Peter says,"That situation serves to sum Len up, he is a very good friend and a great guy".

Coming back to where they were making their home, it has to said that when it came to their living accommodation, Sian had done really well. In fact in Peter's opinion, she could not have done better. The flat that she had found in Caerphilly was on a very pleasant estate, it was set in peaceful surrounding. It had been tastefully decorated and it was very comfortably furnished. The big surprise for Peter when he arrived home after such a long time away was to see how his little boy Simon had grown, since he had last seen him in America. All in all it was a very emotional homecoming, only those people who have been separated by work or military service for any length of time will understand, just how Sian, Peter and Simon felt . Their little family had to get to know each other all over again, before they could slip into the pattern of day to day life. At least they knew that they would not be separated by thousands of miles, Peter could hug his son at bedtime most nights and begin to build a relationship with him.

As always Peter was in good voice and his performances were in great demand, that being the case he was soon working again. On the first occasion that he remembers from his UK comeback days he had been given a weeks cabaret standing in for the excellent performer,

David Alexander. It seems that David Alexander had been had been struck down with the singers curse, a throat infection and it was such a bad one he was unable to perform. Well Peter did the week and as they say in the business, he stormed it, the audiences loved him and the venue had no hesitation in booking him to appear again there again a months time. The TV show with Rosemary Nobel was still pending and Peter was looking forward to doing it. All in all both in his personal and professional life he was settling back in to the UK really well.

One of the gigs that came in at this time was at a very big venue in the area. Peter would be the resident entertainer and by the third day of his tenure, it was his turn to go down with the most horrendous sore throat. It was so bad that he could hardly speak let alone sing. This was a disaster, because as he was just rebuilding his UK career he could not possibly take time off. He was never someone who failed to fulfil his professional obligations but it was even more import that he kept working because, he really needed the money so that he could pay his rent and other household bills. There was only one thing for it, he would have to treat the infection himself. He knew what he needed to do because his mother had her own way of dealing with sore throats. So that's what he did, he made up the concoction that his mother used to give him and as his siblings when they suffered sore throats as children. The concoction sounds really awful, absolutely vile, the ingredients are, a spoonful of butter, half a spoon of sugar and big dash of vinegar when you have drunk all that down follow it with a glass of brandy. After he survived swallowing that terrible medicine, somehow he managed to make it through his cabaret spot.

Len James as we have often said was always working hard on Peter's be half and on this occasion he had arranged for the well known Ian 'Sammy' Samwell to come and see Peter perform. He did this in the hope that Sammy would consider writing a song for him. Now Ian 'Sammy' Samwell had played with Cliff Richards backing group "The Drifters/Shadows during the early days. During his time with Cliff Richard he had written the great song, "Move It" for him. As we know this song has been hailed as a British Rock and Roll anthem, it helped to make Cliff's name as a performer and Sammy's as a song-writer. He had then gone on to write other fine songs. Because of this Len was sure that he would able to write a hit song for Peter. Things seemed to go well he seemed to be impressed by Peter's voice and Sammy gave them a lift after the show in his classic Rolls Royce. He seemed eager to continue the time that they were spending in each others company so he took them for a curry in a restaurant that was situated between Len's home and Sammy's house in Cardiff.

The three men enjoyed a meal together and talked about music an other things for a while. Peter had assumed that Len and Ian were doing some sort of business, so he just left them to it. After all he wasn't good at the business side of things and he knew that Len always had his best interests at heart. Peter has no idea about how the conversation between Len and Sammy that night, as it was never discussed with him again. Clearly Sammy Samwell did not write a song for Peter to record, a pity because such a recording might just have been the one to make it in to the charts..

Authors note: I suspect that Len James found out that night the same thing that I did during my time keeping Tommy Bruce on the road. The lesson learned was that even the best of songwriters do not have any way to fund the recording of their songs, they rely on the artiste or their management to find funding and a record and promotion company to give any recordings the necessary push. Like Peter, Tommy recorded songs throughout his career, *The Reason Why*, *Heartbreak Melody* and *Dancing Cheek To Cheek* being prime examples. There is little doubt that if any one of these songs had any push behind them they would have been even more successful than the song that made his name, *Ain't Misbehavin*. This also the answer to the question Peter's legions of fans have asked themselves for sixty years, "Why hasn't he had a number one record"? It is quite simple, No one promoted the great songs that Peter Wynne recorded, if they had done so there is no doubt his recordings would have topped the charts for months.

While we are on the subject this would be a good time to answer another question that is frequently asked by the fans, "What did this artiste do with all his money"? Well the truth is that artistes like Peter Wynne, Johnny Gentle, Dave Sampson, Danny Rivers, Nelson Keene, Duffy Power, Lance Fortune, Dickie Pride and so many more of the boys who came through in the Parnes era never really had any money. For example Dave Sampson told me how he had to call home to his mum and dad while he was on the Parnes Tours to ask for eating money. Dave's dad confirmed this to me telling me how Dave's mum would send him her weeks housekeeping money, to make sure he could stay on the road. Other artistes have told me similar stories and as we have read one of the things that caused arguments with Larry, was not getting paid on time.

Tommy Bruce was lucky, thanks to Barry Mason's negotiations, Norrie Paramour the A and R man at Columbia Records, gave him an signing on fee of several thousand pounds. Again with Barry's advice Tommy bought two maisonettes, one he lived in and one he rented out, so when he signed for Larry Parnes he had his own income and a place to live. Just a quick word about the wonderful Dickie Pride, Dickie was a very talented artiste a man who could play a variety of instruments. His voice was capable of covering,songs that ranged from Ella Fitzgerald's *There's A Small Hotel* to Little Richard's *Slippin' An' A Slidin* with equal dexterity. Sadly he died without achieving the success his talent deserved in 1969.

Entertainers like Peter Wynne if they had any deal at all got an old halfpenny for every record sold. Now there were two hundred and forty pennies in a £1 in those days, before we were all ripped off by decimalisation. That's another story for another time and another place. This low royalty rate meant that an artiste on the halfpenny a record deal had to sell four hundred and eighty records before they received a £1 in royalties, this at a time when the author was receiving £6 for a weeks wages. Most of the boys did not have that elusive hit record so booking fees for live performances were not so high. Yes they would earn more than a lot of the people who were tied to an office or factory, but it was a short term way of earning money for many of them and sadly their careers in music did not last for most of them.

Many of the artistes ended up with day jobs, Heinz Burt who was the Tornados bass player and had a solo hit with the song *Just Like Eddie* spent time working as a track layer for British Rail, he lived with the author and his wife Margaret rent free for over a year while they got him back on the road, touring with Tommy Bruce on 'The Way It Was Show'. There were hard times for a lot of the artistes, don't forget when Peter Wynne went to America he flew out of the country with just £10 in his pocket. It has to be said that Larry Parnes, Robert Stigwood and Joe Meek gave our generation a fabulous time musically, we saw great shows and fabulous artistes, but there was a downside for many of the acts.

Because what we did not know was the price our talented heroes had to pay for their brief time in the limelight. Peter Wynne and the others deserved more reward for their performances than they ever saw or got. But I never heard one of them complain, they just gave us great times and wonderful memories. They did not waste their money, they were the musical generation who didn't have any. But in my eyes they paved the way for future music stars, to have better and longer careers. Many of the Parnes boys and other artistes who came up at the same time have become the authors personal friends.

People like Tommy Bruce, Dave Sampson, Danny Rivers, Nelson Keene, Lance Fortune, Dickie Pride, Peter Wynne Heinz and Clem Cattini and many more have enriched my life. Some of them like, Dickie, Tommy, Heinz, Dave and Danny are no longer with us but I will never forget any of them.

However returning to Peter's time living and working in the valleys, the week after his terrible sore throat he was booked to appear in Bournemouth. The venue was a only a small intimate club, but the place was always busy. Freddie Starr came in one night and he was very interested to see and hear Peter's impression of one of the artistes that he included in his shows. There was an noisy table during his impression of Elvis Presley, an impression Freddie himself has often been known to perform. Freddie Starr was listening intently and Peter can recall him Starr "Quiet"! At all the rowdy people on that table. When Peter came off stage, he and Freddie sat down and had a drink together and they enjoyed a chat, He found Freddie to be a very amiable guy, but there is no doubt that he did have, as Peter puts it "a very naughty streak".

It seems at this time that Sian, although she had as has been said before a lovely singing voice, had not been singing for a while. In fact she had actually taken a job in a hotel, a job she seemed to enjoy very much. One night Sian surprised Peter by saying she would be going out early the next morning because she had an audition, for a show. This meant that he would be looking after Simon, as he says, "There was no hardship there", in fact he was looking forward to spending time with his son. As he looks back Peter thinks that Sian said that the audition was for a TV show. Anyway, whatever it was for, the inference was that she would be back late that night. He was very pleased that she had an audition, because as singer himself he felt he knew how much she must have missed performing. After all she had put her career on hold while Peter had pursued his American dream.

So Peter looked after Simon and enjoyed the time he was spending with his son. At the same time in mind he was wishing Sian success, he really wanted her to get the gig. The evening came and Peter got Simon ready for bed, tucked him in, told him a story, then went and laid the table. During the day he and Simon had gone out to the shops and bought some nice steak and all the trimmings to go with it. He wanted Sian to see that he was pleased for her and hoped that the meal would be a celebration as he was sure she would come and say that she had got the gig. So the table was set, he had prepared the steak and had it ready to cook. He was still feeling quite happy about the situation even when nine pm came with no sign of Sian returning home. He was sure she was only delayed and would soon be home with the good news, that she had the gig.

But as ten o'clock, eleven o'clock, came and went he started to wonder where she could be. By midnight he was really starting to get worried, thinking, something must have happened to her. Because in those days they didn't have mobile phones he had no way of contacting her, all he could do was worry. This was most unlike her there had to be a good reason why she wasn't home, he just did not know what that reason could be. By this time just to make matters worse, Simon had woken up and wanted his mummy. He was still in bed, so Peter told just told him that his mother must have been held up and not to worry, she would be there soon. During all that time he was hoping that the door would open and there she'd be. Time was passing and he was becoming more and more concerned for her well being.

By one am in the morning Peter knew that she wouldn't be coming home that night. Sitting up worrying was not going to bring her home so he went to bed, but of course he couldn't sleep. He just heard and saw the clock ticking all through the night. In despair he gave up trying to sleep and at 6am he got up and went for a wash and shave. He remembers that it was about 7.30am when he got Simon up, helped him to wash and dress and then made him some breakfast. Peter suddenly decided, that it was pointless to just sit and wait, because he needed help to find Sian, and sitting in the house was just making him feel worse. So he had one thought in mind, he just knew that the person who could help him find Sian would be Len, so he left the house. As he rushed out of the door Peter was clutching Simon's hand together they walked briskly to the phone box down the road.

When he got to the phone box he rang Len's number. When Len answered he asked him if he knew anything about Sian's whereabouts or if he had any news of where she might be. Len was surprised to hear that she was missing, going on to say that he had no idea where she could be but he told Peter to get himself and Simon in a cab and come to his place in Llanrumney. When he got to Len's house they would be able to look for Sian together. They managed to get a taxi and as they were travelling over to Len's house Peter thought to himself, "Well whatever has happened? She can't have had an accident because someone would have come and told him". He tried to console himself with that thought, although it was scant consolation and didn't stop him worrying. This really was a horrible situation.

They arrived at the house and Len was waiting for them outside the front door. Len's wife took Simon through to the kitchen. This left the two men free to discuss and surmise openly about what might have happened to Sian. Len agreed that it was unlikely that she had had an accident, for the same reasons that Peter had thought, mainly that someone would have been in touch with him by now. At 1pm that afternoon the phone rang and Len answered it, It was Sian, she asked if Peter was there, on being told that he was, she asked to speak to him. At last thought Peter, as she told him what was going on. It was not good news for him, in fact he was shocked by what she had to say. It seems that while she had been working at the hotel she had met and fallen in love with a young man. Sian went on to tell him that they had begun a relationship and they really were in love. After much soul searching she said that she had decided that she wanted to spend her life with the young man. This was why she had made the excuse about the audition, she had just wanted to get out of the house without an argument.

So there it was, she was leaving Peter to be with her new love. Peter was absolutely stunned, he just hadn't seen this coming and the news rocked him back on his heels. To say that he was surprised was an understatement it seemed like a sick joke, it just couldn't be happening. Peter asked her questions, trying to make sense of things, hoping to find out what had gone wrong. But Sian had no answers for him none that made any sense to him anyway and it was clear that their conversation was going nowhere.

The whole thing was unbelievable from Peter's point of view because he had thought she wanted them to be together. After all their relationship had finished within a couple of months of Sian asking him to come back from the States. This was a request he had complied with happily, because he believed that they had a future together. It was incredible, unbelievable, because quite simply their relationship, one that Peter truly believed was strong, was over. He had truly believed that he had her support in making his career in America, after all it was only with her help he had been able to go. Their relationship had ended because in that short period of time since he had returned home Sian had met someone else. A someone who she thought could make her happy, in some way that Peter wasn't able to. He could not fight to save their life together because she had isolated him and taken any decision making away from him.

As he resigned himself to what now seemed inevitable Peter felt that he needed a soft shoulder to cry on. What he really needed was the comfort and possibly the companionship of someone he liked and cared for. It was at this point he found himself thinking of a girl called Carrie who he had met while he was working at the Stork Club with Larry Grayson. Carrie was a close friend of Marj, a girl who had been dating Johnny Gentle way back then. Now he knew that Carrie had gone to live in Benidorm after she had left the Stork Club, and he thought that she was working in a bar or a club there. But he thought to himself, you never know she may have come back home. He had a phone number that he could try, so he decided that he would phone her the next day. Who knows, he thought, Carrie might be pleased to hear from him, perhaps they would be able to meet up.

He didn't make the phone call because the next day Simon had an asthmatic attack, he needed medication. So Peter picked him and put him on his shoulders and carried him to the chemist's shop to try and get something that would bring him relief. When he went in to the shop he came face to face with Sian's sister, they spoke briefly, not in a friendly way and they soon parted company. Peter is in no doubt that she informed Sian that Simon was poorly. Because later that day Sian came to Len's and took Simon away with her saying, "He is going to live with me".

As they left in a taxi Peter remembers Simon looking out of the taxi's window as it drove away. His little boy was crying with his arms stretched out towards him, calling out, Daddy, Daddy! All Peter could do was stand there transfixed, despair had him frozen to the ground, he was quite unable to do anything except watch them go. Little did he know that would be the last time that he would see his son forty years. Peter had thought that he would be caring for Simon himself but now he realised that as Sian had pointed out, living in the show business environment as he did, he just wouldn't have been able to cope with his son his own. So he decided that he would not fight for custody of his son. Clearly in the light of the long separation that he and Simon would suffer, it was a decision Peter lived to regret.

Still feeling great despair that night he rang the number that he had for Carrie, to his delight she answered the phone and was pleased to hear from him. She told him that she had returned home after spending some time in Benidorm. She was sorry to hear what had happened in regard to his relationship with Sian and the fact that he had lost his son in the break up. She even went so far as to say that she would have helped him to bring Simon up. Unfortunately that offer had come to late, the decision to let Sian have custody had been made, he hoped that would be the best thing for Simon. Peter really enjoyed his chat with Carrie, and with her input he started to think ahead, he was able to look to the future.

Then he made a big decision, the one thing he had got was a car, it was a Sunbeam Rapier, he decided that he would get in it and head for London. He explained his thinking to Len and his then wife Janet and then he said his goodbyes, packed his belongings into the car and set out on his journey. Once again Peter was leaving his beloved valleys behind in pursuit of his dream of show business success, once again he would put all his effort and energy into finding the elusive path to success. There was only one thing for him to do, he would continue his journey into the Chapel of Dreams. Surely this time he would have the right formula for success, if talent and self belief are anything to go by, he was already halfway there.

Chapter Thirteen

The London Dream Is Alive Again

As he reached his destination, London, he felt ready for what lay ahead, he was looking forward not back he knew the past was not the place for him to revisit. Although he was saddened by the thought that he would not be living with his son, Peter had accepted that Simon would be better living with his mother and he would have to find his way forward on a new path. This new resolve helped to support his belief that he was ready to progress, and he was embracing his ambitions for the future again. Accommodation was not going to be a problem because, with Carries help he had managed to rent nice house near Heathrow Airport. His new landlord was a friend of Carrie's family and he was more than happy to help Carrie's friend in his desire to live in London. This house would give Peter a base to set out from.

So, it was with his usual enthusiasm he prepared to concentrate on his career, Peter is a born entertainer and he always travels hopefully. He would not be starting from nothing because he knew that he had a couple of things going for him, things that should really help him on his way. One of those things was the fact that Len was still in touch with Peter Mallick and he phoned Peter Mallick to tell him to expect a call from Peter. You will remember Peter Mallick was the London lawyer who had promised to help relaunch Peter's career in the UK, if he came back from the USA. Just as important, if not more important the other thing Peter Wynne had going for him was that he was a contact within Leeds Music's, UK branch, one of the guys there wanted to mentor Peter's recording career. This sort of contact is not easy for an artiste to come by so with these two things in place he really felt that he was ready to make a fresh start.

Peter decided that in his persona of Simon Smith he would take every chance that came his way. Surely, he thought with his undoubted vocal talent and his contacts, he would fulfil his dreams this time. As we have said Peter was fortunate to have a mentor at Leeds Music, he describes his mentor as a, 'beautiful guy'. The guys name was Don Agness. Don truly believed that Peter was going to make it very big, he recognised that with a voice like his. Peter really should become a massive star.

So an appointment was made for Peter to go in and see Don, at the meeting they would discuss Don's plans for future recordings. When they got together, after they had discussed the way forward that suited both men in terms of musical direction and opportunities that Don expected would come up when people heard Peter's voice, Don played a selection of songs by various artistes, including Canadian singing star, Paul Anka. He did this so that Peter, would understand his line of thought in regard to what kind of material they should be recording. At the same meeting Don also , significantly in terms of Peter's immediate future played music and songs that had been written by the incredibly talented Roy Budd.

For the benefit of any readers who don't immediately recognise Roy Budd's name, We will just say that he was the guy who wrote, the musical scores for many classic films, including "Get Carter", "The Eagle Has Landed", "Soldier Blue", "Puppet On A Chain" and others too numerous to mention. Anyway Peter listened to several songs, and after some discussion, they came to an understanding, they were on the same page as it were, on the best way forward with Peter's recording future. At the end of their meeting Don Agness asked him to record a demo disc of one of Roy Budd's songs, the song was called, *I'm Going Back*. Peter was in complete agreement with the choice of song, and they were able to end their meeting on a very positive note. Peter came away with happy thoughts about the way things were going for him.

The next thing Peter that thought would need to be done was to actually put musicians together and book studio time. As it happened it turned out that Don was aware of a pre-recorded backing track for the song in question, so they would not be using live musicians, they would use this pre recorded backing track instead. So they both went to a recording studio, that was situated just down the street, from Don's office where he had booked some time. Actually the studio is no longer there it is now at residential address in Hyde Park. When they got to the studio Peter recorded the song using the backing track. It was at that point that he was told that Roy Budd himself had written and produced the track, using an orchestra. It had been recorded in a very low key so Peter decided that the best thing do was to sing it in his lowest register. Then by using his vocal skill during the chorus he jumped an octave, and sang in his high register. When they had finished the recording the resultant demo disc was sent by Don, to Roy Budd so that he could give his opinion Peter's vocal interpretation of the song.

The following day Peter received a phone call from Roy's wife, Caterina Valente, the world famous singing star. He was very surprised that she should want to speak to him and very pleased when heard what she had to say. She wanted to tell him that she was over the moon with his wonderful recording, in the course of their conversation she thanked him for doing such a fantastic job on her husband's song. Peter was moved by her praise and by the enthusiastic way she spoke about his voice. Then before ending the call, she asked him if he would like to come and meet her husband Roy at the office of Leeds Music. Naturally Peter agreed, understandably he was very excited at the opportunity that was being presented to him, to meet the talented songwriter.

When he met Roy they clicked straight away, it was if both men had an understanding of what the other was about. After a while their conversation moved to other songs that Roy had written had written. Roy told Peter that he would like him to record a selection of his songs with a multi piece orchestra. This sounded great, things just seemed to be getting better and better, the early signs were looking very promising, Peter could feel his career moving forward as future plans were being made. Suddenly and once again surprisingly for Peter Roy invited him to join his wife Caterina and himself for dinner at his basement flat. He gave him the address telling him that it was situated just off the Edgware Road. Roy told him what time to arrive and they both went their separate ways until later.

When Peter arrived at the flat Roy welcomed him in and then took him through into the lounge. The first thing Peter noticed was that he didn't have a piano, he thought that was strange, because the piano was Roy's main instrument. Having said that he did have double bass tucked away in the corner of the room. Roy took Peter through to the kitchen where Caterina was preparing the meal for them. He introduced them properly because previously they had only spoken on the phone At some point Caterina realised that she was short of a couple of ingredients for the meal, so she asked Peter to accompany her across the road to a local store to help her with her shopping. Always the gentleman, he was more than happy to oblige, this would also gave them a chance for chat and help them get to know each other.

When they returned from the store, Roy had a chess set out, he asked Peter if he could play the game. Well although it had been many years since he played with his Uncle Bill, they had played on many occasions so he had no hesitation in saying, "Set them up Roy". By this time Caterina was busy with making dinner, so even though the TV was on they started the game. Now up to that point

Peter had always thought that he was a pretty good player, but he was immediately on the back foot having to play defensively. The thing was Roy had a strange approach to the game, he would make his move and then watch TV while Peter contemplated his next move. He did this each time it was his turn, it may have been some kind of ploy, whatever it was it succeeded because, suddenly, very quietly Roy said "Checkmate", Then he said shall we play again"? The very perplexed Peter said. "OK" and set the board again, they played and he lost again, he just couldn't believe it. How could a man who didn't appear to be concentrating win so easily? He wondered, in fact he is still wondering to this very day.

Fortunately he was saved from defeat in the third game by Caterina announcing, "Dinner is ready". Peter was very relieved not to lose again. In the course of conversation over the meal Roy made it clear that he wanted to get down to work on some recordings as soon as possible. Although he was flattered by the enthusiasm being shown, Peter had no choice but to tell him that he was already booked to appear in a Manchester Club, 'The Talk of The North' for a week. "OK then," said Roy, "When you get back we will get together and put down arrangements and sort the keys for the songs, etc.". That was the end of a very pleasant evening, so Peter said his goodbyes and went home feeling more than pleased by the way things were progressing.

As we have said the club that he had been booked in at was The Talk of The North, Manchester. He would be appearing there for a week, it was a club Peter had worked in before so he felt that there was every chance that he would have an enjoyable time. The Talk of The North was regarded by many people as Manchester's premier nightclub for many years, booking only the most talented and well liked performers. The author knew the main men who were involved in making the club, a leading night spot in the north due to his having been Tommy Bruce's manager. Joe Pullen and Roy Mosley were two top men, Joe Pullen in particular did not stand any messing and what he said was law.

There was one occasion when it is said that Shirley Bassey was booked to appear at the club., She was dressed in the most beautiful trouser suit, Joe Pullen was old fashioned in some of his views and he said she could not go on stage wearing a trouser suit in his club. There was some discussion to put it mildly, the upshot being it seems, that Joe got his way. Another legend involves Joe and the Quality Street Gang, who were notorious in the fifties and sixties around Manchester. It seems that The Kray Twins came up to Manchester on the train from London with a view to running the night spots in the Manchester area, in much the same way as they did in London.

Joe and The Quality Street Gang met them on the station platform and explained the situation to them, basically the story goes that if the Kray Twins didn't want a war they should keep out of Manchester. In return The Quality Street Gang would not go down to London an take over their clubs. It seems that the The Kray Twins understood what was being offered and they returned to London the next train. Clearly they must have decided that the club scene in Manchester did not require their attention. Having told you the story I have to say that I always found Joe Pullen to be a smashing bloke. The last time we met was about fifteen years ago in a working men's club in Chorley, where he bought me a drink and we enjoyed a chat about the old days. I wish there were men like Joe Pullen running clubs today, you always knew were you stood and he always in my experience paid and played fair.

It would be fair to say that Joe Pullen liked Peter and the week went really well, because as had happened on all the previous occasions that he had performed for them the Northern audiences took Peter to their hearts. They rewarded him with rapturous applause during and after every single performance. Accommodation had been arranged for Peter at a local hotel, one that was quite near the venue so he had a comfortable week, and there were no problems travelling to appear in the show.

On Peter's last night at the Talk of The North, much to his surprise Roy Budd turned up at the club to see the show. Roy came back stage to see Peter before he went on stage for a quick chat. Then he went out front and watched the performance. After the show Roy waited for Peter to get changed and then went back to the hotel with him, When they got up to the room, Roy played a recording of one of the songs that had been made as a demo. After they had listened to the demo, Roy said how eager he was to get Peter in to the studio and that he had booked them in at the De Lane Lea Studios at Wembley in a couple of days time. Clearly Roy had been busy during the week, because he had chosen the songs that would be recorded and more importantly had also done some great arrangements them. The songs were , "This Is Our World" and "I'm Going Back". Roy told Peter that there would be a full orchestra in the recording studio, and that everything was ready to go, This was great news and working with the full orchestra was an exciting prospect, Peter was really looking forward to the recording session taking place.

When Peter returned to London from Manchester, he received a message that a guy called Chris Morgan wanted Peter to fly out and join him in Cannes in the South of France. He had no idea who this man was but after making enquiries he found out that this guy was an acquaintance of Peter Mallick. It seems that Chris Morgan had been in touch with Peter Mallick and had expressed an interest in meeting Peter, with a view to booking him for a show. Chris had made sure to arrange flight tickets so that Peter could fly out to Cannes straight away. Chris Morgan was clearly not a man who delayed his actions. There was no reason not to go, so Peter went to Heathrow Airport where tickets were issued to him, and he boarded the plane. When the plane landed in Nice, he hired a taxi which took him to the hotel Chris Morgan had booked him into. It was very nice hotel situated on the outskirts of Cannes.

Chris Morgan had left him a message at the hotel desk asking him to come and meet up at the Marine Harbour in the town. After a quick, but refreshing wash, Peter put on some aftershave, then he went back to the hotel reception and asked the person the desk if they could call him a cab, this they were happy to do. When he arrived at the Marina harbour, he enquired of the staff and was told that Chris Morgan was sitting at a table near the water's edge. Peter introduced himself and he found that Chris had a glass of Bucks Fizz waiting for him. After Peter had been made to feel welcome, Chris said to him, "I would like you to sing the new song, *This Is Our World*, at the Marina Club". Peter replied, "Well I don't know what musicians you have here, but I don't have any dots, that is any sheet music for them to play". "No problem" said Chris, "I want you to sing acapella. For those who haven't heard the term before it means, without accompaniment". Peter just nodded, thinking to himself this a bit silly, to sing an unknown song without backing in a foreign country.

So that night he went to the Marina Bar where he found Chris Morgan waiting for him, with a magnum of champagne. "Oh", he thought Chris going to try and get me drunk so that I will sing the new song, that I'm going to record. The evening passed rather slowly and Peter did, unsurprisingly in the circumstances, become a little tight. The band finally stopped playing and Peter took the opportunity to get up on the microphone and introduced the song, Saying to the audience "This a new song, I hope you like it because it is going to be my next record, it is titled T*his Our World*". He then went on to say,"As there is no music available I will sing the song unaccompanied up to the halfway point". This he did, ending the song on the big note.

The audience cheered and clapped Peter's short performance, which was very pleasing for him. Then he went back and sat down with Chris and his magnum of champagne. Chris was pleased that he had sung the song and after a few moments said, "Let's go to the casino, and celebrate some more". They set off together and as they were walking along the promenade Chris suddenly realised, that they wouldn't let him in as he was he wasn't wearing a tuxedo, it seems that there was no admittance without out one. So Peter who was feeling tired and so hadn't been that keen to go in the first place offered him the jacket he was wearing. Saying "I will just go back to the hotel". As he recalls the jacket now, he can remember that it was lovely tuxedo with a velvet collar.

Chris said OK and put the jacket on, saying, "It's a shame that you are not coming but don't go back to the hotel go back to the boat that I am staying on and I will see you there later". Peter later found out that the boat belonged to Roddy Llewellyn, who at that time was Princess Margaret's boyfriend. When he got to the boat he found that the wheel house door was locked, Peter thinks that is what you call the steering area on a boat. Anyway, whatever it was called, he couldn't get in and the weather had turned cold. He didn't know how long Chris would be at the casino, so he lay down on the deck and pulled part of the sail over him and tried to go to sleep, he must have succeeded, because he awoke to sound of someone, it turned out to be Chris, coming on board the boat. He wondered why Peter had chosen to sleep on the deck when there was a perfectly good Cabin with a lovely bed in it, below the deck. After explaining that he hadn't realised how he would get in to the cabin, Peter then asked Chris how he had got on at the casino, judging by the smile on his face , it was clear that he had done OK. Chris confirmed that he had won a few quid.

The next day Chris had to fly back to the UK but, Peter was staying on for another day, because Chris had arranged for him to enjoy a spa session, massage, swimming and all the other things that make for a relaxing time. Later in the day Chris had booked him at a club were he sang a few songs, with just piano backing. He was very tired, in fact he was bone weary after the show so he lay down on a couch and slept the night in the club room, that he had been using as a dressing room.

When he awoke the next morning he was feeling very baggy eyed and confused as to where he was. So he showered got dressed and went out on the large balcony. When he got out there Peter was confronted by a group of naked ladies who were just lying there soaking up the sun. Thinking that they were probably dancers in the clubs cabaret, and would know their way around the place, he asked them if they could direct him to the way out. One of the dancers stood up and without bothering to pick up a towel or clothes with which to conceal herself, walked towards and past him out into the corridor and then she walked with him, showing him the way to the exit. He never knew who these young ladies were or why they were not even a little embarrassed by his presence on the balcony. As he said with a reminiscent smile, "That is just another example of show business and the people in it".

After he had recovered from this unexpected situation, Peter said his goodbyes to the unadorned young lady, Peter made his way to the airport. When he got there he caught the plane back to Heathrow later that day. When he arrived back in London his eyes were still swollen but, he was sure that they wouldn't stay that way, he was proved right. Carrie, now his wife, told him that he had had a phone call from Roy Budd, who wanted to make sure that Peter had not forgotten that the De Lane Lea studio had been booked for the next day. He hadn't and he spent the rest of the day of his return from Nice learning his songs. He was keen to make a success of these recordings, he was determined that this recording session would lead to a major hit.

The following morning full of enthusiasm he arrived at De Lane Lea Studios and found that Roy was already there waiting to welcome him. It seemed that they were both enthusiastic and determined to make their musical collaboration a success. Peter remember thinking that the whole set up was very impressive, there was a massive orchestra and it had a great string section. It also had a brass section with were trombones and trumpets etc. and a lovely rhythm section. Peter went into a small booth just off to the right of the orchestra got himself settled and they were away. He recorded "I'm Going Home" and after a few takes Roy declared himself satisfied with the result.

However "This Is Our World was different, it wasn't just how Roy wanted it to be. So Roy dismissed the band after several takes and he and Peter stayed back to hear those takes and adjust them accordingly. Roy was adamant when listening to the takes that a female voice was needed, to enhance the sound. So he spent some time phoning around until he was finally pleased to say that he had secured the services of the 'Ladybirds' lead singer Maggie Stredder and Roy went into discussion with her and they listened to the song. Much to everyone's disappointment it was not possible due technical reasons for Maggie Stredder to make a meaningful contribution to the recording.

Unfortunately it seems that the key the music had been recorded in was to high, it obviously couldn't be changed the musicians had gone their separate ways so, not to put to fine a point on it, they were stuck with what they had. The next day Roy had the masters transferred on to small tapes that would be played to the producers of TV shows. They were not well received, Roy told Peter that one of the comments that he had received was " that the recordings were too contrived". He thinks that these people were referring to the recording and the arrangements, not the songs as Roy Budd had written them. So there it was, Roy wasn't happy, neither was Peter, they had both worked extremely hard, as he puts it being told a thing like that was a bit of a stomach wrench for both of them. Authors note: Sad to say Maggie Stredder who was dear friend to so many people both in and out of the business is no longer with us, she enhanced many recordings and live performances for so many artistes both here and abroad. We all miss her voice and her bubbly personality, very much.

Opportunity Knocks was coming back on TV at this time and Roy Budd always mindful of an opportunity to promote the singer and the songs they had recorded, said "Why don't you apply to appear on Opportunity Knocks,"? " Apart from anything else if you get on the show it will be free publicity for us all". Peter replied, saying "OK I'll do it then". An audition was arranged for him with Keith Becket the shows producer, who explained that the format of the show was going to be different to that tried by previous talent shows. The idea being that someone would introduce an artiste on to the show as an act that they had seen or heard performing.

Basically they were introducing an act that they claimed to have discovered. Roy told his wife Caterina about their plans she immediately said, "I will fly back from where I am appearing and introduce Peter on the show as my discovery". Peter was extremely grateful to her because, Cat, as he knew her, was famous all over the world and he was very flattered to have her support. Stars of the magnitude of Dean Martin, Perry Como, Bing Crosby and a host of other were all desperate to book her as a guest on their shows. So much so that Dean Martin invited her to appear on his show no less than seven times.

Now as we return to the audition for Opportunity Knocks, It seems that Keith Becket was given the information that, Caterina would be introducing Peter as someone she had heard singing and she had been so impressed that she hoped to able to help in the progression of his career. Keith Becket thought this was a great idea and was quick to tell Peter that he had passed the audition and he just had to wait for a date to appear on the actual show. Well he waited and continued to wait, but he received no news at all. So feeling a little perplexed as to what might have happened he phoned Roy Budd and explained to him that he hadn't had any news at all from the show, no date to appear, nothing.

So Roy tried to find out what was happening even with him making enquiries on Peter's behalf there was still no word coming on the from anyone involved in making the show as to what was happening. To this day Peter never heard any explanation as to why he never received a date to appear on the show. Looking back he finds the whole thing very strange, after all he passed the audition with flying colours. Then added to that he had what he thought would be a great scoop for the show, in the form of a great star, Caterina Valente appearing for no fee, to introduce a relatively unknown singer. Once again as with many other mysteries in Peter's career, the only thing that can be said is, "That's show business"!

So it was time to move on with his career, it was clear there was no prospect of the recordings that he made with Roy Budd being released and promoted, he needed to move on and find work. Because of his popularity as a live performer, he did not have to wait long for an agent to contact him with work. It came in the form of a booking from the Mecca Agency. They wanted him to appear on the QE2 cruise, which would be sailing from Southampton to New York. The agency had also booked Charlie McKay who was the guitarist and singer from the television show, 'New Faces', to appear on the show.

This was good news because Peter and Charlie were old indeed good friends. When they realised they were both booked on the cruise so they decided to drive down to Southampton and meet up at the Customs Control Office. As they were coming out of the office Peter noticed an error on his paperwork the had him down as Peter Wynne born 1949, they had given him ten years grace, as he says, "How nice of them". Charlie and Peter met up with the stewards when they got on board ship, they were pleased to discover that there was a steward allocated to each berth. Peter was even more pleased when he discovered that his cabin was above the water line, this was a real plus point for the journey because it meant he had a porthole that he could open for fresh air. Having a porthole also meant that he could look out on the great Atlantic Ocean during the course of what was his first sea voyage.

When they had settled in to their respective cabin's Charlie and Peter met up for drinks in the bar. There was a casino round the corner from the bar but, because gambling did not appeal to either of them, they never went in there during the voyage. They entertained both first and second class passengers with their cabaret, which meant that they appeared in cabaret rooms on the upper and lower levels of the ship. They performances were very popular and they were greeted to loud an generous applause from all the passengers on both levels.

Peter remembers that the two of them felt a little warm when the ship got near to the Equator. It was to warm for shirts and jackets so they took to walking around in blue, sometimes black vest style sleeveless T shirts. Thinking back now Peter often wonders Why did they do that!! They were probably just doing a bit of posing, nothing wrong with that you might think, but of course back then they hadn't seen Onslow in the TV show, 'Keeping Up Appearances'. If they had the two of them would almost certainly dressed in more formal attire.

In any event the two friends enjoyed some great laughs together, during the cruise. This was especially true when they stopped over in the Big Apple, New York. They took in all the sights they were able to walk everywhere in those days, Central Park and round the streets off Broadway. This freedom of movement is not recommended for tourists today. Returning to the ship for the voyage home, they found things much as before and enjoyed the trip immensely. That is until the last night of the voyage, Peter made the mistake of loaning his berth out for a party, and his steward was not pleased when he saw the mess that the party goers made.

There was only one thing for it he felt obliged to give the steward a bigger tip than he had intended, so that he would feel to grieved by all the extra work involved in making the cabin habitable again. It seemed the only sensible solution if he wanted to have any hope of being booked as an entertainer on the if he wanted on the QE2 again. A sad footnote to this part of the story is that Peter's good friend Charlie McKay passed away on November 2nd 2007, God Bless you always Charlie. Peter is still in touch with Charlie's wife and two children are who now living in Australia.

When Peter came back home from the cruise, to find that things were changing and that Roy Budd was moving to a penthouse property in Kensington. Because he was their friend he offered to help in some way, thank the Lord that there were lifts in place, when they were moving because some of their furniture was very heavy. The property they were moving to was huge so there was a lot of work to do to get them settled in. Caterina was pregnant at the time so she had to be careful about lifting anything, so couldn't help much with the actual move. Needless to say Roy as a new father to be, was over the moon and walking around on cloud nine. Afterwards they had finished moving house they all enjoyed a very pleasant lunch together and then Peter walked back to his house.

Although he wasn't aware of it at the time, the fact was that he would not be seeing much of the couple in the future because, not long after that he got offered the position of Compère at Fagin's night Club in Manchester. Peter talked it over with Carrie and they decided that it would a good move so he took the job. Their son Grant was now 18 months old so they needed to settle down, past experience had shown him how difficult long distance relationships could be. They hired a white van filled it with their belongings and headed of up north. When they arrived they moved into a flat that someone had found for them. They were not there very long as it turned out to be unsuitable accommodation for the family, for a variety of reasons. Luckily heard of more suitable accommodation in the form of a house in Davyhulme. It was situated on the outskirts of Manchester, so they moved in to that.

Fagin's was a nice well placed club that was also on the outskirts of Manchester and Peter was looking forward to being the Compère. He never done that sort of job before but he thought his personality would carry him through and he would still be singing a few songs. One thing he was certain he wasn't going to try and be a comic. As he puts it he just has not got the stand up mentality, he wouldn't be able to tell a joke and get a laugh, he just hasn't the timing required for that job. What he can do is sing so he billed himself as a singing compère. He did very well in that capacity and to this day former patrons of the club speak well of him.

It was an easy drive from Davyhulme to Fagin's each night and he knew that he would able to drive home after the shows and be in the house by midnight, much better. He remembers that the first act that he introduced was a great northern comic called Norman Collier, who had very humorous act involving the microphone appearing to fail. There were other occasions when he introduced some of the great performers that he had worked with in the early days of his career. These acts included stars of the calibre of Billy Fury and Marty Wilde.

The readers of this book will I am sure be able to recall that Peter and these acts had appeared together on TV shows like 'Boy Meets Girl' and Wham. Because of their enduring friendships Peter was able to go to their dressing rooms and they would chat and reminisce about old times. When Billy was appearing at the club he told Peter about his health problems, they were congenital problems that he and his brother Alby had inherited from their late father. It is believed that both boys had suffered from rheumatic fever when they were younger, which certainly contributed to their heart conditions. Billy explained to Peter that in his most recent heart operation the surgeon had fitted a new valve because the other natural one had become clogged and failed. At this point Billy had lifted his shirt to show Peter the scar across his chest, he had clearly been through a lot. There is no doubt he was not a well man, these health problems would unfortunately lead to Billy's early demise. Peter felt very sorry that Billy's health was deserting him in this way.

Marty Wilde on the other hand was still very confident and sure of himself. Added to that he seemed very fit and strong and of course still had his powerful voice. Thinking about those times and conversations, Peter remembers a happy story from their early days together, about himself the boys going down the fish market together in great Yarmouth looking for molluscs to eat, after a while then they found a place that sold shell fish, they bought some and then walked through the town while they ate them. As Peter says, "Happy days and simple pleasures". It is strange to look back and think how popular people like Marty, Billy, Peter, Tommy and many others still were with the paying public when they made live performances, but they were becoming forgotten by television producers and to large extent, their recording companies.

Always an observant man, Peter noticed the different thing that other performers did, for instance Scott Walker had a list of his songs cello-taped to the mic stand, obviously because that was the only way that Scott could remember the order he would be singing them in. The other thing he noticed about Scott was that he wore sandals, not shoes on stage, Peter thought, to himself that's different. Then he thought but so what, if that's the way he likes to do things good luck to him. Everyone is different they have their own tastes and style. Peter did make the odd mistake when he was learning his trade as a compère. There was one unfortunate occasion when he introduced Julie Felix to the audience as Julie Christie. What a fool he felt, realising his mistake as soon as the name left his lips. He corrected his mistake and he apologised, immediately afterwards. Thankfully Julie accepted his apology with good grace It has to be said that Julie Felix is another fine artiste who has not received the plaudits through her career that her talent deserved.

One man who Peter really did admire as an entertainer came to appear and perform at Fagin's, his name was Vince Hill. Vince was they say in show biz a real pro. When he sang he was always true to the melody, he showed real class in every performance that he ever gave. Peter also remembers that Tommy Cooper came into the club one night during his tenure as compère. Tommy did not come to perform, he was just there to relax and enjoy himself. He introduced himself to Peter and they enjoyed a few drinks together. Tommy Cooper was we all know a very funny man and Peter enjoyed his company very much. As always in life all good things come an end, the contract as compère had been for twelve months and the time soon passed, then it was time to move on again. Peter and Carrie had to look to the future and find a home for themselves, while Peter would hopefully continue his career. So with these things in mind they looked towards North Wales for a place to settle and make a home.

The reason for choosing North Wales had a lot to do with the fact that Peter knew that his mother had been born in Ruthin and that is were all his ancestors had been raised. Throughout his life and during all his travels he always felt drawn to that area, really he felt destiny was calling him to live in the area. He knows there is a church in Llanrwst were six generations of his family on his mother's side had been buried, how could he not be drawn there? To this day he often visits the church and it's graveyard, when he finds himself in Ruthin or Denbigh. His Mum's ashes are interred there with her own Mum and Dad, he describes the place where these members of his family are laid to rest, as a beautiful spot, so very peaceful, which as he says, is only right for a cemetery. Both his parents passed away in Australia, but Peter's brother brought their Mums' ashes home so that she could be with her parents.

Returning to the narrative, we find that on this occasion knowing that they had some money saved Carrie and Peter decided that purchasing a property was the way forward. They were helped in this ambition by Carrie's dad who very kindly lent them some cash to supplement their savings. This meant that they started their property search in good spirits. They looked at a nice place in Llangollen, but there was a river, Peter thinks it was the River Dee running through the bottom of the garden. They both knew that this would not be safe for a small child like Grant, do they discounted this property. Then they saw a picture of a cottage that was for sale in Henllan just out side Denbigh, called Bryn y Garn, he asked at the local post office were he could find the cottage. Peter remembers that he couldn't pronounce the name every well, but in spite of his struggle to be understood, the lady behind the counter told him how to find it.

When they arrived at the entrance to the property, they found that it was at the end of a short lane. There was a gate which they stopped at so that they could open it. Then continued up the drive so that they could have a peek at the cottage. They didn't have key yet so they were unable to go inside, they had to had to content themselves with looking in through the windows. The property seemed in good order, there were buildings outside including a garage, that was built from asbestos, they didn't know then but, as we all know now that is not good as there were dangers that came to be associated with asbestos. There was also a brick coal house with a corrugated roof. The garden was about 30 yards long and in the garden they discovered that there was an outside loo, which was no longer in use.

The couple decided that they would stay the night in a Bed and Breakfast establishment that was situated just up the road from the property they were interested in. The next morning they rang the estate agents to arrange a viewing of Bryn y Garn . When they got inside they found that the house had two bedrooms and a good sized bathroom upstairs, there were two rooms downstairs and it had a decent sized kitchen. They had no hesitation in telling the rep that they would take the property, they were more than pleased to have ended their search for a new home. The next task for Peter was to arrange to have their furniture and possessions moved from Manchester. Things were looking very good for the family at this point.

Now Peter was feeling pretty sure that most of his work would be coming from the Lancashire area. The reason that he was feeling this way was because there were so many clubs in places like, Manchester, Burliegh, Blackburn, Bury, Bolton and Swinton to name just a few of the northern towns. He was in no doubt that his work would come from the clubs, as he had arranged with a couple of agents to get him gigs. He turned out to right in his assumption and he soon received his first gig. It was at one of the several Mecca Ballrooms that there were in the north. He found that he was appearing on the same bill as the redoubtable Bernard Manning.

Peter quickly found out as we all did when meeting Bernard, that he was a great chap who was very helpful and not at all sarcastic when he was off stage. After all it is show business and it's just an act, no one is quite what they seem when they are off stage. Some do their spot, take the mickey out of everyone in the audience, but they are as nice as pie off stage. Others might give the impression that they are really nice people when they are on stage, but they are real big heads, when they come off, as Peter said that's Show Biz. After he had done his set that night Bernard came to him and said, "You have just sung the song I finish my spot with". Peter apologised saying, "I am sorry I didn't realise that you finished with a song". Bernard replied "It don't matter, me ole flower, I'll just do another one".

Authors note: I think it is fair to say that many people are aware of Bernard Manning's kind and generous nature but for those who are not, it is worth recounting this true story. It goes back many years now, but at the time in question Bernard was aware that a pensioner from his local area was appearing in court charged with non payment of his poll tax, the man was duly convicted and given a custodial sentence and a fine which of course he was unable to pay. Within hours Bernard had paid the fine and the whole poll tax bill, his actions forced the authorities to release the pensioner immediately. This was I think we would all agree a very Christian act, which some might not find in keeping with Bernard;s on stage persona..

I have heard many criticisms of Bernard over the years by various people, but not one of those people have ever been recorded as carrying out such acts of decency and generosity as the ones that Bernard is known and proven to have performed. Perhaps there are people who should pause and reflect on Peter's very apt comment, It is only showbiz because it is and always will be only Showbiz, we should always only judge the man, and not the act when we look at real life.

The gigs that Peter was doing around the Lancashire area all seemed to be good venues and he was being very well received, during that time he was offered another compères job. He can't for the life of him remember the name the club, only that it was in Burnley, but he does remember that he was offered and signed a six month contract. At this point he was working with acts like Cannon and Ball, they had not hit the big time yet, but as he says, they were clearly very talented. Another artiste who appeared at the club was Stuart Damon, readers may remember him from the hit TV Show "The Champions', he also appeared in the musical 'The Boys From Syracuse' '. Stuart is an absolutely lovely man, he is 80 years old now and for the last 30 years he been appearing in the USA show 'General Hospital', his performances in that show won him an Emmy in 1999. Peter wishes Stuart continued good health and good luck in all that he does

A performer who Peter had appeared with on a couple of occasions was Ken Dodd, so when they appeared on the "Thank Your Lucky Stars' TV show, Peter was very keen to meet him socially. Incidentally Peter sang his own composition "The Wall" that night to great acclaim. The two of them did not meet on that occasion but he lived in hope for the future.

Anyway Ken Dodd came and performed at the club in Burnley and after the show Peter went to the bar and introduced himself to Ken, reminding him of the previous times they had worked together. Ken Dodd just smiled and turned away facing towards the bar. This made Peter feel quite upset at the time. But with the benefit of hindsight he thinks perhaps that some people's memories are not as good as others, clearly Ken did not remember him. Peter carried on with this job until the six months ended, the club management asked him to stay on but he had enough of being a compère. It is a good job because you go home every night with regular money, but he needed the buzz that comes from going on and doing his own spot.

When he arrived home after his last night at the club, he found that there was a letter waiting for him from his brother Charles in Australia. It seems that Charles had done very well for himself, he owned a petrol station and he also sold hamburgers, pies and sandwiches, basically anything that people travelling, could possibly need. Any he was offering Peter' Carrie, who was expecting another baby and Grant a trip to Australia, with all expenses paid. So they garaged their current car, a Singer Gazelle with Carrie's parents, and they packed their bags got ready to fly to Tasmania. It would be a real reunion because that was where the rest of Peter's family had ended up living, he had not seen any of them for a very long time. There is no doubt that he was really looking forward to seeing them all again, Peter is a man who loves his family. He knew that his younger brother Terry, was playing guitar and singing with his own band, so Peter couldn't wait to see him perform. The idea that the two of them were working as entertainers, wow! When they were growing up he could never have expected that. Carrie, Peter and Grant planned to stay over there for six months before they returned home, to good old Blighty.

Chapter Fourteen

The Australian Experience

The family flew with Qantas Airways, it was a very long and tiring flight. At the time Grant was only about three and half and it was especially tiring for him. They stopped off in Bahrain to refuel and then again Singapore. The journey still wasn't over when they arrived in Melbourne because they had to get another flight out to Tasmania. This flight had to cross the 'Bass Straits', they found that crossing to be turbulent to say the very least. So it was with some relief that they landed safely at Launceston Airport, where they were greeted by most of Peter's family.

From there they were then driven to Peter's parents home in Longford, Tasmania. They were very tired after their long journey, so after talking about the good times and bad, that had occurred over the last few years, Carrie and Peter retired to their room. when they entered the room they saw a massive spider, about the size of Peter's hand, crawling up the wall, Carrie screamed and Peter's mother came rushing into the room with a large glass. She had covered the spider with the glass in an instant, then she slid cardboard between the glass and the wall, then she threw the spider outside. It is amazing how calm people become when they get used to living close to nature.

The next day Peter was introduced to his brothers dog, it was called Joe he was a Samoyed, it was a beautiful animal, but he was inclined to bite people he didn't know or like. He must have liked Peter because he was never bitten by the dog during the time he was there. He thinks that it may have been to do with his tone of voice, because he Terry and Charles all speak with a similar tone of voice, so they were accepted by Joe and the other dogs. Before going to Australia Peter had given up smoking but like a fool he decided to have just one, as he says, "This was a big mistake"! One which he regrets to this day.

Later that week his brother played some of Peter's records to the manager of a club in Tasmania, as a result he was able to secure a two week stint at The Launceston Hotel, this was followed by gigs in Sydney and Adelaide, because of the distance between places, this involved quite a lot of flying. The gig in Adelaide,was for the duration of two weeks, he was appearing at a supper club, it was called The Paprika Club The venue served food while the artistes were performing, which can make things difficult, sometimes it is not possible to get audience's full attention. Also it was an unusual line up for the show, a bit like the old variety shows in the UK where very different acts would be appearing on the same bill. There was an exotic dancer who was doing the warm up, after her performance the main act would come on, which of course on this occasion was Peter. His performance went down very well on the first night and he continued to be well received throughout the two weeks that he was in residence. On the first night after receiving the plaudits from the crowd ,he retired to the flat that the venue provided.

When he got into the accommodation he found that there was a lodger already in residence. This lodger took the form of a small tabby cat the two of them soon got to know each other and became good friends. The afternoon following his first appearance at The Paprika Club he found that he had been booked to appear at a rugby club. This was an unusual venue for him at that time, so he wondered how well he would do there. He needn't have worried, the people cheered and gave him a standing ovation, he made a few new friends that afternoon. That night Freddie Garrity's band "The Dreamers" came in to The Paprika Club, for a social evening, Peter thinks that they were gigging in Adelaide that week. He found that the lads in the group were very friendly towards him. They recognised his talent and they were appreciative of his voice and so they made for a very good audience. He enjoyed his time at this venue and his last week there passed by very quickly. Peter had become very popular with the local people who had really become fans of his singing style and performances, so much to his surprise when he went to the airport to board the plane to Sydney, he found that there were many of his new fans from the club, waiting there to see him and give him a memorable send off.

When he landed in Sydney he met up with his brother Terry, now as we have said before Terry is a talented musician and songwriter and they had made plans to see if his career could be advanced. The two of them decided that Terry should take some of the songs that he had written to a music publisher in the hope that these songs could be published and recorded. While he had been looking around for opportunities for both of them to find work Peter had heard of a publisher who seemed to be willing to at least listen to Terry's songs. So with a reasonable amount of hope for success, they went along to meet the guy. They met him settled down for a chat and then played him some of Terry's songs. Well it the meeting could not have gone better because when the guy heard the songs, he liked them and said that he would publish them. Added to that he paid Terry $200 Australian to show good faith, so as Peter says, "That was a good day spent in Sydney".

Just before we leave Peter's memories of Australia he wants to reflect on just how small a place the world can be. As the readers will recall he had spent some time in the Guards so when he learned that his brother was a member of The Old Comrades Guards Association, he was glad to be invited to along a get together that the Association were having. Once he was there the members were quick to tell him that it didn't matter how short his time in the Guards had been, he was still classified as a Grenadier Guardsman. He was in conversation with a Life Guardsman, a Scots Guardsman and a Coldstream Guardsman, they were drinking together and the talk was all about their army days, The Coldstream said "Yes I joined in 1956", "Same here" Peter replied. It turned out this guy had been in at the very same time as Peter and he started telling them about the singer that was in his regiment and the singer that The Grenadiers had, Peter said, "That singer was me". What a turn up that was, it was the key to them all having a really good gossip.

On his return to Tasmania, Peter found that his wife Carrie had been admitted to hospital, to have their baby. She gave birth to a little girl and they named her Daniella, affectionately calling her their little Aussie baby. After the baby's birth the family stayed over in Tasmania for another six months, during that time they were debating whether they should ask the Australian government for permission to stay over there permanently. However after some long distance conversations with Carrie's mother, added to the fact that they were feeling homesick, they felt that they would find it hard to put down roots in Australia. Quite apart from considering the feelings of Carrie's Mum and Dad they had to think about what would happen with the cottage they had bought in Wales. So that was it, they had reached the time when they would have to go home. It was decided that Peter would try to get back to Australia to see his kin when ever he could, but for now he was going home. It was very hard for him to say goodbye to his Mum,Dad and his brothers,Charles and Terry and sisters Pamela and Leo. The family headed back to the UK with an extra bundle of joy, named Daniella.

They arrived back in the UK at Heathrow Airport in the winter of 1977. After landing and going through customs they made their way to Bill and Lou's, Carrie's parents to pick up the car, he had left with them. After spending a little time with them and introducing them to their new granddaughter, they set off on the long journey that would take them home. Peter remembers it was really cold so he was hoping that the Horseshoe Pass would not be closed due to snow drifts. There were no seat belts in cars in those days so Carrie sat in the back of the car, with Grant and Daniellia.

On their way back home they took time out from the journey, to call in on Peters old school friend Brian Instone's parents. Readers will recall that the Instone's daughter Marlene had died at a very young age, several years before and that Peter had helped to carry the coffin, at that very sad time. Mr and Mrs Instone were really pleased to see Peter and his family and offered them tea and sandwiches. However in view of the time constraints with their journey and the anticipated snow, they just had tea and biscuits. Afterwards Carrie and Peter thanked the Instone's for their hospitality and continued on their journey home to North Wales.

When they reached the Horseshoe Pass they were relieved to see that it was open, there were just a few patches of snow here and there, nothing to worry about. However as they got about halfway up Peter saw just one flake of snow fall on his windscreen, it was nature signalling that there would be more. Before long he had the car's windscreen wipers on full speed, but the snow was falling so heavily that he was soon struggling to see where he was going. They were now driving through a real snow storm.

As they drove along they saw a car that had gone off the road, no one seemed to be hurt and Peter could see that there were people trying to push it back on to the road. So held his breath and continued to drive, when he reached the top of the mountain which by now had a thick covering of snow, he breathed a sigh of relief. As they drove down through the winding pass towards, Ruthin, Peter and Carrie could see that other cars were skidding off the road and ending up on the grass verge, or in a ditch. Peter remembers that he was driving with extreme caution and that they were very glad when they arrived back in Denbigh in one piece. They got safely home to their cottage then, got the car unloaded and put the children to bed. When that was done they both dropped heavily into their armchairs, feeling absolutely knackered, but very happy to have reached their destination. They were looking forward to life in back in their home, as always because he such a positive man Peter could see better times ahead.

Three brothers together, L-R Charles, Terry and Peter

Chapter Fifteen

Home again to Wales

Carrie and Peter found that living back in Wales was, to say the very least good, they had settled back in very quickly and soon got back into their routine. They were now the proud owners of six chickens that Peter had bought from a guy down the road, they were good layers, not always the case as people who have kept a few chickens themselves will know, because these birds are very easily stressed. However they must have been content in their environment and it was good for the family to be able to have a fresh egg whenever they wanted one.

The only drawback that Peter had while living there was how far north he was having to travel for gigs. On one occasion he found himself doing a week in Whitehaven, the bookings were not all at the same venue so sometimes he was doing two shows at night, each one at a different venue. Travelling between these places was quite stressful because of the problems he sometimes had getting to the second venue at the time he was required to appear. Very often the club would be hard to find because some of the places were right off the beaten track. As Peter says, "That week was a real white knuckle ride". When he went home he was feeling worn out, and he had a craving for some gigs that were closer to home.

Luckily he was able to find some local work quite quickly. These gigs came in through a DJ called Eddie Green. In the course of his work as a DJ, Eddie had started getting venues,who were looking for a selection of talented live performers and Peter Wynne fitted the bill. Some the venues were good, others not so good, but Peter didn't complain when places were a bit rough, because they were near to his home which meant that he could get home to his family after each show. As he thinks back about this period of time he remembers that he was very busy. This was because not long after Peter had linked up with Eddie Green, he started to do an Elvis Presley tribute. This was not a impersonation, just a few songs performed in the Elvis style, wearing similar costumes to the ones that 'The King of Rock and Roll' as people had styled him, wore. Because of Elvis's popularity work opportunities for Peter, increased.

There were definitely more gigs coming in, and they were coming in the right areas. At one time having got a gig at Rhyl Pavilion, Peter found that he only had to do three songs, his performances were going down great, audiences were seeing that he was and is a very versatile vocal performer. On another occasion when he did a charity gig at a Hotel in Rhyl he absolutely stormed it and more importantly, he was able to make good money for the cause he was working for in the process. As a live entertainer Peter has always been in demand, particularly during they heyday of cabaret and working men's clubs.

The problems came for many artistes not just Peter when the venues that put on cabaret shows started to decline. In only a few years following the demise of cabaret as we knew it, the smoking regulations started to close the working men's clubs and bigger pubs that had previously booked live entertainment stopped some entertainers careers short. Why you might ask did the smoking regulations contribute to the closure of clubs and other venues? Well in those days there seemed to be a lot more people who smoked. These people were used to sitting in the audience drinking a pint and lighting up a cigarette whenever they felt like it, during the live shows. When the ban on smoking in public places came into force, people had to go outside, rain or shine if they wanted to light up. This meant that they might have paid to see an act, but because they craved a smoke they could be outside for up to half of an acts 40 minute spot. During this time people just stopped going out socially, they could not enjoy live entertainment in the same way that they had in previous years.

So like many other performers to a degree Peter's career was affected by these troubled time in the business. In fact there were empty days when work was sparse, so at that time, during what was sometimes months, without a gig, he started to think in terms of getting a day job. He was not alone in this, many artistes never performed in public again because they simply couldn't afford or get permission to take time off from what became their full time employment. An entertainer has to eat and feed his family just like the rest of us and in many cases there livelihood was gone. We know that stopping smoking is healthy, but if more thought had gone into the change in rules many of the venues might have sustained an audience and still been open today. After all it wasn't just the artistes who lost out

, Landlords, Landladies and bar staff were also put out of work by the closure of the venues.

On a personal level there were happy times in Denbigh though, at one point in their time there, Peter's Mum and dad along with other members of his family came over to see him at the cottage. This was a lovely family occasion as is shown by a photo of many of them together his dad has his arm around him. This something that Peter regards as one of his happiest memories. You may recall that in the early chapters Peter wondered if his dad was proud of him, I think that the expression his father's face and the one on his mothers who has linked him, show how proud and happy they both are to be with their much loved son.

As Peter could not find enough gigs to support his family during this lull in the world of show business, he found himself having to take a job at 'The North Wales Hospital for People with Mental Problems'. Employment in this environment opened his eyes to the difficulties that some unfortunate people were suffering in their lives. It certainly gave him another dimension in his own life, being in close proximity to the kind of despair that could prompt people to attempt and in some cases succeed in taking their own lives, Peter found the situation a hard one to exist in. He remembers that one of the guys the hospital was so depressed that he climbed a tower in the hospital grounds and jumped to his death, he was killed instantly. This was indeed a very sad place for anyone to work in, but Peter had a family to support, he needed money to pay bills, buy food and clothes, so he just had to get on with the job. Luckily in comparison to some performers, he still had some gigs so he was still performing in clubs in and around the North Wales area. Added to that he hosted shows and was even on a panel that had been set up to find the best entertainers in the area. So the day job was not preventing him from following his entertainment dream, as the saying goes, 'You have to be in it, to win it', and Peter was definitely still in there wowing audiences with his fabulous voice.

One day while he was working at the hospital he had a phone call from The Delfont Organisation, he was being offered work on a cruise ship, and they wanted him to go to London and audition. So that week he travelled down and as he was walking to the audition room, he met Larry Payne who he had appeared in Camelot with. Larry asked him what he was doing, was he still performing? Peter assured him that he was and he told him about the audition for the cruise. Larry was pleased for him and wished him luck saying rather wistfully that he hoped to be offered a cruise himself one day. As he said "I am finding work very hard to come by". Peter was sorry to hear this and wished for things to get better for Larry very soon.

Well as might be expected Peter passed his audition and was told the format for the show that would be required on the ship. He was pleased, with how things had gone so he went home to Denbigh in high spirits. Of course he would not decide whether or not to accept the cruise until he had talked it over with Carrie. When he told her about the offer she said that he should ask about how long the cruise was and how long the break between docking and going out again would be. He did as she suggested and asked for the information, he was told that the cruise would be up to a month long and that when the ship docked, they would only have a short turnaround, just a few hours before setting sail again. After discussing this at length with Carrie, Peter refused to be away from his family for that amount of time so he decline the cruise lines offer. They tried to convince him to do three months, but they still didn't give him time to get home to Wales and then return to Southampton to sail with the ship, so his answer had to be no!

To this day Peter is not sure whether he made the right decision when he refused the cruise. After all as he asks "Wouldn't it have been better to be performing on a cruise ship, than working in a mental hospital picking up soiled linen"? There were some very unpleasant jobs that he was called on to do during his time at the hospital, one of them was to light the incinerator and burn the rubbish that he and the other porters collected on their rounds. One day one of the other porters lit the incinerator and then heard someone shouting from the inside, they quickly opened the doors and a patient crawled out with his clothes smoking and singed.

When they got him out it seems that he asked them for a cigarette and then just sat on the edge of the incinerator and smoked it, seeming totally unaware of what had just happened. On another occasion there was an interesting admission to the hospital, a famous actress came in apparently suffering from stress and exhaustion, as

Peter recalls she wasn't in hospital for long. In her most recent role she had been appearing in Coronation Street playing the part of Elsie Tanner's daughter, Peter heard that actress in question had died recently. He stayed at the hospital for a few years and then got a job as a postman, the people on his round called him 'The Singing Postman' because he sang everywhere he walked.

When he was out on his rounds delivering the mail he used to stop in the nearby village of Lannys for tea at the home of a lady called Ann. While he was there if he was early enough and could take the time eat it, she would make him poached eggs on toast. On these visits there Ann told him about another lady called Miss Jones, who lived higher up in the village, she played the organ in the chapel It seems that Peter's uncle, Furness Wynne Williams the operatic tenor had known and become friendly with Miss Jones at one time in his life.

With this information in his mind Peter was keen to know more about his Uncle Furness so he made a point of calling on Miss Jones. When he arrived at her door he introduced himself and told him about his desire to know more about his uncle. Miss Jones invited Peter into her home and she was more than happy to tell him about her friend Furness, who had been the principal tenor at Covent Garden. The man who among other things had been a friend of Enrico 'The Great' Caruso. There was a photograph of Peter's uncle on the sideboard, in it he could be seen to be a very handsome man, he had long flowing grey hair, he was wearing a homburg hat and he had a black cape draped over his shoulders. Apparently Furness would take Miss Jones out for drinks in the local pubs around Ruthin. As Peter listened to her, it was clear that she held a great affection for Furness, in fact Peter gained the impression, that Miss Jones and his uncle were almost certainly having an affair. Although he respected her privacy to much to ask for his impression to be confirmed.

Time is as always relative and as such can control decisions and how life and ambition is approached. Peter was only fifteen at the time of his uncle's death, but oh how he wishes that he could have met him before he died. Because he wanted to ask a question that he felt only his uncle could have answered, "Was his own voice good enough for operatic training"? If his uncle had given a positive answer, then he would have followed, that path and not sung rock songs and ballads the way he did. Having said that Peter takes a philosophical view about the path he chose to follow, because he believes that fate is fate, basically what will be, will be.

During this period of time Peter read in "The Stage", this a very useful and informative paper for people in the entertainment profession, that they were looking to audition actors/singers to appear in a forthcoming production of '42nd Street'. At this time he thinks that he must have been in his late forties, perhaps pushing fifty, but he knew that he still had great enthusiasm and more importantly that he was still in fine voice. He was positive that he could and would obtain a part in this production. So filled with his usual enthusiasm he called a cab to take him to the train station in Rhyl. When he got there he caught the train to Manchester, where the auditions were being held. He arrived at Victoria Station, from there he made the short walk to 'The Palace Theatre' for the audition. When he arrived at the theatre he met a few of the other guys who were waiting to audition for the production. Finally getting backstage heard someone who was already on the stage, singing the audition piece that he intended to perform. "Damn", he thought, "I haven't brought anything else with me, oh well never mind I will just have to sing and perform the song better than I have ever done before".

A chap who had travelled from Cornwall was up next, he performed his song and then it was Peter's turn, when they called him on stage he apologised for having the same song that they had already heard, to perform for them. They said, "Never mind sing it anyway". So he did, he had chosen a lovely song from the musical 'Carousel', titled, "If I Loved You". The people who were holding the auditions listened to the song all the way through, then they said, "Thank You Peter, would you mind waiting until we have heard the rest of the people who have come for the audition"? He didn't mind waiting at all because, he knew that this was a really good sign. Not put to fine a point on it he felt elated! Because he knew he must have given a stellar performance during his audition in order for him to be asked to wait.

In the event he had to wait until the last person had sung and then he was called back on stage. One of the crew asked the question,

"Will you read for us"? Of course he would! They brought a young lady on and handed Peter a script saying we want you to act this part with -----, sadly he is unable to remember the actresses name. Knowing that the show was about Broadway in New York, he asked if they would like him to perform using an American accent. It doesn't matter was the reply, but he used an American accent anyway, his time in the USA had not been wasted.

After he had done the reading they asked him which stage productions he had been in recently, because most of his recent performances had been in the clubs and in cabaret, he could only tell them about 'Camelot' and the Pantomime at The London Palladium. So he told them about those appearances and the parts that he had played in those shows. For good measure he also mentioned the places he had performed as a solo artiste, highlighting his theatre performances with the big bands. They okayed everything and said, "Don't take any bookings for the next few weeks, as we may have a part for you in the show".

Peter remembers feeling that he was floating out of The Palace Theatre on a cloud and went home to North Wales, feeling really enthused about show business again. This seemingly successful audition was just what he needed, because he had always loved theatre, he has always felt that was his forte. Once again he allowed himself to dream, with good reason that he was on his way to major theatrical success and stardom. Well the weeks went by and heard nothing from the shows producers, when at last he was unable to contain himself any longer, he rang the producers office and was told that, they had chosen another performer for the part he had auditioned for as this other guy seemed ready made for the show.

They then went on to tell him, "It's a pity you didn't audition for the other lead role, because we feel that would have suited you more. That role would have been the role that Frankie Vaughan had played, the part of the impresario. Peter was completely and utterly deflated, another great opportunity missed, through no fault of his own. He felt ill used and unwanted, they hadn't even called to say that he hadn't got the part, they just left him hanging in the air.

However as he says himself "Life must go on". Even so it was a very hurt and disillusioned Peter who continued to work as a postman for the next seven years. During that time he also did one nighters in venues around Denbighshire. One of those venues 'The Night Owl' was owned by a friend of his Alan, he has lost touch with him now, he living abroad as far as he knows. Peter had a couple of videos made there, on one of the videos the audience is singing along loudly to the Elvis songs that they knew, not really listening to Peter's voice. Very disappointing, this kind of audience participation, really was a far cry from the days when he was in Florida headlining at 'The Fontainebleau Hotel'. After all this prestigious venue had Frank Sinatra and Elvis Presley performing there in the fifties and Peter had more than lived up to the reputation of these top line entertainers during his own time there. Nevertheless on the positive side of things he had built up a strong following around the clubs in North Wales and was more than well received wherever he appeared.

Other things were not going as well as he would have hoped, for one thing he had started to suffer health problems in the form of arthritis and the pain and restricted movement resulting from the condition meant that he had to leave the postal service. Sad to say this a condition that he still suffers with today, although ,the pain is a hundred times worse, than when he retired from the Postal Service. However never having been someone who would just give up, when faced with adversity, Peter then went and found employment in a tile manufacturing factory. An international company they were making and exporting tiles to customers in places like Dubai and other areas in the Far East.

One of the memories Peter has from when he was living in Denbigh was of trying to arrange to go and see his old friend Ricky Valance perform at Denbigh Town Hall. He was pretty sure that he would be able to arrange this through his then agent Eddie Green, who lived in the town. He had spoken to him but Eddie didn't get back to him to confirm that any arrangements that had been made, so he was a little apprehensive about just turning up at the gig. After some thought he decided that he would not to go, in case Ricky said he didn't remember him.

Then while he was sitting watching TV the doorbell rang, he thinks that his son Grant got up and answered the door. When he came back the room Grant told him that Ricky Valance was waiting outside for him. Peter very surprised to hear this, so he got up and went out and found that Ricky was sitting in his car waiting for him. He greeted Ricky like the long lost friend that he was, and in response Ricky replied in his Welsh accent, "What the hell are you doing sitting here? You should be at the Town Hall, not sitting here watching TV!" Peter tried to explain about not being invited by Eddie, and Ricky replied, "You are invited by me, so get your coat on" Ricky then drove them both to the Town Hall.

Peter says that Ricky gave a fantastic performance, that night going down really well with the crowd. The audience still remembered Ricky's big hit, 'Tell Laura I Love Her", and they loved hearing him sing it. When Ricky was leaving theatre he invited Peter and Carrie to his home,. Unfortunately Carrie said that wasn't able to make it, Ricky was very disappointed because he had wanted them to come down and spend a weekend with himself and his wife Evelyn. Peter promised him that they would come when they could. The visit never took place and it would be quite some time before they would be in touch again, due other things in both their lives taking precedence.

The time that they spent living at the cottage in Mill Lane, with it's long garden, with an Ash tree an Oak tree and the Victoria Plums on the tree at the end, was really good for Peter. As he says, "It was a relaxing place to be, a place where his old friend Brian 'Lic' Locking from The Shadows would come and visit him and talk about old times. They had great chats on these occasions and 'Lic' would say

"You and I were there mate, at the start of Rock and Roll in the UK, no one can take that away from us". It is true no one can. Brian was still doing gigs here and there, sometimes meeting up with Bruce Welch or Brian Bennett for trips abroad to The Shadows Appreciation Society gigs. As Peter says, "He is brilliant, my old mate Brian, better known to us all as Lic, he really is", he is one of the good guys".

Peter Wynne courtesy of Denbigh free press 1985

Tribute to Elvis in Denbigh in 1984

2008 Asaph with Lic Locking

Having a laugh with Lic Locking reading the Beat magazine, 2013

Chapter Sixteen

Back To Australia

1975 was also a time of great happiness for Peter because his Mum had come over from Australia, she was staying with him and his family for a few months and they were all really enjoying their time together. Things were going along fine until one day there was an unexpected phone call from Australia, it not good news, Peter's brother Terry had been admitted to King Georges Hospital in Sydney. It seems that he was in a serious condition, so serious that he was waiting for a Liver transplant. Their Mum was really worried about her youngest son and so she quite naturally, started arranging her return to Australia. As she prepared to go she asked, indeed she begged Peter to travel with her, or at least follow her because she was sure that Peter's presence would help Terry through the waiting process. He really thought that he should go and when he asked Carrie what she thought about him travelling to Terry's side she had no hesitation in saying, "If you are needed and you clearly are, you should go".

Peter made his decision to go, knowing that he would miss Carrie and the children, but he felt that he was needed to help and support Terry, and his wife Dawn. Terry and Dawn also have a daughter, her name is Eloise and at that time she was being looked after by a close friend of theirs so that Dawn could spend time at the hospital with her husband. Of course Peter needed to speak to his bosses at the Tile Company were he was working and explain the circumstances to them. As he said, at the time his bosses were very kind to him, understanding his position perfectly, When he left they gave him an excellent written reference in case he found himself in need of one.

So in the company of his mum Peter quickly found himself on his way back to Missenden Road, Camperdown, Sydney, Australia. As they were flying into Melbourne he enjoyed the privilege of being taken on to the flight deck a remarkable experience. They were also treated to glasses of Aussie champagne, in between sleeping and eating food. When they arrived in Melbourne he was feeling slightly worse for wear, so he took the opportunity to sleep for a little while at his younger sister Pamela's house. When he awoke feeling refreshed they booked a coach trip to continue their journey to Melbourne. It had been a marathon journey made more tiring by the stress that both he and his mum were quite naturally feeling.

When Peter arrived in Sydney early the following morning after travelling overnight through the outback. He was amazed that he had no real idea of where he had been travelling. As he says he doesn't remember any of the towns he past through in the dark, because Australia is such a vast country it would be very hard to get your bearings from a seat on a coach. The first thing he did when he left the coach was find himself a cab he asked the driver, "Please take me to St Georges Hospital in Camperdown please". He was so pleased to able to say that after such long journey, most of the time he was travelling he was so far from his ultimate destination, at last he was there. When he got there he asked him the driver to drop him off at the nurses home, because Dawn, his brother Terry's wife was staying there, while Terry waited for his operation.

When Peter arrived he found that Dawn was waiting to meet him on the steps outside to nurses home, the family had phoned ahead to let her know of the approximate time of his arrival. Dawn greeted him warmly and then asked him if he wanted anything to eat. Peter declined saying he that he was fine because he had eaten during the coach journey. Telling her that the coach had made a few stops at eateries along the road to Sydney. So he just said, "A coffee will suffice please, because I am a little thirsty" After they had drunk their coffee, Dawn showed to Peter to the room he would be staying in. He left his luggage in the room and then he went across the road to King Georges Hospital once there he made his way to the ward Terry was in.

Even though he was aware how serious things were with Terry's health it still came as a shock to see how ill he really was. He was not anything like his normal self, the colour of his skin had taken on a slightly orange/yellow hue, although Peter didn't know it at the time this normal. Because when someone needs a liver transplant, as they are getting to the later stages of the illness, and a liver transplant is critical, it is the only thing that will save the patient's life, so the orange yellow hue is a clear indicator of the seriousness of the patient's condition. It was plain to see that Terry had reached this terrible stage, he would clearly have very little time left if he didn't get a transplant, it was urgent and Peter was dismayed by what he saw. It has always been clear that he loves his brother and in this situation he found it difficult to hold his emotions in check.

The brothers quickly got over the initial difficulty that was caused by Peter's shock and soon became comfortable in each others company. They talked about music and the songs that Terry had composed, Somehow rather than just lie in bed Terry had somehow managed to accompany Peter around the hospital grounds while they were chatting. During this time Peter noticed how swollen Terry's stomach was, when he asked he was told that this condition is called ascites, this a very debilitating condition that was adding to Terry's parlous state, That night Peter went back to the room that the hospital had loaned him and wondered how long Terry would have to wait for a liver transplant. He was very worried, he did not wish to contemplate the possibility that a transplant donor might not be found in time. As he lay on the bed in the room that he was staying in, about seven floors up he found that the sounds from the street below, reached his ears easily. He could hear the ambulances coming and going from the hospital through his window, they were not comforting or restful sounds.

The surgeons and the nursing staff were fantastic though, really lovely people. The operating team were really laid back and friendly and after Peter had been introduced to them as Terry's brother they always found time to speak with him. In order to try and put his mind at rest one of the team told Peter that he would be told as soon as there was a liver available. True to his word that night the team member came to tell him that a liver was available. When heard the news Peter, after his initial joy and feeling of relief felt really sorry for the donor's family. This was because they were losing someone that they loved. But he had to put that sadness aside as he was feeling real happiness because his brother Terry was getting another chance of life. Even so it was impossible not to think about the fact that this chance came at the expense of someone else's terrible misfortune. That night was a long one spent wondering about the operations outcome. Eventually Dawn came and told Peter the good news, the operation had gone well and that Terry had come back from theatre, he was now asleep and back intensive care. Filled with relief Peter went back to his own room for a short nap.

A couple of weeks later having seen that Terry was recovering well, Peter decided to take time out to visit his sister Pamela and her husband John. He would also go and spend some time his older brother Charles and his wife Jean in Tasmania. Since the last time Peter had visited Charles had bought a restaurant in Launceston and he was keen for Peter to sing there. So he boarded a flight and was quickly on his way to Tasmania. On arrival he was met by his Charles who Peter remembers was wearing a suede Aussie / Western type of hat, he looked very well and Peter was pleased to see him again. Amazingly it had been nearly ten years since his last visit. Together they walked to Charles's Land Cruiser and threw what little luggage that he was carrying into it, and Charles drove them back to the house in Whitemoor.

The house was called Long Range, it was a fantastic four bedroomed bungalow with a field to the rear. Charles had a workshop and just past the workshop he kept chickens in a run. Off to one side of the bungalow he had logs stacked, ready for the winter, there was an axe close to the stack that was kept to chop the wood for the fire. It really was a great place to live. When the Land Cruiser pulled up at the door, Jean, Charles's wife came out to meet them with their three dogs, two Alsatians, and a third dog, he was a Labrador cross, and he had the nickname, Kimbo Warrior. The dogs gave them an enthusiastic welcome. Charles then showed Peter to the room that he would be staying in. It was very impressive, it had a king size bed and plenty of space to move around in. Like many of the residents out in Tasmania Charles had a couple of guns, one being a Magnum Pistol that he showed Peter. Incidentally it came about that the Magnum would later be stolen during a break in. After showing him the guns Charles and Jean wined and dined him and they all enjoyed a very cool and relaxing evening, then they all retired to their beds.

The next day the two brothers went down Launceston to open Charles restaurant. It was in Peter's opinion very aptly named, 'Squires' it really was a top of the range venue. Charles employed three chefs in the kitchen, although Peter believes one was just a cook, not a qualified chef, like the other two. For the first week Charles put Peter in charge of his accounts in 'Squires'. One of the other tasks he voluntarily undertook was to help wash the kitchen utensils in the huge wash sink. This made him feel that he was at least earning his keep during his stay. Speaking of doing things to earn his keep, he also helped out with work at Longrange. One thing he took on was the task of mowing the grass. The lawns in front of the property were at least fifty yards long, Peter walked with push mower to do that job. For cutting the grass in the field he had the use of a sit down mower.

Peter also spent some time refurbishing and repairing a metal bench that he came across in the garden. He rubbed it down and then repainted it with black metallic paint, if he says so himself, it looked ace when it was finished. He also climbed on the roof so that he could clean the fire flue and the chimney. There was always one chore or another to be done but Peter enjoyed doing these things. Sadly later in his life his arthritis would become worse and he would have great difficulty walking, which also meant that climbing ladders and other things that he had always found easy and taken for granted, became hard if not impossible to do. He will tell us more about the pain he has suffered and efforts to help the condition surgically later in the book.

While he was staying in Launceston he was made aware that his bother Charles had a speedboat and liked to go fishing now and then. So it was that one day Charles suggested that they take the boat up to The Great Lakes and do some fishing. Now Peter quite fancied the idea so he said, "Lets do it". Without delay they hitched the boat to the back of the Toyota and set out on their journey to The Great Lakes. When they arrived they found a decent landing area from which to launch the boat from and slid it down into the water. Peter still remembers how vast the lake was, he is sure that it must have been many miles from one end to the other.

Anyway they started to fish, they threw their lines out and waited, for something to bite. After they had been fishing for about half an hour or so Charles got a bite, he reeled the fish in, finding that it was a good catch, a nice big Salmon. Peter kept trying but he had no luck at all, not even one that got away, which all fishermen like to talk about. They decided to go further out across the water to see if Peter would have more luck, still he had no success. They stayed anchored in their new position for hours, occasionally shouting to campers that they could see on the shore. These people who seemed to be day trippers, with their barbies on their fires and their beer bottles clinking musically together, were having a great time. The time passed the sun was disappearing from the sky and dusk was falling, they were not catching anything so Peter turned to Charles saying, "I think we should go back to shore, it starting to get dark". "Yes" Charles replied, "You are right, I think it is time that we were making our way back".

They started the boats engines and made some speed as they cut a course across the big lake back to their intended landing area. They had a problem though, it was dark and neither of them could remember where they had set out from. Peter was straining his eyes trying to see something that resembled the area of the bank that they had set sail from, without success. It seemed that they had no chance of finding the place, because by now it was absolutely pitch black and completely silent. The brothers weren't helped by the fact there was no moon. To make matters worse everyone seemed to be gone from the bank and the brothers were alone. It really seemed as if they were the only two people left in the world. They were stuck in the middle of the lake and all they could do was wonder where they had put the Toyota. Suddenly they saw some little lights shining in the distance, so Charles suggested that Peter swim to the shore and find the place that they had launched the boat from .

Peter's immediate reply was, "No way not a chance". He gave this reply because he is not the greatest of swimmers and the idea of swimming in a very large lake in pitch darkness was not something he felt able to do. They could see one light in particular, so they headed hopefully towards it. As they got closer to the light and to the shore Peter could see the outline of a motor vehicle, hopefully it would be their Toyota. When they had got nearer to the shore, they both felt a sense of relief , because it was the Land Cruiser, soon they would have the boat out of the water and be on their way home. This was a very stressful end to what, up to the point it went dark,had been a very pleasant and enjoyable day for the brothers.

Moving on with the story, we recall that Charles had expressed the wish that Peter would perform at his restaurant, 'Squires', naturally he had complied. He remembers one night in particular when things went very well. Always wanting to provide versatile performances Peter had planned a cabaret set which included some soft quiet ballads, mixed in with some up tempo songs. At one point he even sang one song, "Memories", from the musical 'Cats' while he was sitting in an easy chair. All in all that night he performed for 45 minutes at which point he thanked the audience for their applause, then he retired to table that had been laid for him and relaxed. At the end of the evening Peter and Charles began harmonising with some Elvis ballads, both they and the audience had a great time. The next day there were some photographs with captions describing a fabulous evening at 'Squires' in the newspapers, this was very good publicity for Charles restaurant.

The weeks were passing by very quickly and as much as he was enjoying his time in the company of Charles and his wife Jean, Peter decided it was time to fly back to Sydney. He needed to see for himself how well Terry was progressing following his operation. So he booked a flight then said his goodbyes to Jean and Charles, boarded the plane and flew back. When Peter arrived at King Georges Hospital Camperdown he was sent to the nurses home where he was surprised and pleased to find Terry lying on the bed waiting for him in the room that had provided for Peter to stay in.

Terry was eager to show Peter just how much he had improved since they were last in each other's company. Although he was still on the drugs that he had to take to stop the liver being rejected, he was clearly restored to his old self. At one point he got out his guitar and played and sang one of his own compositions, a real favourite of Peter's, called, "Manchester In The Rain". Peter thinks that it is a shame that Terry had written so many great songs, that most people have never heard, but would certainly enjoy if they did. He thinks the reason for the lack of commercial success is that Tasmania, indeed Australia itself was just to far away from the real world of show business razzmatazz to allow for international success.

Peter feels that is the only way to explain why Terry had not enjoyed real success with his music, is to say that there was just no where for his talent to go that would showcase it. Peter really believes and wishes Terry had stayed in the UK, then he is sure that it would have been a different story, in the UK Terry would have had the success that his talent deserved. Problems with promoting his music aside, the good news was that Terry was on the mend meaning that it was time for Peter to go home. After all he needed to sort out his own life, not the least of his problems were his mortgage payments, he had been in Australia for three months and there had been a lack of funds to pay the family bills. So telling Terry that he would see him again before he actually left, Peter began to make his arrangements.

So after quick trip back to Tasmania to once more say his farewells to Charles and Jean, he then flew back to Sydney to say goodbye to Terry and Dawn. Then he made a trip to see his Mum who had been staying with his nieces husbands Mum and Dad. It was sad to leave everyone behind, but he was really looking forward to seeing Carrie and the children again. Peter really hoped that he had been of some help to Terry, during his stay, his brother was looking a lot better. He remembers that it was a lovely day in Sydney when he flew out to Melbourne to see his younger sister Leonora and her husband Ade. They were living Melbourne now because Ade's job as a sharpshooter kept him there. He thanked all the family for thelp they had given him while he had been in Australia and then they said their farewells. He didn't manage to see Pamela and John, he thinks they were away on holiday in Hawaii.

So with conflicting emotions he caught his flight back to the UK, happy as he thought of seeing Carrie and the children, but sad as he wondered when he might see his mum, his siblings and their families again. He still remembers just how long a flight it was coming home, it seemed to take a year and a day just to fly over Australia.

L-R Bill, Lou, Grant, Carrie holding daughter Daniella, Jean, Mum and Dad, Peter. Denbigh 1980

Peter holding Daniella, ex-wife Carrie and Grant 1977

Chapter Seventeen

Back In The UK
And On To Pastures New

Eventually the journey home came to an end and early one morning Peter landed at Heathrow Airport, back in the UK again. After the usual delays coming through the queues in baggage handling and customs, he got out of the airport then he took a cab to his mother in laws house in Longford. Once there he gave her a present, a bottle of brandy, that he had bought for her in the duty free area. Peter stayed for a while and had breakfast with her and then he got his car out of the garage where he had left three months before, thanked her for a lovely brekkie and set off on the long drive over the Horseshoe Pass to Wales, at least it wasn't snowing blizzards this time.

When he got to the top he pulled over stopped and got out of the car and took a deep breath of Welsh air. Damn he thought, that is really lovely, the air was fresh and clear and there was a wonderful smell of heather being carried to him on the breeze, it felt so good to be back. He drove further on through Ruthin, to Llanbedr so that he could see his old friend, Len, as always Len was delighted to see him. He also stopped for a quick word with another friend, Alan Hughes, the potter, before continuing his journey to Denbigh. He finally arrived home and was delighted to see Carrie and the children. Daniella was looking really well, she looked great to her Dad, Grant had really grown and he was looking very fit, they were pleased to see their dad home at last.

Peter really loved Wales but unfortunately the work just wasn't there for him any more. So he took the decision, after talking things over with Carrie, that they should move nearer to the big cities. Having said that they decided that they should still look for a home in a rural setting, for the benefit of the whole family. His daughter Kareena and her partner Chris had offered to help them with the move so that would make things easier when they actually found a place. After looking around at various properties they found a really secluded lodge in the heart of The Wyre Forest, they made an offer on it and it was accepted. So even though they were sad to be leaving their current home, this place really looked like the ideal home for them all and they couldn't wait to move in.

Chris hired a van for moving day and working together as a family they loaded most of their furniture in to it. Sadly there were some things that they had to give away, carpets and other items that they simply couldn't take with them. It was such a shame having to leave things behind, but it was necessary to get rid of these things as they had no place for them in their new home. Peter was driving a Ford Granada at time so they loaded that up as well and they set off on the journey to a new life. They were not travelling without some trepidation, because as we all know moving can be both traumatic and stressful. Nevertheless Peter was sure that there were good times ahead,

They arrived at the outskirts of the Wyre Forest late that night, then it seemed that they were driving for what seemed like an age, until at last they reached the Lodge. It really was a lovely building it was built from stone had a tiled roof. Inside there were three bedrooms, a large lounge, there was also galley kitchen and not always the case back then in rural properties, the lodge had a bathroom. The family had acquired three cats while they were living in Denbigh and they loved their new home. They couldn't wait to climb all the trees that were growing just outside their door, they also hunted in the undergrowth, searching for voles and mice that they could return to door of the house with. It had the makings of an idyllic paradise for both the family and their pets.

In the morning Peter was able to take a proper look at their surroundings, he found as he walked around the immediate area that their lodge was situated in a circle of other lodges. There was a lake in the centre of the circle. There were lots of lots of ducks and other water fowl swimming on the lake. He thought to himself God, Carrie and I are going to love it here, they did and so did Grant and Daniella. The only worry Carrie had was one shared by them all, how far was it to the nearest food store. They needn't have worried because there was one not too far away in Bewdley.

Bewdley is a lovely little town with several shops that stocked all the items that the family required. The family quickly settled into the lodge and made acquaintance with a couple of people who lived near them. Peter used to walk in the woods and look for fungi, they had moved in the autumn so it was the right time. There were many deer that he could see were living in the woods, there one in particular that caught his eye while he was out walking. On that particular day Peter had walked deep in the forest, as he walked he came to a clearing in the trees, and stopped as he saw this lovely creature. The deer didn't move it stood and stared at him as if to say, "This my place, what do you want here"? Then without a backward glance it just trotted off and disappeared into the trees. As Peter thinks and often asks "Isn't nature a wonderful thing"?

Quite soon after their arrival Peter drove in to Bewdley with Carrie, to look for a large food store, they found one that they used regularly a place where they could buy produce for the week. But he really loved to forage around in the forest looking for edible food. With this in mind Chris, Kareena's partner had lent him an air rifle in case he saw a rabbit that he could shoot for the pot. Money or the lack of it was an issue at this time, because Peter wasn't earning anything at all. They had paid four weeks rent in advance plus a deposit. This outlay had used up all of the money that they had made on the sale of certain items before they had left Wales. They needed to know the area they lived in and were Peter might find employment so from time to time they would get in the car and drive out looking to find their bearing and the distances from different towns. Of course these trips out were using up petrol that he couldn't afford to replace.

On one of these trips they hadn't travelled very far when they passed a small shop which sold all the basic necessities, milk, bread, butter, cheese and various cans of food such as soup and corned beef. Peter thought to himself I could walk through the woods to this place. When they returned he set off on a walk to see how far it would be from their lodge to shop if he walked through the woods. He also needed to know how long it would take him to walk there and back home again. He set off at a brisk pace and soon discovered it was much further than he had anticipated, in fact it took him half an hour to get there, so it was a round trip of over an hour by the time he had shopped. Still it would save on his use of petrol so he decided that he would make the walk when needed.

Grant and Daniella liked the environment but did not like being so far away from everything, so he made a point of taking the family to visit Kareena and Chris at their home, which was close by, in Stourport-on-Severn whenever it was possible. They would spend time by the river and visit the local fish shop. The family always started the journey home before it went dark, because everyone felt that driving in the woods at night was really spooky. Having said that Peter says that none of the family ever heard the cry of a wolf, Ha Ha!

One day one of the family's cats Smudgie, went missing Peter thinks although he could never prove it, that one of the neighbours took him away. His reason for thinking this was that the neighbour in question also had a cat, which Peter's cat, a tom, always took every opportunity to boss around. These folk didn't like that happening, so he thinks that they took Smudgie away in their van and dumped him. Peter and family have never known to this day if that really was the case, but one day after Smudgie had been missing for four weeks, they heard a rattle at the door, they opened it and low and behold, there was Smudgie their cat! He made a great fuss of them all meowing and asking for food and drink. None of the family could believe it, so Peter rightly or wrongly worked out a solution, to explain to them about where the cat could have been for all that time and how he could have found his way home.

His story as he told it to the family goes like this, it is well known that cats have an uncanny ability to find their way home. Incidentally before we proceed with his story, it is important to say that the people who he believes took the cat, had moved away the day he went missing. So it had to be assumed, in Peter's mind that they had taken Smudgie with them in their van and dumped him somewhere on their journey. The presumption must be that they were the kidnappers, sorry Cat nappers! So Smudgie displaying that legendary homing instinct, after he had been thrown out of the van must have walked day and night until he found his way home to his family. I doubt any of us can come up with a better reason for his long absence and miraculous return, so I think we must agree that Peter's story makes sense.

As they got older Peter's children made friends in the Bewdley area who would visit them on occasion. When their friends arrived they would very often walk with them through the forest, to the pub, even though it was an hours walk away. The whole family really enjoyed living in the Wyre Forest but Peter realised that it really was too far off the beaten track for Grant and Daniella now that they were getting older and had the need to socialise on a regular basis. There would have to be changes made for the sake of the children's futures, also there might be the chance of an upturn in Peter's musical career in a more populated area.

So after living in the lodge for some time they started to make enquiries about alternative accommodation, somewhere nearer to the towns. Grant was looking for work now, he had ambitions to be a hairdresser, it just didn't make sense for him to somehow get from the forest, where they were living, to wherever he found a job. After they had made an extensive search of the area the family found a place in Stourport-on-Severn and Grant, having now left school, was able to find a job. The happy days spent living in this lovely setting of The Wyre Forest had to be put behind them. Once again there would have to a new location for Peter's dream to find fulfilment in a musical sense, it would be a new start for them all.

Chapter Eighteen

The Musical Dream Is Revived

When the family had got over the stress that always goes with moving house and location they quickly settled into their new surrounding. They all realised that they would probably be living in Stourport for some time, so they took the opportunity to make the most of their time there. In this new environment there would be more opportunities for them all to have a social life. With that in mind Peter used visit a local pub, as he says it was a good way of meeting people. On one occasion he got in to conversation with a guy who turned out to be a musician, he was a guitarist who was playing in a local band called 'The Crestas'. Naturally the talk swung to their mutual interest in the world of Show business. Peter was very interested in the band the style of music they played.

He also wished to know who this guy was and also who the other band members were. He was told that the line up consisted of Nigel Turrell on Drums, Brian Glass on Bass, the Keyboard player was Dave Mansfield, and Nigel Bache was on Guitar. Although they were a bit younger than Peter, it turned out that the keyboard player Dave Mansfield and the drummer Nigel Turrell had attended the same school as Peter had, all those years before. There was a difference of a few years between their attendance but, they shared similar memories of the place.

The five of them became great friends and they all spent many enjoyable hours together, mostly in the back room of the pub rehearsing numbers and talking about things they had done or dreamed of still doing. As Peter says. "I really did have some great times with those lads in 'The Crestas'". Really the lads in the band made his time in Stourport most enjoyable and they also gave him the opportunity to rehearse a few songs with them and perform, locally.

One day while they were rehearsing Peter was singing a particular song, and a face from the past came into the room saying, "I recognise that voice". It was the Bass Player from 'The Rockin' Berries', who Peter had done the summer season with in 1967-68 in Lowestoft. It turned out that this guy was also living in Stourport. Although Peter doesn't remember the guy's name at the time it was good to have a catch up and talk about old times with someone who was there and part of the music scene. As he says, "It really was a pleasure to meet up with him again".

Authors note: Although Peter does not remember the bass players name, I can be fairly sure that it was one of two people. It would either have been Geoff Turton who has a life long association with 'The Rockin' Berries', or Rod Clarke who came in to replace Geoff sometime in 1966. Rod Clarke came in after spending some time with the 'Move' I believe. He was and is a very talented vocalist and bass player. However he only stayed with the Rockin' Berries for a few months, and then Geoff Turton returned to the group at that point. Given the time frame it is my strong suspicion that it would have been Geoff who came into the pub while Peter was rehearsing and recognised his voice.

Geoff Turton did leave the band again being replaced on that occasion by Clive Lea, but I am not sure of when, and of course there was a period when the group were not performing. I am aware and the readers may be interested to know that Geoff enjoyed some chart success as a solo artiste, under the name of Jefferson, both in the UK and the USA after 1968. Using that name he recorded a song called *Colour Of My Love* which reached number 22 in the charts. Then his recording of *Baby Take Me In Your Arms* achieved number 23 in the American Billboard chart. I am aware of these things due to the more than forty years spent as Tommy Bruce's friend and manager. I am sure that there are others who will know more about Geoff Turton's career, but I feel that this, is just enough information for Peter Wynne's book.

Another person who Peter met during his time with 'The Crestas', was Joe Smit. Joe Smit had been the lead singer with 'The Dallas Boys', this was someone who Peter knew from the TV show 'Oh Boy'. Joe who also lived in Stourport, was quite a shy man and had been keeping himself to himself. He told Peter that he had given up singing, but he didn't say why. Out of politeness Peter didn't pry into why Joe had given up singing or what had led to him was living in Stourport.

Carrie and Peter had met two other people who lived in the area who had become good friends. Their names were Alan and Mary Sinclair and they were often invited Carrie and Peter to their home. The couple were talented musicians in their own right, in fact Mary possessed an excellent contralto voice and Alan was a fantastic banjo player, they were very professional in there approach to their music. Because it seemed that Alan and Mary's other friends were also musicians, guitar players, banjo players, etc. Carrie and Peter were able to spend many happy times in the company of the couple and their other friends.

There was someone else that the readers of this book will remember Bob White who had been Peter's best friend at Sladen Secondary School. We also remember that the two lads had joined the police force together when the left school. Well unlike Peter who as we know had left the police force to join The Guards, Bob had stayed in the police force and made his career there. Showing great aptitude for the job he had been steadily promoted having now achieved the rank of inspector. Well after some investigation of his own Peter discovered that Bob White was living quite close to Stourport. So he was very keen to meet up with Bob and have a good old chin wag about how they had both fared in their lives. Sadly it was not to be, because Bob was not in the best of health and he died before they could get back in full contact. This upset Peter very much at the time because he is a loyal and caring man and when they were young the lads had enjoyed good companionship, being close friends and he had hoped that they would be good companions again .

Carrie and Peter had managed to acquire a property in Wolverley, just outside Kidderminster. It was a bungalow with a biggish garden and it was a very pleasant environment for the family to live in. Their daughter Danniella was seeing a nice chap from Stourport and the two of them were buying a house a in Kidderminster, so they would soon be living there. Then their son Grant found himself a girlfriend who he decided to go and live with so it seemed that every ones life was very settled. Peter was still singing and using his voice to great effect, he is admired by everyone who hears him sing to this very day. He is a man who clearly has a very artistic nature and he took the opportunity to develop two hobbies. He can make very fine walking sticks and he has a real gift for painting.

One year his sister Leo and her husband Ade came over to the UK from Australia on a couple of occasions in the 1990's and the early 2000's. It was wonderful to see them and they enjoyed lovely times together. There were frequent visits from brother Terry who came over as often as he could afford to, these were special times because Terry and Peter shared that musical dream. Although Terry was younger than Peter, they both shared a musical dream. There was one musical occasion that really stands out in Peter's memory, this event took place at his daughter Danellia's, house in Kidderminster with his son Grant on lead guitar, Daniellia playing bass and Terry providing rhythm and vocals, he was entertained to a fabulous jam session. He was thrilled by the performance and just sat clapping and cheering,for once he had no desire to sing himself. Those happy days in Wolverly were great, really good but time passes so quickly and everything changes. Peter's eldest sister Pamela would visit occasionally when some of her friends were still alive, when they died she stopped making the trip. Sadly she herself passed away a few years ago, Peter never really saw much of her over the years, once she moved away. One thing is true he loved her as he loved and still loves all his family. The one Peter really misses is Terry, he was a lovely man and a great musician Peter sends this message out to his memory, "I love and miss you bro, I always will, you were my mate and my brother

But as he looks back these were happy times and one year when his birthday came round, his daughter Daniella surprised him by buying him a computer and that gift open new avenues for him. The computer helped him to do things that would otherwise would have been impossible. For example he managed to obtain backing tracks for songs that he had always wanted to record. It also opened up ways for him to learn covers, that is songs by other artistes that he had always liked. His interest in music really came back to life with this gift.

It wasn't just the musical aspect of the computer that lifted Peter's spirits Peter, because found himself able to access something called 'My Space' and Danniella's boyfriend Andy was able to teach him the basics of how to make the best use of a computer. This technology enabled him to get back in touch with some of the people that he had known during his time in America. Peter became really absorbed by the new possibilities that were being opened up for him by the computer. Exciting times were upon him and as always Peter embraced any opportunities that came his way.

Peter has always been very proud of his son Grant and was so pleased that he possessed a natural ability to sing and play guitar. He might well have enjoyed a career in the music business, such was his talent. More to the point Grant enjoyed playing and singing, so he wasn't just doing it to please his dad.. But suddenly right out of the blue things changed and Grant's talent took a backward step. Peter and Carrie were confused, asking themselves a question that first seemed to have no answer, "What had gone wrong"? The answer was one that would really upset them, for some reason as yet unknown, Grant had become dependant on alcohol.

Peter was so disappointed to think that all of his son's talent had been virtually put one side, because of the demon drink. As his parents both Carrie and Peter naturally rallied round doing all they could to help their son, even sending Grant into rehab not once but twice. This was very expensive thing to do and if it had not been for the gentleman who ran the facility, Nik Charles O.B.E, they could never have afforded the treatment offered. Nik Charles was a man who Peter knew from his school days and also from later on during in his own recording and television career. Nik very kindly adjusted the payments for him as a favour, if this had not been done he would have been unable to afford to send Grant this rehab clinic. Incidentally it may be interesting for readers to know that Nik had been a member of the famous 'Tornado's' before they recorded "Telstar"

When Grant came home things seemed to be going well for him, that is until he was unfortunately invited to a barbecue. Obviously people were drinking there, so Grant decided to have a half of lager, a terrible decision if you suffer from alcoholism, because that one drink will always lead to another. Alcoholism is a terrible disease, if you suffer from it, you must not ever take a drink if you do all your previous efforts are so easily destroyed. Always trying to help, when Carrie and Peter heard in the late eighties that a new Rehab Clinic had opened in Stourbridge, they went down and looked the place over, they found the place very sound and well organised so they sent Grant there.

They had high hopes of him being helped there. Three weeks later he was doing really well, he hadn't had a drink for nearly a month and wanted to come out of the place. Unfortunately he had split up from his girlfriend and so had nowhere to live, so he asked his Mum and Dad if he could come home to Wolverley and live with them in their bungalow. They agreed that he could stay until he got back on his feet, as long as he didn't drink. Grant assured them that he wouldn't, so they made their dining room into a bedroom for him and he stayed.

Peter was really into his computer by this time and he was making friends with people, on line. One person in particular, a lady called Amanda from York, became a really good friend. By this time he was in his sixties and he and Carrie had been together for thirty odd years and they had without realising it, slipped into a very quiet life. His days seemed to pass where the only things he did were eating, drinking, sleeping and painting, this was not enough for Peter. He wanted more from his life, he felt that time was passing him by and he still had ambitions to fulfil.

They sat down together and discussed the situation, but those discussions only served to show just how far they had drifted apart. Putting it simply they realised they both wanted different things out of life. To make the situation worse they couldn't find any common ground. Peter wanted to sing again hopefully perform and at the very least record a new CD. Carrie had different needs from her life, she wasn't interested in Peter reviving his musical career her life revolved around home and family. She was spending more and more time with their daughter Daniella who along with boyfriend Andy was bringing up her two lovely children, Carrie just wanted to be with her grandchildren. After spending those thirty years together, somehow Peter and Carrie had lost touch with each other, it was clear to them both, that they needed to go their separate ways.

At the same time they were both finding that it was really hard to live with an alcoholic son, it made there lives very stressful. Not that Peter himself had been angel when it came to drink, over the years he had drunk his share, but it had never overpowered him, or prevented him from fulfilling his obligations. Added to that he had smoked a lot and this lifestyle had resulted in him getting C.O.P.D. This condition now found him having difficulty breathing, not a good thing for a big ballad singer, or any other singer for that matter.

But at that time the condition was not so severe as it has since become, having talked about his C.O.P.D. We are also aware that Peter has other health problems, he has let us know that added to these difficulties with his breathing, he does suffer from other life threatening conditions. But as he says, "I really doesn't want to dwell on those at this point in time". What he really needed a new challenge, a dream to pursue, something to get the blood racing through his veins again. Because Peter is a man who spends his life looking beyond the horizon, he always climbs the next hill to see what is in the valley below. When he sees what is there he invariably goes down and takes it on.

Peter and daughter Catrina

Peter and Chloe

Peter with songwriter and mate, Laurence Harrington playing songs they've written together.

Peter, Amanda and Daniel

Peter with mother-in-law, Anita

Peter, Simon and Grant

Teena, Daniella, Peter, Simon and Grant

1995 with the Crestas with superb guitarist Nigel Bache and Nigel Turrell on drums

1995 fronting the Crestas with Dave on keyboards and Brian on Bass

Chapter Nineteen

Amanda and a new lease of life

Getting back to the story. In 2008 Peter travelled to meet Amanda, the lady who he had been getting to know on the internet, who is as he says, "A lovely looking woman, with a great personality". Amanda would be the catalyst for change and provide the support that would help him with the new challenges that he was starting to reach out for. Although at the time that they met he was sixty nine and she was fifty, they soon found that they shared an affinity which meant that the two of them got on as soon as they met. Peter made the trip to where she lived in York to meet her by train, as he didn't posses a Sat Nav with which to plot the journey by road. That being the case the train seemed the best and easiest way to travel.

As soon as they met and got together Peter thought, "This lady will give me something to aim for, she will not let me just sit around cogitating and turn into a very old man before I am ready". They were very comfortable in each others company and as they chatted the conversation moved on to how they felt about their respective lives. Peter found out that Amanda had been married but was now divorced from her previous husband. She has four grown up children, Daniel, Brook, Michelle and Chloe and as of 2017, two Grandchildren Henry and Meadow. The important thing from Peter's point of view was that Amanda was a very attractive and vivacious single lady with a wonderful personality, he just knew that he would enjoy getting to know her. All to soon their first meeting had come to an end and it was time for him to start making his journey home, but they both knew that they would be seeing each other again soon.

Peter and Amanda on the Thames

Peter's journeys over to York soon became a regular thing and during these trips to visit Amanda, she introduced him to people that he likes very much. They are Amanda's sister Jackie, her husband, Laurence and their family, Peter enjoys spending time in their company. Indeed since those early days, Laurence has become a really good and honest friend to Peter. He is a friend who writes songs and plays great guitar, It has to be said that Laurence is a very fine musician. Having a shared interest in music meant that they were able to get on right from the start.

Now Peter was returning home after each time he visited York but he was starting to feel that he was using people, especially Carrie.

He knew the time had come to make a fresh start in his life. He could not continue to live two lives, and that is how it seemed to be for Peter now. If we have learnt anything during our time spent with Peter it is that he is too honourable a man to keep anyone dangling on a string. So it was at this point he resolved to make a clean break and start again. After all the situation as it was just couldn't last, he felt that he was being unfair to both Carrie and Amanda. There was only one honourable course of action, he left Carrie to the life that she loved with her daughter and grandchildren. Then he broke free of the home they had shared in Wolverley and set off on the long drive to a new life in Yorkshire.

When he had completed his journey he was able to find himself temporary accommodation in a hotel in Scarborough. Not the most salubrious place that he has ever lived in but as he says, "No names no pack drill, it was not a nice place, but it would have to do". One thing he did find rather off putting during time there, was that the proprietors had a cat that they allowed to walk around on the breakfast table, while he and any of the other guests were eating. There would be open packets of cornflakes, milk, sugar and other foodstuffs left on the table, so having a cat on the table was not very hygienic. Having said that Peter had lived on a farm years ago so there were a lot things that he let pass or possibly weren't noticed by him. But as he thinks back to his time living in that hotel, the things, like furnishing and paintwork, were a little faded and tired, it really was not somewhere for him to stay when he wanted to start a new life. So he looked for alternative accommodation and when he found somewhere else, ever the gentleman he made his apologies to his hosts and left.

Peter had got to know Amanda quite well by now and had started to meet her family. One the people he met was her daughter Chloe, at the time they met she was eighteen and did not seem like Peter being at the house. Chloe felt that he was taking what she thought was her time with her mother. So knowing that he wasn't as yet very popular with Chloe, he decided to rent a mobile home near by. In fact it was about fifteen minutes from Amanda's house, it was a very new dwelling and it had two bedrooms. Heating was provided by calor gas which as we know comes in bottles. He was told by some one else who lived on the site that they had found that the bottles emptied quickly and that they were very expensive to replace. This was not something that he worried about too much when he moved in, because the weather was warm. That being the case he was able to be very frugal with his use of the calor gas. He found that the mobile home suited him very well as accommodation for a short period of time. Having said that he quickly realised that it wasn't the kind of accommodation that he wanted to live in permanently.

After more searching for and looking at properties, he was relieved when at last he found a suitable flat. This was quite a spacious property with two bedrooms and a nice living room/lounge area. There was also a big light bathroom and the well appointed kitchen suited him. It was in a lovely little village/town and it gave him the benefit of all the amenities. He moved in and soon found that he had made a very comfortable choice for himself, As he settled in and got to know the area he soon found his way around and discovered places of local interest.

One of the things that he discovered that there was a local theatre / arts centre which would host a variety of different shows. Much to Peter's surprise and pleasure at one point Marty Wilde came to appear there. Peter was pleased to have the opportunity to take Amanda to see his old friend perform in what turned out to be a great show. Marty's performance was a great credit to him given that he is the same age as Peter, so he is not as they say, in the first flush of youth.

Because Peter knew Marty Wilde, after having toured with him, on all those Parnes shows years ago he made a great effort to meet up with him after the performance. As often happens in these cases when you look forward to seeing someone after many years, something important came up and prevented them getting together. Peter doesn't remember what it was but he felt it was a real shame not to have seen and spoken to Marty again after all those years. However he would live in hope that he and Amanda would have another opportunity to meet up with Marty in the future.

As a result of seeing Marty Wilde perform, Peter could feel that spark that made him want to be out on stage again had been reignited. That being the case he had no hesitation in speaking to the manager of the Arts Centre about available dates, he would promote his own show at the venue. Once he had the information he required, he then made a tentative booking to appear there himself. The old fire was burning again and he was filled with enthusiasm. Of course Amanda was eager to assist him in his endeavours, this support was just what he needed to spur him on.

Peter had already met some guys who had a nice sounding rock band, so he asked them if they would be interested in appearing on the show with him. They were very excited at the prospect of performing in a theatre, in fact they seemed very keen to be part of the event. They soon got together with Peter and they rehearsed different tunes, mixing rock, pop, standards and some country music. This was something that they had done with him before in jam sessions so he was confident that they were up to the job. They were all for it and seemingly they couldn't wait for the big day. Peter wanting them to be confident in their own abilities, told the band members that he was sure if they got together for a couple of months and worked hard on the act, they would have a good show. Convinced that they would achieve the standard that he expected Peter confirmed the booking with the Art Centre.

The next few months were hard for Peter physically, because he had to go into hospital for a full hip replacement, this operation left him first on crutches and then walking sticks, for a considerable period of time. There was another problem, for some years Peter had been suffering with spasmodic throat pain, not directly in the larynx, more off to the right side of his throat. He didn't know what caused it but he knew that the pain was unbearable. To make things worse when he suffered an attack he was unable eat, drink or even speak clearly, let alone sing. Then and this was inexplicable to him, after a few days the pain would disappear completely as if there was nothing there. This problem needed to be sorted out if he was going to enjoy doing the show. He spoke to the manager of the Art Centre again, who agreed to hold the date, pending the outcome of Peter's medical examination.

So Peter then did what he should perhaps have done sooner, he sought medical advice for the problem. At this point he was given some answers, although not answers that he wanted to hear. Apparently the medical people he consulted thought that he had a condition known as Eagles Syndrome. Trying to explain the condition simply, this condition is caused when the Styloid bone at the base of the neck becomes overgrown and calcified. When this calcification occurs it causes the symptoms that Peter was suffering from. An operation to shorten the bone, to relieve the pressure so he was told, was the only way that the problem could be alleviated. Worried about the possible outcome of such an operation, he decided to seek a second opinion. Putting it bluntly he was not keen to have such an operation unless there was no alternative. So he made further enquires and found another specialist in York. He contact this man's office and when he got an appointment he went for an examination.

Based on the finding of that examination, the new specialist said that he was of the opinion that the problem was not Eagle's Syndrome at all. In his opinion what Peter was suffering from, was, some damaged nerves in his throat. For this condition the specialist said that he would prescribe medication, something called Pregabalin. This medication proved to extremely effective. In fact it stopped the pain that he had been suffering almost immediately. Having said that Peter does still feel a twinge now and again, but nothing like as severe as he had been suffering previously.

Once he found that the treatment was working, Peter started to feel really good about the prospect of doing the show again. He was sure that with medication that worked, he would be able to sing properly again. So he got the band together and they ran through the numbers that he wanted to perform. The rehearsal went really well and enthusiasm was really high for the future of the band. They got a booking to appear at a local fête, This performance was a great success, their performance really pleased the audience, this meant that they would carry on preparing for the big show. After the reception they had received at the fête Peter was sure that last they were ready, so he went back and confirmed the booking with the manager of The Arts Centre.

As usual the vagaries that can occur with bands, came back to haunt Peter, they told him that even after all the rehearsal time they would not be available for the show. This was a week before the big day, meaning that he didn't have a band. He was in a dilemma, he didn't want to cancel because proceeds from the show were being donated to charity and he felt obligated to perform, but where could he find a band at short notice? Some how he managed to contact his old friend, Brian 'Licorice' Locking, who as we have mentioned before had been a bass player with 'The Shadows' and prior to that Marty Wilde's 'Wildcats'. Brian said "Don't cancel the show, I know a great band who do a Shadows tribute, they come from York, if you give them half an hour's rehearsal before the curtain goes up, they will be able to back you. This was great news for Peter because it meant that the long anticipated show would go on!!

There was even better news because in a very poignant and unexpected way someone very special had come back in to Peter's life a few weeks before the show. After forty years of not knowing were he was, his son Simon, who was now a Metropolitan Police Officer, had found Peter and made contact. More than that Simon introduced his dad to his wife Rachel and joy of joys, his own son Fletcher, Peter's grandson. When they had both got over the initial shock and come to an emotional understanding about their parting all those years before, Peter invited Simon to come to theatre and see the show. Simon agreed to attend and be part of the audience, so there was an added frisson of excitement in the air on the night of the show, for Peter.

When the big night arrived, it was an unusually nervous Peter, who had a band call with the tribute group, he was hoping for the best. The group did not let him down, they did very well in the time available. Although understandably in the circumstances, there were some numbers that had to be dropped from the programme. The arrangements of some of the songs were difficult for the musicians to get their heads round in such a short space of time. Amanda's son Dan (Daniel) Spiller opened the show with his partner Ciara, they received a great response from the audience. It has be said that they are great and a very professional duo. Then Laurence Harrington went on stage and during that part of the show Licorice played a great harmonica medley. Peter closed the show ending his set on his old favourite, "It's Only Make Believe" Then there was a rousing rock and roll finale, with vocals from Dan, Laurence and Peter.

The audience was in raptures, it was a very emotional night for Peter, especially with his son Simon being there in the audience, seeing his dad perform for the first time. In that moment he knew if he hadn't know already how fortunate he was to have Amanda in his life, sharing his musical dream. Peter and Amanda are the soul mates that we all hope that our partners will become, but only the lucky few are able to find.

After the show the dressing room was packed with people, They were all saying, "What a great show, amazing performances from all concerned". All the people went on to say how much they had enjoyed themselves. Once he was in the dressing room Peter introduced Amanda to all his colleagues from the show. Then there were photographs taken and then the cast and their supporters all started to say their goodbyes and return to their homes or hotels. When Peter and Amanda returned to their hotel, Daniel and Ciara who had appeared in the show under the names of 'Belle and the Busker', and surprised them by saying that were staying in the same hotel. Peter wanted reiterate the point that to them that Ciara has wonderful singing voice and in his eyes is a star of the future, which he did. With the four of them being unable to calm down the excitement lingered in their conversations right through breakfast the next morning.

This would be a good time to let the reader know that apart from appearing on the show at Pocklington, and going down great with the audience, Daniel is an excellent singer, musician and songwriter. He and Ciara have both been on Radio 2 and appeared on several television shows. Daniel has his own recording studio and Peter had talked with him about the fact that Peter himself has the desire to record some new songs and in the process produce a CD. Daniel when heard Peter's ideas thought that they had a good deal of merit and offered to help. So they arranged a date to go in to the studio and lay down the tracks for the new CD.

Things have moved on quickly and only week later they were in Daniel's studio, Peter was very eager to start work. After they had done a mic check and it sounded good, everything was OK and in place for the session to begin so they set to work laying down the first track. It was a great song called "I Need You Close Again". This song had been co-written by Peter, with, David Firmstone a close friend of his and Bob Barratt, who was a lovely guy and another close friend. The three of them met when they were at EMI in the sixties and it is clear from this song that they worked very well together. Sadly both of these men passed away quite some time ago and Peter misses them both very much and wishes that they were still around.

The next track would be "You're Mine" Peter wrote this song one night when he was travelling home after a show at the Stork Club.

As he has never been able to write music, just lyrics Peter has developed a remarkable ability to compensate for this. He writes down the words of the song, then remembers the feel of the music he has imagined in his head until he is with a pianist, who will then follow Peter's remembered melody. The other songs that were laid down in Daniels studio were a mixture, of Elvis covers. As fans will know Elvis was not well known for writing his own material but he did some fantastic covers of other people's songs. Also included were a couple of Perry Como tunes and then they finished on "Smoke gets In Your Eyes", which was the B side of Peter's great song 'Chapel of Dreams with Dand Ciara adding some harmonies to the backing. The CD came out with the title "As Time Goes By". The reason for the title being that Peter was seventy two years old at the time that it was recorded and as he says himself, "Time waits for no man".

Judson's pub, Pocklington May 2012

Judson's pub, Pocklington May 2012

Poster for Pocklington Centre

Peter with record labels

Tottenham Studios, London with Daniel Spiller, record producer, 2009

Cover shot for the CD, 'As Time Goes By'

Recording session 2009 in Tottenham

Peter at the former site of the 2i's coffee bar 2013

Peter the artist showing off his talent for painting

Marty Wilde

Robert Plant

Mohammed Ali

Mark Wynter

Tommy Bruce

George Michael

Joe Brown

Amanda's daughters: Michelle, Brooke, Chloe and her son Daniel

Amanda and Peter in Bridlington, 2012

Peter, Amanda, Linda and Chris Ely

Chapter Twenty

Inspiration and Innovation Continue

Because Peter has sung Elvis songs and intends to sing more in the future, it is important to say at this point that when Peter first heard Elvis singing "Heartbreak Hotel", he didn't understand why anyone would sing in that way. From his point of view the song had a strange beat. After all Peter had grown up listening to singers of the calibre of Al Martino and David Whitfield who as we all know had many hit's singing in a fine tenor voice, and this was the sound Peter in his younger days hoped to achieve. Added to that he had really studied the way Mario Lanza sang, because he was and is one of his great favourites.

These fine singers and others like them influenced Peter as he was learning to express his own timing and phrasing. Then he was trying ally what he was able to learn from listening to their recordings to the phenomenal power and range that he possesses in his own voice. However it was when Peter was in Nashville doing the rounds and performing there, he began to wish that he had been lucky enough to meet Elvis, sadly the nearest he would come to fulfilling that wish was, having one of Elvis's drummers play for him on his recordings of *The Hole That Holds The Bones* and *My Kind Of Love*. As Peter says himself, "I now realise what great performer and singer Elvis was, I'm sorry I was slow in understanding his style of music".

Going back to the present time after theatre show Peter's son Simon came back stage and told his dad, that he had really enjoyed the show. He said that it had been a thrilling experience because he was seeing his dad on stage for the first time. Sadly this would be the first and last time he would see his Dad performing in a show because he, along with his wife Rachel and their son Fletcher, (Peter thinks that this a really great name, for his grandson!) all left to live in Australia at the end of 2013. Peter now misses them all very much and he found their parting to be, a very emotional farewell. Having said that he was happy for Simon who had served in the Parachute Regiment and The Metropolitan Police, because Simon was going out to Australia to continue his career in the Police Force over there.

A great event that took place before Simon and his family left to make their journey to Australia, was Peter' marriage to Amanda in 2012. Amanda had wanted her Dad to attend but unfortunately he was to ill with cancer to attend, which was sad for all the family. They have been married for six years now, the time since they met ten years ago has Peter says, "Quite simply been wonderful". He wishes to describe his wife Amanda to the readers of this book in his own words, saying that "Amanda is stunningly beautiful, she has the most electrifying blue eyes and when she smiles she takes his breath away". He goes on to say, "I am so glad that I met her because she has gives me hope for the future". Because she is seventeen years younger than Peter who is now seventy nine years young, he realises that when he feels a bit down she knows the way to lift his spirits, As he said, "She is great"!!

Because of their age difference Amanda never saw Peter perform on stage at the height of his career. She would really love to have the opportunity to see some old film footage of any of the TV shows that he was on. So for that reason Peter has been searching high and low for film recordings from those days, without success. He even enquired of the news station in Nashville who reported on his outstanding success on the country music show that was filmed for Canadian Television, so far he has heard nothing, from them, Because of the difficulty he has been having in his search to date, he would be extremely grateful if any reader of this book would contact him if they know where there are any recordings of his TV appearances in the UK. He worries that the TV companies back in those days would have wiped the tapes, so that they could use them again.

Amanda and Peter enjoy their time together and share their happy lives with other people. They lived for a time in a house on the outskirts of York. While they were living there Peter enjoyed many rehearsals with his previously mentioned friend and brother-in-law Laurence, who is a great Beatles fan. Something that has pleased Peter very much is that Amanda's daughter Chloe who prior to him marrying her Mum had never paid any attention to him, has become like another daughter to him since the marriage and they really get on well.

Following the show that they put on in Pocklington, Peter asked to appear on another show at The Empire Theatre in Halstead on the 25th of March 2012. On the bill that night were Graham Fenton, originally the lead singer with the group 'Matchbox' who had several hit records one of which was a song written by a guy called John Longo who does a show that is a tribute to the songs of Elvis Presley. Not an impression just a tribute to the man and his songs. Much to Peter's delight Danny Rivers his old friend from the days that they were doing shows like TV' 'Wham' and numerous others in the same style was there. These shows included the ones that they had appeared in with Billy Fury, it was great for the two of them to get together again.

During his rehearsal with the house band, what terrific musicians they were, being led by Johnny Spencer on lead guitar. Peter heard a voice saying. "You've still got that great vocal range Pete" He looked down to where he had heard the voice, but didn't see anyone that he recognised, mind you the spot lights were very bright. So he walked down the stage steps in to the auditorium and walked up to the man who had spoken, at that point he realised it was another old mate from the 1960's who had performed on many shows with him, a man with a fabulous voice Dave Sampson. People reading the book may remember Dave Sampson for his self penned top thirty hit, "Sweet Dreams, performed with his backing band The Hunters.

Authors note: The Hunters were a great band, formerly known as the Parker Royal Five. This band who had the amazingly talented

Brian Parker on lead guitar had hits in their own right. 'Golden Earrings' and 'Teen Beat' being two that I remember. The line up was Norman Sheffield who died in 2014 on drums, Norman Stacy was on Rhythm Guitar, on Bass was John Rogers who was tragically killed in a car crash in 1961 after leaving The Hunters to join Adam Faith's Roulette's. Billy Kuy would take John's place when the band played together on any future occasions.

Incidentally Brian Parker and Norman Stacy also played with the Roulette's on different occasions. On one occasion that I know of The Hunters backed Cliff Richard at 'The London Palladium', when The Shadows had another contractual commitment, due to the success of *Apache*. Brian Parker and one of his former band mates from the Parker Royal Five, David, 'Buster' Meikle formed the vocal harmony band Unit 4+2 in company with Tommy Mouler and Peter Moules. They later asked Robert Bob Henrit to be their drummer, he went on to replace Mick Avery in The Kinks, and Russ Ballard, who would later form the great band 'Argent' join them. With this lineup they had a number one hit record, *Concrete and Clay*. Sadly Brian who had a heart attack while playing tennis, died in 2001. These are my memories of dear friends who shared this knowledge in conversations with me, over many years. As the author, I would not contradict anyone who believes any part of these memories to be different.

So there Peter was, delighted to be back in the company of his two old mates from the sixties. The three of them hadn't met up for more than fifty years and while they were all pleased to be there they had grown somewhat older. In spite of this Danny's hair was still dark brown and Peter's was jet black, Dave's was white as snow, Peter wondered why, although as he says he knew that his hair and Danny's were coloured from a bottle. They all hoped to see each other again soon.

When it was time for Peter to go on stage all was going well until during one of his songs, he was interrupted by a woman was clearly under the influence of alcohol, She wasn't being abusive, but she was shouting out silly things. The other members of the audience asked to her to quieten down as she was spoiling their enjoyment. At this point the woman turned nasty and started to become abusive, shouting threats. Thankfully at the interval she was escorted from the auditorium.

At the end of the show Peter came back on stage with a rendition of that great rock and roll song, written by Johnny Kidd and his bass player Brian Greig *A Whole Lotta Shakin'* the whole cast joined him on stage for the finale. Now Dave Sampson had not been on the bill but Peter brought him up on stage and he sang a verse of the song, Dave sounded great, as good as Peter remembered from the sixties. Danny was also in great form. Sad to report that both Dave Sampson and Danny Rivers have left us for that great Rock and Roll party in heaven. Dave passing away in 2014 and a couple of years later the lovely lady in his life Wendy also died. They were smashing people.

Danny sadly went in 2016, his wife Emily is still our good friend and is always in our thoughts.

Peter really enjoyed doing the show especially as he was seeing his old mates again. Back in the dressing room they had photos taken, then carried on chatting about the great times they had enjoyed on the Rock and Roll shows with their dear friend the late Tommy Bruce, a man who enjoyed great success during his long career, and had hits, including *Ain't Misbehavin* and *Lavender Blue*, using his unusual, deep gravel voice. There were many others to be remembered including, Lance Fortune and Georgie Fame and Johnny Gentle. The list,of the performers they remembered if it were written down would go on forever. There is a book that could be written just using the names of all the people Peter has shared a stage with, during his career, describing their lives and many performances. After a while Peter's wife Amanda joined them all in the dressing room and his old friends, Danny and Dave were delighted to meet her.

Although they had been happy in their home, after a relatively short period of Peter and Amanda moved to a place in the Cotswolds. During their time there Amanda fostered children for a few years. Peter enjoyed his painting, finding this pastime very relaxing. At first he painted landscapes then he tried animals, including Horses, Elephants, Zebras and various other species. Later on when he got into portraits, he painted Marty Wilde, Mark Wynter, George Michael, Robert Plant and his latest Joe Brown. He has been to see Marty, Mark and the others to present them with their portraits.

He is he has now caught up with his old 'Idols on Parade buddy Joe Brown and handed him his portrait, he was very pleased with Joe's response and they hope to get together for a catch up soon. Another portrait he painted was of Chris Cornell, who has sadly died recently, that one was done for his daughter Daniella, who had always admired this performer. Sad to recall that the fine artiste and entertainer George Michael has also died.

Authors note: Peter also painted a portrait of the late Tommy Bruce, which he kindly gave to me. Margaret and I have hung it in our entrance hall. It is the first thing people see when the come to visit. They always comment on it because they know how much I loved Tommy, I am proud to tell them that the artist is Peter Wynne. Another note of sadness while Peter was living in the Cotswolds, he had to have a complete knee replacement. During the operation he suffered a stroke, the stroke has left him with impaired vision, mainly affecting his peripheral vision his left side. His normal vision has also been limited by the stroke and he now has the problem falling over things as a result of this limitation.

This loss of vision has resulted in Peter having to hand back his driving licence. This has been one of the worst things that has ever happened to Peter. He feels that his independence and freedom to come and a go as he wishes has been taken from him. He has always really enjoyed driving and in those early days with Amanda, they were able to drive out on the Yorkshire moors and take a picnic with them, they enjoyed these outing and made trips out on several occasions. This something that they are still able to do, but of course Amanda has had to take over the driving, he still offers his not always welcome advice to her. Amanda is a strong minded lady who when driving as in all things makes her own decisions.

To make matters worse the knee operation was not a great success although it did ease the arthritic pain that he had been suffering. It did not however improve his mobility in the way that he had been hoping. The replacement knee is very painful and he still has to climb stairs one at a time, having to get both feet one step before he can go up the next one. He also had to have a complete new hip on his right side, the consultant has told him that sometime in the future he will need the left one replacing.

That as Peter says, "Is never going to happen". The reason being that he is fearful of having another stroke while under the anaesthetic, possibly even worse than the last one. It is not at all surprising in the circumstances that Peter never wants to have another procedure of any kind. Because of the stroke he now travels any distance, that would normally require him to walk, on a mobility scooter. Amanda now has the task of driving him to any appointments in the car. As Peter points out it is not a job she relishes because he has taken on the role of her driving instructor. As those of us of an age all know it is not easy to be a passenger when you have driven for most of your adult life.

There has been an invitation that Peter was more than happy to accept, it came from Chris Ely and his wife Linda who really are wonderful people. They are good friends and they work tirelessly to help us all in any way that they can. As Tommy Bruce would have said and did in his lifetime, "Lovely People". Chris runs "The Sound Of Fury" which is the official Billy Fury Fan Club. As we who are fans know there is a regular get together where we all meet up at Billy's grave in Mill Hill Cemetery to pay our respects. Afterwards everyone proceeds to a booked venue for refreshments and entertainment. Peter was invited to be the Guest of Honour at the most recent event. Chris and his wife Linda are great hosts and they treated Peter and Amanda with great courtesy. It was a most enjoyable event and several acts got up and performed their tributes to Billy Fury. As Peter commented, "There were some excellent impersonations of his old friend Billy".

Something else happened in 2013, Peter took a trip down memory lane and visited the place in London were so many of the stars of the British music scene, in the late fifties and early sixties found their way into the business. The iconic 2i's Coffee Bar, holds great memories for our generation because between 1956 and 1962 our own music was being performed there. Peter had photographs taken beside the commemorative green plaque that has been placed on the site at 59 Old Compton Street where the venue stood, he has so many memories of the people who met up and performed there. Paul Lincoln and Ray Hunter the two Australian ex wrestlers who took the place on in 1956 could never have dreamed of the great musical scene that would be created their. When the author of this book visited the coffee bar in 1962 it was being run by Tom Littlewood, who had I think previously been on the door there. The venue was coming towards the end of its heyday by then, although I did see a group who I think were called 'The Jury' or a name very close to that, perform. I thought that they were quite good, but I never heard any more about them.

Peter at Graham Hunter's house

Peter with Danny Rivers, Halstead Empire, 2012

Peter with Graham Hunter & Mark Wynter
Windsor Theater 2014

Lic Locking (left) on Bass

Peter with Graham Hunter

Peter with Joe Brown
March 2011

Peter with PJ Proby
Dec 2014

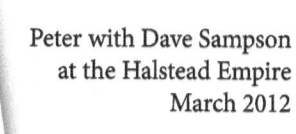

Peter with Dave Sampson
at the Halstead Empire
March 2012

London Charterhouse studios 2016

Chapter Twenty One

A Conclusion But Not The End

At one point having made their home in Berkshire, Peter and Amanda asked the local residents of the complex where they live, if they would like some entertainment over the Christmas period. The response came back, from all the residents, that they would love some. So Peter asked Daniel and Ciara if they would like to put on a show for the residents, of course Peter would sing on the show as a guest star. They agreed, this was very good of the couple because as they live on the other side of London, they had to travel rather a long way for the show and bring all their own equipment, Speakers, Microphones and a Lighting System with them. They were doing the show completely free of charge, as a favour to Peter. They would not have benefit of a roadie, so that also meant that Daniel had to set up the PA and lights himself, this entailed a lot of work for him, before he could go on stage and perform. Of course he also had to take the equipment down again after the show, but as Peter says, "Daniel is just a lovely guy"!

The Community Room was packed, it was a full house, Dand Ciara took to the stage for the first spot. They performed brilliantly and they received a tremendous ovation from the folks in the audience. After the interval when refreshments had been served, It was

Peter's turn to take to the stage. Not surprisingly with his tremendous voice he went down very well, the applause he received was lifting the roof. For the finale he was joined by Ciara and Dan on stage and they sang some country songs and then some carols, with everyone in the audience joining in. The event had been a great success and Peter agreed to put on another show the following Easter.

During the following May they performed at the wedding of Peter's sister-in-laws daughter, Mandy and her partner Simon. They also provided musical entertainment at the christening of his stepdaughter Michelle's, new little boy Henry. This was very enjoyable period of time for the whole family. The next thing that happened was that Harry Whitehouse expressed the wish to produce and release a CD of every song that Peter had ever recorded. This was very exciting news as it would give a whole new generation of people the chance to hear why all those years ago The Daily Express had dubbed Peter "The voice of the Sixties"! So he put every recording that he could find together and then sent them to Harry Whitehouse. When the Album is released, it will be titled, 'The Life of Peter Wynne in Song', he hopes that Harry is doing well with it.

At this point Peter would like to mention a great performer by who he has known since 2012, Graham Hunter. Graham has been a real stalwart and uplifting friend to Amanda and Peter during the last six years. During that time Graham has also been of help with Peter's stepson Daniel's career. Daniel as we have said before is a very talented artiste, who it is hoped will one day aspire to reach the very top in his chosen career. Recently Graham wrote a great piece covering Peter's recording career for The Beat Magazine. Graham Hunter is known to all of us who have an interest in sixties music, indeed he has met and got to know many of the artistes from that era. Added to his literary skills we would like to let any readers of this book who are unaware of this fact he is also a fine singer in his own right.

Graham Hunter is now putting his weight behind a big release for another old mate of Peter's the much loved and talented performer Mark Wynter. Speaking of Mark Wynter, Mark has been performing as part of the Dreamboats and Petticoats show and when the show was in Windsor a couple of years ago, Peter along with wife Amanda enjoyed going backstage to see him. They had never actually spent much time together before, although Mark and Peter have been in the business for a similar length of time. They had a lot to catch up on and they really enjoyed chatting together. Sometimes it seems that promoters have caused confusion over the years between their two surnames, so they were able to have a smile about that situation.

They have kept in touch since then and Mark had the opportunity to showcase his talent as actor, as he was on tour with a play the last time they spoke. Mark has also out on tour again for Flying Music appearing with Marty Wilde, Eden Kane and Mike Berry. Peter and Amanda went to see him again during that tour. Peter has not as yet met either Eden Kane or Mike Berry, but of course he has known Marty for more than fifty years. We have spoken about Peter's talent as an artist and the fine portraits that he has painted, well he is grateful to Graham Hunter for making it possible for him to get the portraits that he painted of Mark Wynter and Marty Wilde to them. I am pleased as the author to be able to say that Peter will continue to paint portraits. Not only does he find this a relaxing way to pass time, it is something that he is very good at. Of course he is far to modest a man to tell us that himself.

It is strange how life as we are living it today, can revive memories from the past. In Peter's case he has been thinking about a clairvoyant who he visited while he was living in Florida. He had been persuaded to go by a friend to go and see this woman, so he thought he would go along for a laugh as he was not really a believer. Anyway the woman asked him to remove a ring that he was wearing and put it in her hand, This he did and while she was holding it she spoke of certain things which he knew to be correct. Then she told Peter that he was going to be a star on both sides of the Atlantic. She said this stardom would involve religion. Well that was way back in 1970 nearly fifty years ago!! As he says, "I am still waiting".

But now strangely or perhaps not so strangely, given his love of fine music in any form, Peter has just recorded a religious song at Andy Edwards recording studio. Andy is his son-in-law, he a very talented drummer, who has good musical knowledge and expertise. As a result of Andy's input, Peter is now thinking of releasing an album of songs with a religious meaning. Life as we all know can move in mysterious ways so who knows what may come of this venture? The song that he has recorded in Andy's Studio is titled "One Pair of Hands", this a beautiful and very emotive song about God as the creator of all things and it encourages us all to keep the faith when things are not going well in our lives. The song is paired with is anti war hymn that Peter recorded in Nashville, it was written by a Native American called "The Hole that Holds the Bones", this hymn tells us that we are all one people, so we should put down guns and weapons of war. It goes on to tell us that each person should believe in their God as we will all become equal at the end of our lives. Authors note: Neither my wife Margaret or I have been able to listen to either of these songs without being reduced to tears. The words in both songs are so emotive and Peter's wonderful expression and interpretation of the words is an inspiration as to how we should all try to live our lives.

Peter believes and I believe that he is right in his belief, that he has an affinity with uplifting ballads, He has always sung this type of song during his stage performances, also he has recorded some great versions of the songs that have become standards over the years. Remember songs like *I Believe, The Day That The Rains Came Down, Didn't It Rain Chillun* the list is endless. Those of us that were born during and just after the war years can all remember David Whitfield, singing "The Book " this was about the gift of a bible his mother had given him, Then Frankie Laine sang *Make Me A Child Again*. These songs and hundreds like them inspired all of us during the fifties and sixties as we were growing up. Indeed we are still inspired when we hear the lyrics of these wonderful songs today.

Not to long ago Peter and Amanda went to one of PJ Proby's gigs. They arranged to meet him after the show. But while they were in the bar before the show, a very well spoken man came up to Peter saying, "I hope that you are singing *Maria* tonight Jim, it is one of my favourites". Peter felt that it would make the guy look silly if he said he wasn't Jim Proby, so he just said, "I'll be singing it no problem". After the show they went back to PJ's Winnebago to spend some time with him. It is really well laid out inside and he has decorated it with things like, Buffalo Horns and Indian Headdresses and other western country memorabilia. They spent a good hour talking with him, Jim knew Peter as the guy who had toured with Eddie Cochran. Peter likes Jim Proby and he certainly admired his talent as a recording artiste. We are agreed when Peter says, "Long may PJ Proby keep on singing".

During the time spent in Pocklington, Peter enjoyed performing at some open mic nights in a venue called 'Judsons. He also did a one nighter with his friend and brother-in-law Laurence Harrington at Boston Spa, they both enjoyed a great evening. They have started writing songs together, Peter wishes that they had done this sooner, because they are writing a good mix of blues and big ballads. He is painting again he has done an acrylic of a boat on a beach with a storm brewing in the background this was his first attempt at his art for some time, he has got back the bug for painting again and looking forward to his next project.

During 2016 he did some recording at Charter House, Peter's step daughter Brooke treated him to a couple of studio hours. At that session he recorded, *Somewhere* from 'West Side Story', an Elvis cover, *If I Could Dream*, A Matt Monro Hit, *Softly I Will Leave You, Love is a Many Splendored Thing*, which was a hit for 'The Four Aces' *I Dreamed A Dream* from "Les Miserable' finishing off with Elvis Presley's *Love Me Tender* He will add these to a CD that Peaksoft intend to release of every song that he ever recorded. The CD has now been released and benefits from having some of the older tracks remixed and remastered by the redoubtable skills of Graham Hunter.

There has also been time to keep in contact with buddies from the music business. One of them, Brian Licorice Locking who is a really close friend always keeps in touch. There is another, Ricky Valance, who recently gave Peter a call and they talked at length about the good old Rock and Roll days. For some reason Ricky has stopped phoning and Peter wonders if it is something that he has said, If it was he says, "Sorry Rick, remember all the traumas we have been through together and please phone again" He has known Ricky for years and he knows that Rick is a very outspoken man, who speaks his mind, but is prone to feel the hurt himself.

During his many years in the business Peter has met and worked with some very likeable and talented people along the way. Of course there have been those who were not so likeable or talented. But the least said about them the better, this a book about the positives in Peter's life. Many of the great guys he has met are no longer with us, he would not try to list them all here, but he will never forget them. As Peter says we are approaching the end of the book now and at the age of seventy nine, hoping to be eighty and more, there are still many ambitions that are waiting to be fulfilled. Peter wants to thank all the people who he has been acquainted with during his life and career to date. These are people who have always been willing to help and who have stayed friends through the good times and the bad, he will always be indebted to each and every one of them.

Times have been hard for Peter health wise, in recent years, he has suffered with COPD for the last fifteen of those years. Also during that time he has endured knee and hip replacements and he suffered a stroke. The stroke has left him with sight problems and cardiovascular disease. But through it all he still loves to sing and thrives on the sound of the audiences applause. In a perfect world he would have embraced his love of opera and followed his uncle, Furness Wynne Williams who sang in all the major opera venues all around the world, as a principle tenor. It was not to be, but he will forever be associated with the youth culture of British Rock and Roll, how could he not be? Because Peter Wynne was there at the start, he will be forever remembered by the generation that matured through that era as the "Voice of the Sixties". Although he is not a Rock and Roll singer, the Rock and Roll shows were the vehicle that took him to his place in history, but that music did not and does not define him.

That is because over the years vocally, Peter evolved into the consummate artiste, someone who, could and did cover all types of music. He loves the blues rock style, he has been influenced by Muddy Waters and Etta James the list of great performers whose music Peter appreciates, is endless. He has the ability to feel all types of music and when he sings that rare quality still shows in his voice. Unfortunately when he is given dates to perform or record, he finds that his voice is hoarse because of all the different medications he has to take for his emphysema. But that is not always the case, sometimes it is clear and his voice is still sensational on those occasions. There can be problems sustaining the last big notes in a song, because he hasn't got the lung capacity of yesteryear. But that doesn't stop him trying, it never will because it has been clear through every page in this book that Peter Wynne is no quitter, he never has been and he never will be!

In this time for reflection, Peter pauses to remember the mates who have passed on to join, 'The Big Band" up there in heaven, it is a long list, Duffy Power, Danny Rivers, Dave Sampson, Lonnie Donegan, who Peter worked with during that summer in Great Yarmouth, Bert Weedon, and of course his dear old friend, as he puts it, "The incomparable Tommy Bruce. Going on to say that "Tommy was a lovely man, he never had anything nasty to say about anyone, unless they really deserved it. He used to hold audiences spellbound with his deep gravel, yet enchanting voice". These guys and many more from those early days of Rock and Roll seemed to have unending talent and they are really missed, God bless them all.

Of course Peter is still a performer, we hope he will be for many years, with this in mind he has been planning some new recording to take with him on a nostalgic trip back to Nashville that he intends to make in the near future. The songs that he has plans to record include "Gentle On My Mind" and "Wichita Lineman", two great songs which he will add to as it gets nearer to the time of the trip. He will be recording the songs with his son-in-law Andy Edwards, as we have mentioned before Andy is a very talented teacher and player of percussion instruments, including the drums and he will record and produce the tracks for him.

Peter has already taken up his pen to begin writing some new songs that he will be including on this album. He will have the skills of his great mate and brother-in-law that most accomplished musician and song writer 'Laurence Harrington' to assist him, (As Peter says, "With a name like that Laurence should be a star in one of the big soaps like 'Dallas' or 'The Colby's'",) Anyway he is pleased that he will be able to rely on these skills when writing the new songs. He is always looking to the future still believing in and following his musical dream.

He will be accompanied on this journey by his wife Amanda and his stepson Daniel. Peter truly believes that Daniel, who is a great musician, singer and songwriter, has the ability to become a big success over there in Nashville. While he is in Nashville Peter will try to look up some old acquaintances who, even if they are no longer active in the business he hopes will still be alive, One such person is the record producer Russ Aldrich who has been in touch with Peter recently, so he is really looking forward to seeing him and his wife in September 2019.

Incidentally it is worth mentioning that Russ Aldrich did the arrangement for the Jerry Reed Song *My Kind Of Love*, the song that Peter enjoyed such success with during his time in Nashville. We should not forget what a great and talented guy Jerry was. Bud Reno also produced that song which as readers will remember was on the flip side of *The Hole That Holds the Bones*. These two tracks were not given much playtime for reasons that Peter doesn't want to go into now, because he wouldn't want people to think he was making excuses for the tracks not making it into the charts. Rest assured Peter, that the author and the people who will be reading this book know that your talent and song interpretation were outstanding on these and all your other recordings, any failure to chart can be firmly laid at the door of the people who failed for whatever reason to promote your excellent recordings.

There are other recordings in the pipeline, his family team are working on more and Peter will definitely be taking quite a selection of songs with him when he makes his journey over to Nashville. He hopes that someday far in the future he will leave many musical memories that hold so much of him in the melodies, not just for his family but for his countless fans as well. He hopes his children and grandchildren realise just how much he loves them all, that they are in his heart all the time. He knows that he has not been there for them as much as he would have wished but, he has always tried to do his best for the people he loves in the only ways that he knew. Since writing this part of the book, Peter has been advised by his respiratory doctor that the requirement for him to have oxygen regularly means that he and it is to risky to fly on long haul journeys, Sadly this means that he and Amanda will be unable to make that trip to Nashville.

Most of all he wants people to know that he has really loving thoughts for Amanda, the lovely, proud stubborn blue eyed girl, who has honoured him by marrying him. As he says, "Amanda is now and always will be my beautiful, special lady". Peter has so much that he wishes to say about Amanda, she is, "As straight as a die", always there for him and guiding him along the road that is best for them both, He adds, "She has put up with me being a grizzly old git for years now, she just sticks by me". Amanda of course has her own view on these things, As she says, "I just love him and we are happy together".

Peter who has briefly touched on his health problems as we have gone through the book, would without dwelling on them just like to share with us the things he that overcomes on a daily basis. These are the things that as he says have, "Slowed him down", don't forget he was a schoolboy athlete of some renown and he was a 10.6 police cadet sprint champion. Who knows what more he might have achieved in the world of athletics if he had not chosen to share his musical journey with us all? A question which will have to remain unanswered.

He has suffered with arthritis particularly in his leg joints since he was in his fifties. This has resulted in him having a successful hip replacement operation, but a far from successful outcome to a full knee replacement. This operation has sadly left Peter with several problems, he suffered a stroke while under the anaesthetic and when he came round it was discovered that there had been damage to the peripheral vision in both his eyes. This deficiency in his eyes led to him having to surrender his driving licence, this was a terrible blow to him.

Peter really misses the freedom he had, he loved been able to just get in the car and go for a spin. Driving was something that as he says, "Gave him great pleasure". The very worst thing that has happened to Peter, in his own opinion was being diagnosed with C.O.P.D. He feels that this was caused by more than forty years of smoking and performing in night clubs that had smoke billowing out everywhere, from the patrons cigarettes. This condition can on occasion, prevent him from holding his notes at the end of his songs and obviously he becomes breathless when he sings more than a few songs. When he is recording and performing, he has to take the time to prepare properly so that he can control his breathing during each song. Also as if he hasn't already suffered enough, Peter has recently spent time in hospital recovering from Sepsis. This most debilitating condition is one which the author can sympathise with, as he spent two weeks in hospital and several months afterwards, recovering from Sepsis himself in 2014.

On the subject of his health Peter is currently having to wear an oxygen mask to help with his breathing. He hopes this will be a temporary situation because at this moment in time it means that he is unable to fly. Because of this he will be unable to attend his stepdaughters wedding. Also his planned trip to Nashville to meet up with old friends will have to be put on hold until he recovers a level of fitness. All his friends and family are giving him their full support and Amanda will be ensuring that all the right things are in place to help him with his recovery. On the face of it doesn't look as if the trip will take place, but it would be a brave man who counted out Peter Wynne, ever! Because he always looks for second opinions and makes the best out of every situation.

Peter would like to make an apology to all his readers at this time, for covering what he terms, "The boring bits of his life". There is no need for this apology because it is clear that there is nothing boring about Peter Wynne or any part of his life. He is a determined and likeable man who continues to overcome the obstacles that life has put in his path. He is an inspiration to many people and well liked because of his fortitude and attitude to life. Having reached the age of seventy nine on the 30th of April 2018, he straight away thought of an old show business acquaintance, Gerry Dorsey who was eighty two on the 2nd of May 2018 and sent him an email to congratulate him. Peter hopes that he has received it.

Of course we all know that Gerry Dorsey is better known as Englebert Humperdinck and as Peter says, "Englebert, more power to his elbow, can still carry off a song with great panache, hats off to him it is great that he is still performing". Although they have known each other for fifty eight years, it has to be said that the two of them were not the greatest of friends back in the day. That said they both had great respect for each other, the thing to be remembered is that they were rivals in their quest to become singing stars. Peter says, "Englebert as we all know made it, he is star"! Well Peter there are people in the USA, Australia and the UK who know that you did too, you are a star to everyone who has ever heard you sing. You are still remembered by so many people. As the Daily Express said all those years ago, you are 'The Voice of the Sixties'. Your fans will say that you have a voice that will be remembered for all time. Your place in musical history is assured, we your fans, of which you know there are many, all wish for you to enjoy that acclaim for many years to come.

A lovely thing has happened for Peter recently, right out the blue he received an email with a phone number, it was from his old buddy Bernie Burgess, the man who as you will all remember was married to Ruby Murray. It seems that Bernie has now returned from Spain after many years over there and is now living in Sutton Coldfield. Naturally Peter when Peter received the phone number, he got straight on the phone to Bernie and spoke to his old friend at great length. They were reminiscing for some considerable time about the old days, which for them both are filled with happy memories. Bernie has now reached the age of ninety, but Peter says that he sounds virtually the same as he always did, it was fantastic to be speaking with him again. Amanda and Peter are definitely going to stay in touch with him and they hope to go and visit him soon. As we say good things just keep on happening for the popular and likeable Peter Wynne.

So here it is the fabulous story of Peter Wynne's journey into The Chapel of Dreams, so far. I say so far because he is still in that chapel of dreams and not surprisingly because of his hard work and talent, dreams are still coming true. As he points out himself, good things just keep on happening. He is now living in the home counties with his lovely wife Amanda, special lady that she is Amanda keeps the dreams alive for him, as he says, "She is brilliant because she does the things that he feels he can't". Amanda encourages him and helps him to be positive about all the things he can do, so that he never needs to worry or have negative thoughts about any aspect of his life.

Peter is still tall, still good looking and he still has a full head of hair not to mention his own teeth. As he puts it himself, "I am grateful for small mercies". On a personal note as the author I can tell you he is an amazing man who is still worth the admission fee. Sixty years or more since people first stood up in theatres and clubs and shouted to acclaim the talent of this lovely man audiences are still shouting for more. Long may Peter Wynne continue to prove that dreams really do come true, for talented people like him, who put the work in and try hard to follow their dreams.

Peter Wynne / Simon Smith Discography

1959
A side: Chapel of Dreams
Parlophone UK R 5597
B side: Twilight Time

1960
A: Ask Anyone In Love
Parlophone UK R 4668 July
B: I Need You Close Again
A: Our Concerto
Parlophone UK R4705 Nov
B: Your Love

1962
A: The Wall
Parlophone UK R 4884
B: You're Mine

1964
A: I'm a Fool To Want You
Polydor NH 52*316
A: It's A Lonely Town

1967
A: And This Is My Beloved
Colombia DB 8213
B: Just Can't Live Without You

1969
The Hole That holds The Bones
GWS USA
My Kind Of Love
2012

CD
Peter Wynne - As Time Goes By. Shoot The Dog Productions
2016
CD Double Album
The Story Peter Wynne. Peaksoft Media PEA028
Unreleased

1965
Another Tear Falls

1966
The Love In My Heart

Excuse Me Dear Martha
1968

Windmills Of Your Mind

Research on the above recording believed to be correct at time of publication.

Larry Parnes UK Tour 1960

April
13th 14th and 16th
Venue: The Hippodrome Bristol
Cast:
Gene Vincent and The Wildcats
Eddie Cochran
Peter Wynne
Tony Sheridan Trio
Georgie Fame
Johnny Gentle
Billy Raymond

May
6th
The Gaumont Salisbury
Cast:
Gene Vincent and The Wildcats
Eddie Cochran
Peter Wynne
Tony Sheridan Trio

Georgie Fame
Davy Jones
Nero and the Gladiators
The Beat Boys
Billy Raymond

16th to the 21st
Venue: The Hippodrome Brighton
Cast :
Gene Vincent
Jerry Keller
Peter Wynne
Colin Green and The Beat Boys
Nero and The Gladiators
Lance Fortune
Georgie Fame
Billy Raymond,
Note, Sally Kelly replaced Jerry Keller on the shows dated 19th and 20th of May, Jerry Keller back in the line up on the 21st. Sally Kelly retained.

June
1st
Venue: The Gaumont Rochester
Cast:
Gene Vincent

Jerry Keller
Sally Kelly
Nero and The Gladiators
Lance Fortune
Georgie Fame
Colin Green and The Beat Boys
Billy Raymond

2nd
Venue: The Gaumont Norwich
Cast:
Gene Vincent
Jerry Keller
Lance Fortune
Peter Wynne
Nero and The Gladiators
Davy Jones
Georgie Fame
The Beat Boys
Billy Raymond

3rd
Venue: The Gaumont Ipswich
Cast:
Gene Vincent
Jerry Keller

Lance Fortune
Peter Wynne
Nero and The Gladiators
Davy Jones
Georgie Fame
The Beat Boys
Billy Raymond

4th
Venue The Rialto York
Cast:
Gene Vincent
Jerry Keller
Lance Fortune
Peter Wynne
Nero and The Gladiators
Davy Jones
Georgie Fame
The Beat Boys
Billy Raymond

6th 7th 8th 9th 10th 11th
Venue: The Glasgow Empire
Cast:
Gene Vincent
Freddie Cannon

Jerry Keller
Lance Fortune
Peter Wynn
Nero and the Gladiators
Davy Jones
Georgie Fame
The Beat Boys
Billy Raymond

There a change in the line up after the first night at The Glasgow Empire, Freddie Cannon and Jerry Keller stepped out and Billy Fury and Keith Kelly stepped in.

13th 14th 15th 16th 17th 18th
Venue: The Theatre Royal Nottingham
Cast: Gene Vincent
Billy Fury
Vince Taylor
Lance Fortune
Keith Kelly
Peter Wynne
Davy Jones
Georgie Fame
Nero and The Gladiators
The Beat Boys
Billy Raymond

After the first night at The Theatre Royal Billy Fury stepped out and Duffy Power stepped in.

21st, 22nd 23rd 24th 25th
Venue The Empire Theatre Liverpool
Cast:
Billy Fury
Joe Brown
Lance Fortune
Keith Kelly
Peter Wynne
Davy Jones
Georgie Fame
Nero and The Gladiators
The Beat Boys
Billy Raymond

27th 28th 29th304th
Venue: The Hippodrome Birmingham
Cast:
Billy Fury
Joe Brown
Lance Fortune
Keith Kelly
Peter Wynne
Davy Jones

Georgie Fame
Nero and The Gladiators
The Beat Boys
Billy Raymond

July

1st

Venue: The Hippodrome Birmingham

Cast:
Billy Fury
Joe Brown
Lance Fortune
Keith Kelly
Peter Wynne
Davy Jones
Georgie Fame
Nero and The Gladiators
The Beat Boys
Billy Raymond

8th 9th

Venue: The New Theatre Cardiff

Cast:
Billy Fury
Joe Brown
Lance Fortune
Keith Kelly

Peter Wynne
Davy Jones
Georgie Fame
Nero and The Gladiators
The Beat Boys
Billy Raymond

November
27th
Venue: The Gaumont Bradford
Cast:
Billy Fury
Joe Brown
Lance Fortune
Keith Kelly
Peter Wynne
Davy Jones
Georgie Fame
Nero and The Gladiators
The Beat Boys
Billy Raymond

28th
Venue: The Gaumont Coventry
Cast:
Billy Fury

Joe Brown
Tommy Bruce
Nelson Keene
Dickie Pride
Peter Wynne
Red Price With Jimmie Nicol and his 15 New Orleans Rockers
The Valentine Girls

29th
Venue: The Odeon St Albans
Cast:
Billy Fury
Joe Brown
Tommy Bruce
Nelson Keene
Dickie Pride
Peter Wynne
Red Price With Jimmie Nicol and his 15 New Orleans Rockers
The Valentine Girls

30th
Venue: The ABC Dover
Cast:
Billy Fury
Joe Brown
Tommy Bruce

Nelson Keene
Dickie Pride
Peter Wynne
Red Price With Jimmie Nicol and his 15 New Orleans Rockers
The Valentine Girls

December
1st
Venue: The Odeon Llandudno
Cast:
Billy Fury
Joe Brown
Tommy Bruce
Nelson Keene
Dickie Pride
Peter Wynne
Red Price With Jimmie Nicol and his 15 New Orleans Rockers
The Valentine Girls

2nd
Venue: The Granada Shrewsbury
Cast:
Billy Fury
Joe Brown
Tommy Bruce
Nelson Keene

Dickie Pride
Peter Wynne
Red Price With Jimmie Nicol and his 15 New Orleans Rockers
The Valentine Girls

3rd
Venue: The Ritz Cinema Cleethorpes
Cast:
Billy Fury
Joe Brown
Tommy Bruce
Nelson Keene
Dickie Pride
Peter Wynne
Red Price With Jimmie Nicol and his 15 New Orleans Rockers
The Valentine Girls

Authors Note: The dates venues and cast members for these shows have been researched to the best of Peter Wynne's and Dave Lodge's ability. While every care has been taken, it should remembered that this tour took place 58 years ago at time of writing. If there are any errors please forgive us. The main thing is that Peter Wynne was right there with Eddie Cochran, Gene Vincent, Joe Brown, Tommy Bruce and all those other much loved performers on the Larry Parnes Tours.

International Praise for the authors previous books:

Have Gravel Will Travel

Dave Lodge's biography about Tommy Bruce *Have Gravel Will Travel* is an excellent book. The reason it is an excellent book is because it doesn't just tell the very moving story about the life of sixties recording star Tommy Bruce. It also tells about what happened to some of the other sixties recording stars and where they are now. Artistes like Michael Cox, Lance Fortune and Nelson Keene, are in my minds eye again. I am reading *Have Gravel Will Travel* for the fourth time!!
Svein Sorlie Norway.

I believe Dave Lodge's book *Have Gravel will Travel* is more than just a fine tribute to our old mate Tommy Bruce. I think that in time it will come to be regarded as a reference point for the history of Rock and Roll history.
Brian Poole Hit Recording Artiste and Entertainer England

Dave Lodge with *Have Gravel will Travel* has written the best book about an entertainer Tommy Bruce, that I have ever read. The book made me see Tommy Bruce as a great guy who I would really like to have known. You just can not put this book down, page after page it just got more and more interesting.
John Eckert Talent Consultant, California, USA.

Have Gravel will Travel is a great book. Written by Dave Lodge I really enjoyed learning about sixties recording artiste Tommy Bruce. I just couldn't put this book down.

Manfred Kulman Author, Drummer, Rock and Roll Promoter. Beilfield, Scholenesh, Germany

Lucky A Dog's Tail

This book received special mention at the 2016 Lakeland Book of the Year awards! Lucky a Dogs Tail could move you to tears, I recommend that you read it.

Fiona Armstrong TV personality and book of the year judge.

Lucky A Dog's Tale is a read that will touch your heart, This time Dave Lodge shows the loyalty and friendship he and his dog Lucky shared for sixteen years. It is a clever piece of writing as Dave has written it from Lucky's perspective, as though Lucky had written it himself. **Great work. John Eckert. Talent Consultant. California. USA**

The Long Road

This a great read we get to know the people Dave Lodge has met as he journeys through life.

John Eckert Talent Consultant. USA

The Long Road also received special mention at The 2017 Lakeland Book of The Year. 'A very interesting read'

Hunter Davies. Event Judge and internationally respected author.

Tin Pan Aspirations

Tin Pan Aspirations I always look forward to Dave Lodge's books and I have to say that *Tin Pan Aspirations* The Golly Goulding Story is one of Dave Lodge's best works to date. A very good read.
John Eckert. Talent Consultant, California USA.

Dave Lodge writes the kind of books that I enjoy reading. *The Long Road* and *Tin Pan Aspirations* open up the world of show business and the people in it. These two books follow on well from, *Have Gravel will Travel*. His book *Lucky A Dog's Tale* is different but still a good read.
Svein Sorlie Norway.

Crane The Left Handed Gun

Entered for the 2019 WWA Golden Spur Award.

Chapel Of Dreams - The Peter Wynne Story

Peter Wynne was not only there at the beginning with the great names of British Rock and Roll in 1960, but he naturally possessed the kind of semi operatic vocal range that the likes of Elvis had to work on over two years in Germany! There is no doubt that Peter Wynne was one of the great voices of the sixties. He was the one to listen to, his effortless renditions of classic songs like "More" and the beautiful ballad "For Your Love" Both of these songs were attempted in 1964 by Billy Fury, with whom Peter worked, will surely convince any sixties music lover of the excellence of this man's compelling voice.

Chris Ely-The sound of Fury

If like me you like to hear and read of people with great talent making their way in life with what seemed to be impossible dreams, then this book is the one for you. *Chapel of Dreams* gives you an insight to life of a man who knew he was born to make his way in life as a singer a man who will never give up, a man who will always be remember by that first Daily Express headline, 'The Voice of The Sixties'. I am sure that as you read and enjoy this very personal story, you will find that reading it, is worth every minute of your time.

Dave Lodge
Personal manager to the late Tommy Bruce.

Peter with Dave Lodge,
the author 2018

Amanda, Margaret, Dave and Peter

Dave Lodge's books range from novels to biographies and are available online and from good bookshops.

Have Gravel, will Travel
The Official Tommy Bruce Biography

The amazing story of how a young cockney lad went from 'barra boy' to a teen singing idol. A unique insight into the 1960's rock 'n' roll scene when Tommy Bruce and contemporaries such as Billy Fury, Johnny Kidd and Joe Brown were doing the rounds together. In this fickle world of show business many friendships don't stand the test of time. Not so that of Tommy Bruce and Dave Lodge, his manager, friend and author of this biography. We see how their partnership has endured since the 1960's unhampered by contracts, surviving on friendship through the highs and lows. The book is a testimony to Tommy's affable style both on and off stage making him a well-loved character in the industry for the past five decades.

Price: £6.99

Paperback: 280 pages / 100 B&W photographs
Publisher: Pixel Tweaks Publications (July 2015)
ISBN-13: 978-0992751487

THE LONG ROAD Dave Lodge

ONE MAN'S EPIC JOURNEY THROUGH THE WORLD OF SPEEDWAY, SPORT AND SHOWBUSINESS

Starting from the rural backdrop of Cumbria, as a young man, Dave ventured South to Manchester. There he was involved in Speedway at the world famous Belle Vue track, he played Rugby for TocH, and competed in Marathons, Triathlons and even Quadrathons! In 1973 a chance meeting with Tommy Bruce, the sixties rock 'n' roll star, started him on a path into the world of showbusiness. As manager and promoter for Tommy, Dave mixed with the great rock 'n' rollers from the Sixties and the world of entertainment of the day. This book is a warm recollection of these times, a celebration of the people behind the celebrity – never in a negative or salacious way, simply a reflection of the warmth, camaraderie and teamwork of the people he encountered whether on a Speedway Track, a Rugby field, a Marathon or Backstage.

£9.99

Paperback: 360 pages / over 300 B&W photos
ISBN-13: 978-0-9934679-4-3
Available from local bookshops, Amazon & Bertrams
or directly from the author at: davelodgeauthor@gmail.com

Pixel tweaks
PUBLICATIONS
ULVERSTON · CUMBRIA
WWW.PIXELTWEAKSPUBLICATIONS.COM

Lucky, a Dog's Tale

The story of a remarkable dog, whose loyalty and love for those in his life may have been equalled but never surpassed. From the moment he came into our lives, abandoned and dishevelled on the Mancunian Way, he was an amazing and unexpected addition to our family. A Newfoundland, Labrador cross, he grew to be a gentle giant who surprised us every day of his life.

This book will appeal to those who have enjoyed the company of wonderful pets of their own; they will understand how much we loved Lucky. I can't say he was the best dog in the world; I haven't known enough dogs to make that assumption, What I can say, without fear of contradiction is, "I have never known a better dog"!

So I leave it up to you, read and enjoy Lucky's book and see if you can answer his question, "A dog can have a life story, can't he?"

Price: £4.99

Paperback: 72 pages with B&W photographs
ISBN-13: 978-09956190-3-6

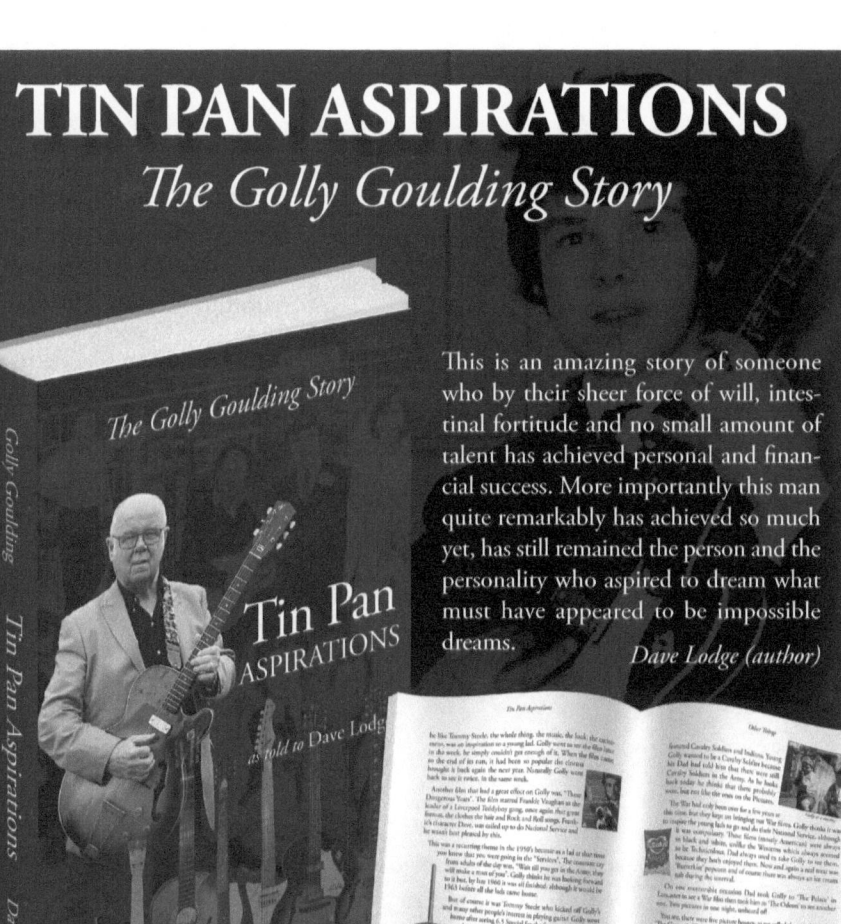

Born on a scrub farm on the Texas border, Crane is forced by circumstances to set out on the Vengence Trail.

He has his own code that he would live and die by.

Loyal and determined he finds hope and love and friendship as he rides his lonely trail.

With his horse Devil Dancer and his dog Bruno, he wreaks havoc among the lawless men who stalk the land.

In this his fifth book Dave Lodge manages to capture the spirit of the Wild West and has created a brand new hero in the form of Tony Crane - the left handed gun!

Paperback: 350 pages
Publisher: DML (9 April 2018)
Language: English
ISBN-13: 978-1999893682
Product Dimensions: 12.7 x 2 x 20.3 cm

www.ingramcontent.com/pod-product-compliance
Lightning Source LLC
Chambersburg PA
CBHW031054080526
44587CB00011B/680